CLOTHES CLOTHE
MUSIC MUSI
Y S B O Y

V   grew up in London. In 1976, while studying at
C   ool of Art, she formed the Flowers of Romance with
Si   , and later joined the Slits. After a career as a filmmaker,
sh   back making art and music. She lives in London with
h   ghter.

F   praise for *Clothes, Clothes, Clothes. Music, Music, Music.
B   Boys, Boys*:

'E   cit, traumatic and moving in equal measure.' *Mojo*

'F   y, rude, tender, and superbly written.' Ian Thomson,
Spe ator

'A t   ific read . . . Gripping and moving.' Ian Rankin, *Guardian*

'A st   y of femaleness, of feminism and of a fascinating life, which
sho   Albertine to be a memoirist of great skill, wit and humour .
. . A ertine is a natural writer, and this story soars in her hands,
shak   g off rock-biog clichés.' Sinead Gleeson, *Irish Times*

'I've   ways loved Viv Albertine and I love her even more now that
I've   ad this affecting, oddly beautiful memoir.' India Knight

'A n   holds barred, poignant, touching and funny account of her
life   at finally gives a woman's view of the punk rock boys club
as w   l as the rest of her adventures in art and music. . . A riot of a
read   John Robb, *Louder Than War*

'With a title that is an incantation and a picture of the gorgeous
author on i   te something . . . A   they talk

about what it is not to be a Typical Girl.' Suzanne Moore, *Guardian*

'Not only the best book about punk but one of the best books of any kind I've read.' Greil Marcus

'Unflinching, candid, revelatory: the perils of being a pioneer.' Jon Savage

'A frank and fearless account of sex, drugs and life on the cultural frontline.' *Esquire Weekly*

'Pithy, hilarious and smart, this is a wonderfully observant account of the life of a woman who made her dreams come true.' Leyla Sanai, *Independent on Sunday*

'Fabulous, exciting and cool . . . An eyewitness account of love, chaos and reflection: a gender-slashing, guitar-smashing report from the radical front.' Thurston Moore

'Love or hate the punk movement this memoir of those turbulent times by the Slits' guitarist is infused with humanity and vulnerability that gives it far broader appeal.' *Sunday Express*

VIV ALBERTINE

CLOTHES
CLOTHES
CLOTHES
MUSIC
MUSIC
MUSIC
BOYS
BOYS
BOYS

ff

FABER & FABER

First published in 2014
by Faber and Faber Ltd
Bloomsbury House
74–77 Great Russell Street
London WC1B 3DA

This paperback edition first published in 2015

Typeset by Ian Bahrami
Printed in England by CPI Group (UK) Ltd, Croydon, CR0 4YY

A CIP record for this book
is available from the British Library

ISBN 978–0–571–29776–4

2 4 6 8 10 9 7 5 3 1

For Arla

CONTENTS

Introduction ix

Side One

INTRODUCTION

If you don't want to slip up tomorrow, speak the truth today.
Bruce Lee

Anyone who writes an autobiography is either a twat or broke. I'm a bit of both. Once I got going, I did make myself laugh a couple of times and learnt a few things, as patterns emerged that I hadn't noticed before. Hopefully you'll have a bit of a laugh and learn a few things too.

The title comes from something my mother used to say to me: 'Clothes, clothes, clothes, music, music, music, boys, boys, boys – that's all you ever think about!' She would chant this refrain when I came home from school every day with no clue about the content of my lessons but able to describe in minute detail what the teacher was wearing, raving about the boys I fancied and predicting which records were going to be hits.

This is an extremely subjective book, a scrapbook of memories. The experiences documented here left an indelible emotional imprint on me; they shaped and scarred me. And I was present at every one. Let others who were there tell their versions if they want to. This is mine.

Some names have been changed to protect the guilty.

For those in a hurry . . .

Sex references: pages 3, 32, 38, 113–5, 370–2, 380
Drugs references: pages 54–5, 147–9, 230, 376–7
Punk rock references: pages 84–6, 89–90, 136–8, 142–3, 153–4

Side One

1 MASTURBATION

Never did it. Never wanted to do it. There was no reason not to, no oppression, I wasn't told it was wrong and I don't think it's wrong. I just didn't think of it at all. I didn't naturally want to do it, so I didn't know it existed. By the time my hormones kicked in, at about thirteen years old, I was being felt-up by boys and that was enough for me. Bit by bit the experimentation went further until I first had sex with my regular boyfriend when I was fifteen. We were together for three years and are still friends now, which I think is nice. In all the time since my first sexual experience I haven't masturbated, although I did try once after being nagged by friends when I complained I was lonely. But to me, masturbating when lonely is like drinking alcohol when you're sad: it exacerbates the pain. It's not that I don't touch my breasts (they're much nicer now I've put on a little weight) or touch between my legs or smell my fingers, I do all that, I like doing that, tucked up all warm and cosy in bed at night. But it never leads on to masturbation. Can't be bothered. I don't have fantasies much either – except once when I was pregnant and all hormoned up. I felt very aroused and had a violent fantasy about being fucked by a pack of rabid, wild dogs in the front garden. I later miscarried – that'll teach me. This fantasy didn't make me want to masturbate, I ran the scenario through my head a couple of times, wrote it down and never had a thought like it again. Honest.

(Please god let that old computer I wrote it on be smashed into a million pieces and not lying on its side in a landfill site somewhere, waiting to be dug up and analysed sometime in the future, like Lucy the Australopithecus fossil.)

Here we go then, (genital) warts an' all . . .

2 ARCADIA

1958

My family arrived in England from Sydney, Australia, when I was four years old. My sister and I had three toys each: a Chinese rag doll, a teddy bear and a koala bear. We were not precious about our toys. The dolls were repeatedly buried in the back garden, eventually we forgot where they were and they perished in the earth. The teddies we would hold by their feet and smash them at each other in vicious fights until they were torn and mangled, with eyes and ears missing. We didn't touch the koalas because they were covered in real fur and felt creepy.

We sailed from Australia to England on a ship called the *Arcadia*, according to a miniature red-and-white life-belt hanging on a nail in the bathroom. It was a six-week journey. One of my earliest memories is of my mother and father tucking my sister and me up in bunk beds in our cabin. They told us they were going to dinner, they wouldn't be long, and if we were worried about anything, to press the buzzer by the bed and someone would go and get them. This all sounded perfectly reasonable to us, so we snuggled down and off they went.

About thirty seconds later, we were gripped by terror. I was four, my sister was two. Once the door was shut and my parents had gone, the reality of being alone at night in this strange place was unbearable. We started crying. I pressed the buzzer. After what seemed like ages and quite a lot of pressing, a steward appeared and told us everything was fine and we should go back to sleep. He left. Still scared, I pressed the buzzer again. For a very long time no one came, so I carried on. Eventually the steward came back and shouted, '*If you press that buzzer once more, the ship will sink and your mummy and daddy will drown.*' I didn't stop pressing and Mum and Dad didn't drown, they came back from dinner to find us bawling.

Mum and Dad

At four years old I learnt an important lesson: grown-ups lie.

3 PET SOUNDS

I wish I were a girl again, half-savage and hardy and free.
Emily Brontë, *Wuthering Heights*

My sister and I were quite feral little girls. We weren't like girls at all for a few years, quite unemotional, verging on cruel. We had a dog called Candy. She was a white Yorkshire terrier and she ate her own poo. Her breath smelt. After she had an operation (so she couldn't have puppies), she lay in her basket trying to chew the scab off her wound. I suppose we all do that in a way.

My sister and I taught Candy to sleep on her back, tucked up under a blanket with her front paws peeping over the top. On Guy Fawkes Night we dressed her up in a bonnet and a long white dress (one of our christening gowns), sat her in a doll's pushchair and wheeled her round Muswell Hill Broadway asking for 'a penny for the guy'. We didn't get much, but that wasn't the point.

We got bored with Candy quite quickly and stopped taking her for walks. The only time we called out 'Walkies!' and rattled her lead was when we couldn't get her in from the back garden at night. Eventually she caught on and wouldn't come in at all.

One day somebody put an anonymous note through our door, 'You don't know me but I know your poor little dog . . .' Telling us off for being mean to Candy. We gave her away.

We had a cat too, Tippy. We used to build traps for her in the garden. We would dig a pit, cover it with leaves and twigs, then wait for her to fall into it, which of course she never did. So we tried to push her in instead. She ran away.

Lastly we had three goldfish, Flamingo, Flipper and Ringo, all

With my little sister

from the local fair. Flamingo died after a few days, Flipper died a couple of weeks later and was eaten by Ringo. Ringo had a nervous breakdown (no doubt guilty about eating Flipper) and started standing on his head at the bottom of the fish tank for hours at a time. Eventually I couldn't stand it any more so I flushed him down the loo. When the bowl cleared, he was still there, standing on his head. It took lots of flushes to get rid of him. That image of Ringo on his head at the bottom of the loo still haunts me.

4 BAD BOYS

1962

The classroom door opens and in strides our headmaster, flanked by two identical, scruffy boys. Mr Mitchell announces to the class that the boys' names are Colin and Raymond and they've been expelled from their last school for bad behaviour. He looks down at the twins and says:

'St James' is a church school: we believe in redemption and we are going to give you another chance.'

Colin and Raymond scowl up at him; they are not happy to be here or grateful for their second chance. They look at us clean-haired, well-behaved children in our maroon blazers, starched white shirts and striped ties with contempt. Their holey grey socks are crumpled around their ankles, they don't wear silly short-shorts like all the other boys in my class – their shorts are long, right down to their scabby knees. They have greasy brown fringes hanging in their eyes. One of them has a scar on his freckled cheek. I think to myself, *Thank goodness, two good-looking boys at school at last.* I want to clap my hands together with glee. I don't know where this thought comes from. I don't recognise it. I've never cared about boys before, up until now they've been invisible to me, not important in my world. No one's ever told me about bad boys, that they're sexy and compelling, or to stay away from them. I work all this out by myself, today – at eight years old, in Class Three.

As our class marches in a crocodile through the leafy streets of Muswell Hill to the dining hall, I can't take my eyes off these two delinquents. I want to drink them in. I screw my neck round and

In junior-school uniform, 1963

end up walking backwards just to stare at them. I'm disappointed that we're not at the same table at lunch, but at least I'm directly behind Colin, sitting at a long trestle table with my back to him. I feel excited, a new kind of excitement, a bubbling, choking, gurgling feeling rises up from my navy-blue regulation school knickers into my chest. The effort of keeping this energy contained is revving me up even more. There's only one thing I can think of doing to release the tension and get Colin's attention: I poke him in the back. He takes no notice, so I poke him again. This time he spins round and snarls at me, baring his teeth like an animal under attack, but I'm buzzing on this new feeling and once he's turned away from me, I poke him again.

'If you do that again I'll smash your face in.'

I've never been threatened by a boy before and I don't like it, I think I might cry. I have a feeling that this is not how it's supposed to go if you like someone, but the adrenalin coursing through my blood obliterates my common sense. I can't believe what I'm doing, I must be out of my mind, I risk everything, pushing all feelings of fear, pride and self-protection aside – I stretch out my arm and poke him again.

Colin swivels round. Everyone stops chattering and stares at us. I look for a teacher to come and save me but nobody's near so I grip the bench tightly and stare straight back at Colin, waiting for the punch. His mouth twists into a sly smile.

'I think she likes me.'

From this moment on, we are inseparable.

5 THE BELT

1963

> But the child's sob in the silence curses deeper
> Than the strong man in his wrath.
> Elizabeth Barrett Browning,
> 'The Cry of the Children'

I live with my mother, father and little sister, on the ground floor of my grandmother's house in Muswell Hill, North London. The house smells of moth balls and we have to be quiet all the time, even in the garden – *I really identify with Anne Frank tiptoeing around her loft* – because of the nerves of Miss Cole, the tenant living on the top floor. Our flat has no living room and we share a bathroom with my grandmother. There are no carpets, just bare boards and a threadbare oriental rug in the kitchen. The only furniture we have is three beds, a mottled green Formica-topped dining table with tubular steel legs and four dining chairs covered with torn yellow plastic with hairy black stuffing poking out of the slits. This dining-room set was shipped over with us from Australia.

I can't imagine what a happy home is like: parents cuddling and laughing, music playing, books on the shelves, discussions round the table? We don't have any of that, but if Mum's happy, I'm happy. The trouble is, she isn't happy very often because my dad is odd and difficult and not as quick-minded as her – and also we're poor. Every night I lie in bed listening through the wall to Mum tidying up the kitchen. She opens and closes cupboard doors, bangs pots and pans, and I try to interpret the sounds, to gauge by the strength of the door slams, the ferociousness of plates clattering together, the way the knives and forks are tossed into a drawer, if she's in a good mood or not. Usually not. Occasionally I think, *That door was closed gently, that saucepan was put away softly, she's feeling OK*, and I go off to sleep, happy.

Tonight, my eyes are swollen from crying and there are red welts across the back of my legs; the marks hurt so badly I have to lie on my side. Mum's tucked me and my sister up in bed, given us both a kiss and turned off the light but I'm wide awake, straining to hear through the bedroom wall. I close my eyes, concentrating on the sounds to see if she's got over the upset earlier. I can hear Dad talking to her. *What's he doing in our home, this big hairy beast?* Lots of dads seem like that to me: awkward, in the way, out of place, filling up the rooms with their clumsy bodies. They should've gone off into the wild to hunt bison after their children were born and not come back; that's how it was meant to be. My dad's not like other dads though, he's worse: hairy all over his body, with a stubbly chin that's sprinkled with shaving cuts. He sticks little bits of toilet paper onto the nicks to stem the bleeding. Most of the time his neck and chin are covered in tiny white petals with red specks in the middle of each one. Halfway through the day, little red dots begin to reappear on his chin and he goes back to the sink for another shave. His deep voice, made even stranger by his French accent, rumbles and reverberates through the walls and he's always clearing his throat of what sounds like great gobs of phlegm. He's so . . . masculine, so . . . foreign – a cross between Fred Flintstone and a French version of Stanley Kowalski from *A Streetcar Named Desire*.

Earlier today two things happened, one that's never happened before and one that happens a lot. We had people round, not friends – I don't think Mum and Dad have any friends – but a couple of aunties and uncles. I was so excited, rushing round picking all the bits of fluff off the threadbare rug under the table – *Oh no! it's so bare you can see right through to the strings* – as we don't have a vacuum cleaner, straightening the chairs, making the beds. That's the first time I'd seen our flat through other people's eyes and I realised we lived in a dump.

By about three o'clock, everyone had arrived. I was in the kitchen putting homemade rock cakes onto a plate when I heard my dad telling a story about how him and Mum ran a fish-and-chip shop when they lived in Canada and everything that went wrong with it. They burnt the chips, made the batter out of the wrong flour, couldn't feed a coach party that came in, told them to come back tomorrow. Mum and Dad laughed their heads off about it. That's the thing that's never happened before: Mum and Dad laughed together.

I stopped what I was doing and went to have a look. Standing in the kitchen doorway I gaped open-mouthed at them. Tears poured down my face and ran into my mouth, as I drank in this extraordinary sight. I was so happy and so scared, scared that I would never see such a wonderful thing again.

I never did.

Four hours later I'm lying in the dark, listening. I can tell from the noises coming from the kitchen that Mum is angrier than usual and I know why. After everybody left, me or my sister, I can't remember which, said something that irritated Dad, just something silly, but he flipped.

'Go and get the belt.'

This happens a lot. I go to the cellar, open the door – no need to switch the light bulb on, I know this ritual by heart – and unhook the brown leather belt from a nail banged into the bare brick wall. As I breathe in the brick and coal dust, my throat tightens. Then I walk back to Dad, trailing the buckle along the floor behind me, letting it bang and clunk against the furniture. This act of defiance makes him even angrier. I hand the belt over. He tells me to turn round with my back to him and hits me three times across the back of my bare legs. It's my sister's turn next. We howl with the unfairness and the pain of it all. We cry as loud as we can, hoping Mum will stop him or the neighbours will hear us and come round and tell him off or have him sent to prison. But no one interferes once you've shut the front door of your home. The house next door could be in a different country for all they care.

Dad orders us to our bedroom as extra punishment. It's always freezing in there. As soon as he's gone, we root around in the bedside-table drawer, find an old biro and draw around each other's swollen red welts in blue ink, so even when the marks heal, the squiggly blue outlines will be a record of what he did. We promise each other: we'll never wash the biro off and we'll draw over the outlines every day. Our homemade tattoos will be permanent reminders – to him and to us – of what a bully he is. Yep, we'll show him.

A bit later Dad comes in to see us. We're sitting on our beds drawing, having got over the worst of the pain and the tears. He cries and hugs us, tells us he's sorry and asks us to forgive him.

'Yes, we forgive you, Daddy!' we chorus.

We have to forgive him, we've got to see him every day, life's going to be even more uncomfortable if we don't forgive him; it's a matter of survival. We just want everything to be all right, or seem to be all right. Mum calls out that tea's ready, Dad tells us to wash off the silly biro and come and sit at the table.

We leave a few blue traces behind on our red skin on purpose, not enough to get him worked up again but enough to salvage our pride, then troop into the tiny steamed-up kitchen to eat stew: lumps on our plates, lumps in our throats, red eyes, red legs. Dad makes a joke and we laugh to please him, then we all chomp away in silence. When no one's looking, I spit the chewed-up meat into my hand to flush down the toilet later. The radio's on, the theme

14

tune of *Sing Something Simple* with the Swingle Singers seeps into the room, the vocal harmonies – sweet and sickly – pour out into the air and fill up the silences.

I still can't stand the sound of those 1950s harmonies – like a drink you got drunk on as a teenager, just the smell of it brings back the nausea.

6 YOU CAN'T DO THAT

1964

I'm at my babysitter Kristina's house, my first time in a big girl's room. There are no dolls or teddy bears anywhere. On her bed is a 'gonk', a round red cushion with a long black felt fringe, no mouth, big feet. Her bedspread is purple and she's painted her furniture purple too. In the middle of the floor is a record player, a neat little box covered in white leatherette, it looks a bit like a vanity case. Flat paper squares with circles cut out of the middle are scattered around the floor. Kristina opens the lid of the record player and takes a shiny liquorice-black disc out of one of the wrappers, puts it onto the central spindle and carefully lowers a plastic arm onto the grooves. There's a scratching sound. I have no idea what's going to happen next.

Boys' voices leap out of the little speaker – 'Can't buy me love!' No warning. No introduction. Straight into the room. It's the Beatles.

I don't move a muscle whilst the song plays. I don't want to miss one second of it. I listen with every fibre of my being. The voices are so alive. I love that they don't finish the word *love* – they give up on it halfway through and turn it into a grunt. The song careens along, only stopping once for a scream. I know what that scream means: *Wake up! We've arrived! We're changing the world!* I feel as if I've jammed my finger into an electricity socket, every part of me is fizzing.

When the song finishes, Kristina turns the record over – *What's she doing?* – and plays the B-side, 'You Can't Do That'.

This song pierces my heart, and I don't think it will ever heal. John Lennon's voice is so close, so real, it's like he's in the room. He has a normal boy's voice, no high-falutin' warbling or smoothed-out, creamy harmonies like the stuff Mum and Dad listen to on the radio. He uses everyday language to tell me, his girlfriend, to stop messing around. I can feel his pain, I can hear it in his raspy voice; he can't hide it. He seesaws between bravado and vulnerability, trying to act cool but occasionally losing control. And it's all my fault. It makes me feel so powerful, affecting a boy this way – it's intoxicating. I ache to tell him, *I'm so sorry I hurt you, John, I'll never do it again.* I have a funny feeling between my legs, it feels good. I play the song over and over again for an hour until Kristina can't stand it any more and takes me home.

I already know 'You Can't Do That' by heart and sing it to myself as I trail my hand along the privet hedges, pulling off the leaves and digging my thumbnail into the rubbery green flesh every time I get to the chorus, 'Ooooh, you can't do that!' I can still hear John Lennon's voice in my head. Not a scary rumble like my dad's, but familiar and approachable, a bit nasal, like mine. That's it! He's like me, except a *boy.* Through tree-lined streets, past the terraced houses, I float, catching glimpses of those other, happier, families through the illuminated squares of their little brick boxes. But today I'm not jealous, I'm not looking in windows for comfort any more. Under lamp posts and cherry trees I glide, stepping on the cracks between the paving stones and squashing pink blossom under my Clarks sandals – I no longer have time for childish things. Until today I thought life was always going to be made up of sad, angry grown-ups, dreary music, stewed meat, boiled vegetables, church and school. Now everything's changed: I've found the meaning of life, hidden in the grooves of a flat black plastic disc. I promise myself I will get to that new world, but I don't know how to make it happen. What, or who, could possibly help me get closer to that parallel universe? I look up and down the street as if someone might pop out of a doorway and whisk me away, but all I can see are houses, houses, houses, stretching off into infinity. I feel sick. I hate them.

7 CHIC

1965

It's a Sunday afternoon, I have long, straight, light brown hair and a fringe tickling my eyelashes. I'm wearing a purple corduroy mini skirt, my grey school jumper, knee-length white socks and black school shoes. I am eleven years old and my dad and I are walking along Muswell Hill Broadway, past the Wimpy Bar, where I always stop and look longingly at the faded, greenish photos of Wimpy burgers and chips in the window. I've only been in there once. I loved everything about it. The red plastic chairs all joined together, the plain white tiled walls, which look so modern and clean compared to my home. The chips, so thin there's no room for any potato inside, just crispy golden sticks. The rubbery meat of the burger, I liked that it wasn't like real meat, didn't look like part of an animal. My teeth bounced off the brown disc in a very satisfying way. It was like eating a toy, made-up and fun. Fantasy food. Perfect for a picky eater like me, uniform, bland, no surprises.

Next we pass the toyshop, where I choose my Christmas present every year, and the school-uniform shop, where we buy the maroon skirt, yellow blouse and grey jumper every September. Muswell Hill is my universe. Today we've been to Cherry Tree Woods to play on the swings and Dad has bought me a *Jackie* comic. I feel relaxed with him for the first time in ages, I slip my arm through his and say:

'Daddy, I want to be a pop singer when I grow up.'

There, it's out, I've dared to voice my dream, to say it out loud. Dad is the only adult I know who has some interest in music, even if it is Petula Clark, and now I've told him, I've taken the first step towards making my dream real. Dad will know what to do, how to get me started, point me in the right direction.

'You're not chic enough.'

I don't know what the word *chic* means but I know what *he* means. I understand from the tone of his voice that I'm having ideas about myself that are way above my looks, capabilities and charms, and I believe him. He must be right, he's my father.

Dad and I walk along in silence. I think, *He didn't ask me if I can sing* – but obviously that doesn't matter. I'm just not chic enough.

8 JOHN AND YOKO

I grew up with John Lennon at my side, like a big brother. When I first heard him sing, I had no idea what he looked like, what he wore, that there was a group of cool-looking guys in the band with him: nothing. The music and the words said it all.

Year by year, he unfolded to me, and he did not disappoint. He just went on getting better and better. He kept changing his clothes and hair, experimented with drugs, spiritual enlightenment, religion and psychology, and the music got more sophisticated, record by record. Then he met Yoko Ono. At last there was a girl in my life who intrigued and inspired me. The English press hated Yoko, but I was fascinated by her and so were my friends. We thought she was fantastic. She wore a white mini dress and white knee-length boots to her wedding. I read her book, *Grapefruit*, she had ideas that I had never encountered before; her thoughts and her concepts were like mind-altering drugs to me. A poem would consist of one word. Simple doodles were art. Her philosophical statements and instructions made me think differently about how to live my life. I liked that the Beatles – well, John and Paul (who was with Jane Asher then) – dated women with ideas, who had interesting faces and strong personalities (the Stones were all dating dazzling beauties). When John and Yoko took their clothes off for the *Two Virgins* picture, their sweet, normal bodies all naked and wobbly were shocking because they were so imperfect. It was an especially brave move for Yoko; her body was dissected and derided by the press. But I got it. At last, a girl being interesting and brave.

I thought John was funny, clever and wise. The only problem

with him being my muse was that he was so open about his emotions – he wrote and talked about his mother, Yoko, even his *aunt*, all the time, acknowledging how important women were in his life – so I assumed all boys were like this – and to my huge disappointment, almost none of them were or are.

9 GONE

1965

My mother, sister and I arrive back home on a Saturday afternoon in late August after staying with my aunty for two weeks. Mum and I dump our plastic bags and rucksacks in the hall whilst my sister races upstairs to say hello to Dad. We hear her charging in and out of rooms and banging doors: she's very excited, it's the first time we've been away for years. Then her voice, a little panicky, shouts from the top of the stairs:

'He's gone!'

I run up, Mum follows, all three of us stand staring at the door to my father's study, which is always kept locked, but today is hanging open. We are never allowed in there, so it takes us a moment to shuffle forward and peep round the door. His precious study is completely empty. The wooden desk with sharp corners he made, the turquoise Anglepoise lamp, the books on engineering, the ties hanging on the back of the door, all gone. We walk back into the hallway and look around. Pictures have disappeared from the walls, the big trunk with all the photographs has vanished, and gradually we realise loads of stuff is missing – it feels like a robbery. My sister and I look at Mum, waiting for her to make sense of it. We have no doubt she will make sense of it: she makes sense of everything.

'Oh thank goodness for that, he's gone,' she says, smiling. 'What a relief.'

My sister and I laugh nervously. We are not convinced. We don't take our eyes off Mum's face for a second, looking for a flicker of doubt in her expression. When we're sure that she's OK, we relax and agree, yes, it's great that the big hairy nuisance has gone. It's all perfectly normal and right. Let's go and make a cup of tea!

Mum must have been so shocked to discover Dad had done a bunk – even if things were going badly, it's never nice to be deserted. I wonder how much self-control and acting (mothers are very underrated actors) it took for her to quickly arrange her features into a composed expression and modify her voice so she sounded calm and reassuring. Or maybe it was all planned? Maybe it was arranged that we'd go away for two weeks whilst Dad packed up and left. When I ask Mum she refuses to talk about it. I don't want to upset her, so I'll just have to live with the not knowing.

10 THE KINKS

The Kinks were a guiding light to me when I was young. I went to the same schools as them, junior, secondary and art school. As I went into Year One of secondary school at eleven years old, the bassist Pete Quaife's younger brother was just leaving, so there was quite a big age gap, but I followed in their wake, and I was very aware of every move they made ahead of me.

Everyone in Muswell Hill seemed to have a vague connection to them, even my mum. She worked at Crouch End library and Dave Davies's girlfriend – a beautiful natural blonde – worked there too. Mum used to come home with tales of how volatile Dave was.

In junior school I'd ask the teachers, 'Did you teach them? What were they like? Do you think you might have any of their old exercise books at home?' I was extremely curious, much more so than I was in any lessons. I didn't aspire to be a musician – there wasn't that equality at the time, it was inconceivable that a girl could cross over into male territory and be in a band.

When I got to secondary school, people were much more interested in them: the older boys dressed like them, long hair in side or front partings, very low-cut hipster trousers – we called them bumsters – and stack-heeled boots. The young male teachers dressed like that too. To Muswell Hill kids, the Kinks were heroes, they came from the same place as us and they made something of themselves.

11 SHIT AND BLOOD

Shitting and bleeding. Always had a problem with shit and blood. The English love to talk about shitting, so other nationalities can skip this bit. Also any potential boyfriend, anyone who fancies me, please skip this bit too.

When I was four I started school, a year earlier than normal, I don't know why. Everyone in the class was a year older than me – a couple of years later I had to be kept back a year to be with my own age group. I kicked and screamed from the moment my mother and I reached the school gate, all the way through the corridors, to the door of my classroom. Every morning I did this, because I was scared: I didn't want to leave my sister and my mother. It was too soon, I was traumatised, but I couldn't express this in any way except through tears.

Because I was so young and so shy, I was too nervous to put my hand up and ask to be excused to go to the lavatory during class, so after trying to hold it in as long as possible, I did it in my pants. The choice between raising my hand and my voice whilst the teacher was talking or quietly soiling myself was not an easy one, but I chose the option I could bear. I was such a baby that I didn't think anyone would notice. This happened often. When I got home, Mum would be sympathetic, clean me up and give me a cuddle – except one day she didn't. This time she was cross; there was no sympathy, she stormed out to the garden, picked up a rough stick and scraped the poo off my bum and legs, telling me that she'd had enough. That scraping really hurt my legs, my pride and my feelings. I never did it again.

I was a hypersensitive child – always watching and listening out for people's moods and their fluctuations – and a small thing like the anticipation of school every morning would set me off with diarrhoea, right up until I was sixteen. I wasn't bullied at school, thank god, it was just that tiny little things made me anxious, like if someone was walking behind me as I walked in – I was self-conscious, it made my gait stiffen and I couldn't walk properly, that sort of thing.

My period started the day before my thirteenth birthday. I went ballistic. I howled like a banshee, I shouted, I slammed doors – I was furious, crazed, ranting and murderous for days. This thing that had happened to me was totally unacceptable. I hated it, I didn't want it, but I had no control over it. I couldn't bear to live if it meant going through life bleeding every month and being weak and compromised. It was so unfair.

I went on creating a scene every time I had a period for the next four years until they only appeared a couple of times a year. I don't know if this was the triumph of my will over my body, or if it would have happened anyway. I thought my cycle was affected because I was so traumatised. I still went mad every time it showed up, even though it wasn't that often. Having periods changed my personality: from the first one onwards I was resentful and angry inside, I felt cheated and I knew to the core of my being that life was unfair and boys had it easier than girls. A burning ball of anger and rebelliousness started to grow within me. It's fuelled a lot of my work.

As I got older and started having sex, I would anxiously be looking for blood to come instead of wishing it away. Eventually I went on the pill, but was hopelessly undisciplined and always forgetting it. After the pill, I had the coil (it was called a Copper 7). I could feel it wedged there inside me at the top of my cervix. It hurt. I hobbled around for months, because I couldn't be bothered to sort it out and I thought maybe this was what it was supposed to feel like. About a year later I went to the Marie Stopes Clinic in Soho – you could ask for a female doctor there – and they removed it. The doctor said it had become dislodged. I felt a wave of relief pass through my whole body as soon as the coil was removed, like I was returning to normal, the first time I'd felt like myself for a year.

Shit and blood (I'll get on to them again later) have dominated and punctuated my life since I was a child. I'm still scared of blood, seeing it, not seeing it. 'Is it old blood or fresh blood?' the doctors always ask. Is there a right answer to that question?

12 TOO COOL FOR SCHOOL

1969–1971

Music lessons at my comprehensive school are so boring that we liven them up by trying to make the teacher run out of the room crying. We bang the desk lids and chant, 'Out out out.' Works every time. There are individual music lessons as well; we have the choice of nursery rhymes on the recorder or classical music on violin. Only the uncool kids play an instrument. I'm not interested. I don't connect music lessons with the music I'm listening to, they're worlds apart.

The only teacher who makes music interesting is the RE teacher, a Peter and Gordon lookalike with thick ginger hair, black horn-rimmed glasses and a polo-necked jumper. He tries to get us interested in moral issues through music. Sometimes we're allowed to bring a record in and spend the lesson dissecting the lyrics. People bring in all sorts of stuff: King Crimson, Motown, 'She's Leaving Home' by the Beatles, anti-Vietnam songs by Country Joe and the Fish, Hendrix and the Byrds.

Musicians are our real teachers. They are opening us up politically with their lyrics and creatively with experimental, psychedelic music. They share their discoveries and journeys with us. We can't travel far, no one I know has ever been on an aeroplane. We can't meet the Maharishi, but we learn about him through music. We hear Indian musical influences by listening to George Harrison's sitars, discover Timothy Leary, R. D. Laing, Arthur Janov and *The Primal Scream*, acid, California, Woodstock, riots . . . whatever they experience, we experience through their songs. It's true folk music – not played on acoustic guitar by a bearded bloke – but about true-life experiences.

The thing I like most about school is my group of girlfriends. They're a mixture of girls from my year, the year above and the year below. We're a gang. We roam the streets together or go to each other's houses. There's Paula, Sallie, Kester, Sue, Martha, Angela, Judie, Hilary, Myra, and sometimes there are a couple of boys, Toby and Matthew. Most of them come from shabby, bohemian, stripped-pine-furniture houses with Che Guevara posters on the walls; their parents are communists, artists and intellectuals. We're always at someone's house – not mine, my house doesn't fit in, not the right atmosphere – lounging around in someone's bedroom, stretched out on the bed or cross-legged on the floor, smoking a bit of hash pinched from an older brother or a parent. We listen to

The gang. Front: Judie, Su, Angela, Sallie. Back: Me, Paula, Kester. Note psychedelic summer uniforms. 1969

records, talk about school, music and boys. If the parents are out, we go downstairs and cook an omelette, sometimes we go to the cinema but usually we wander round Hampstead Heath: it's free.

We wear very short skirts, just six inches long, or jeans and a T-shirt. None of us has many clothes. We all have long hair parted in the middle and don't wear makeup; there are no grooming sessions, nail-painting, hair-dyeing parties, none of that sort of thing. Our feet are black and hard from walking around Muswell Hill barefoot, our fingernails short and functional.

In my fourth year of school I'm allowed out of school at lunchtime, so I go round my friend Judie's house every day. She has an older brother called Reuben and he has a friend called Mark Irvin. Me and Mark fall in love. I'm fifteen, he's seventeen, my first proper boyfriend. We kiss and cuddle on Judie's bed and listen to music all the time: Syd Barrett, Motown, King Crimson, Pink Floyd. At the weekend we go to gigs in pubs and take acid and Mandrax ('Randy Mandies') on Hampstead Heath. We're known at school as a cool couple, we go everywhere together. One day I'm on my way to school early because I've got an exam. I see Mark walking ahead hand in hand with my friend Cathy. It's so early in the morning they must have spent the night together. I feel like I've been smacked in the chest with an iron bar. I choke, I can't breathe. It can't be true. I turn and run. I run and run. I run to the other entrance of the school, about half a mile away. I'm late for my exam. I try to concentrate. Mustn't let them ruin my future.

I manage to avoid Cathy and Mark for a couple of days. I'm devastated – the first boy I've ever loved, ever trusted has betrayed me. Cathy comes up to me in the gym, 'I'm sorry, it was a terrible mistake. He loves you not me, he talks about you all the time. It's over.' Me and Mark get back together. We haven't had sex yet so it's easier to forgive him.

We go out together for years, we go to youth hostels, visit Cathy in Wales (she's moved there with her new boyfriend). We take acid on the Gower Peninsula; once when the drug was just kicking in, 'Here Comes the Sun' by the Beatles was on the record player and I sang along with it. Mark said, 'You have a beautiful voice.' That's the first time anyone ever said something nice about my voice. I'll never forget it, although I'm not sure it counts, seeing as he was tripping on acid at the time. Mark took my virginity, I bled a tiny bit. It felt right, though, that it was him. He also took my art O level, did all the preliminary drawings for me. I felt a bit guilty afterwards because I got an A, a higher mark than he got for his own art O level. Love.

Mark (Magnus)

When I get to the fifth year at school, I have the terrible realisation that I've left it too late to do well. I've mucked about, bunked off and not done my homework for so many years that the teachers won't put me in for some of the exams. The boys I like are clever and in the top streams, and I'm a wastrel. At night I'm haunted by anxious recurring dreams, I'm wandering the school corridors not knowing where the rooms for my lessons are and arriving at the school gates in my pyjamas as everyone else is leaving: an outsider, a failure, always going against the flow.

Eventually I'm expelled. I foolishly admit I smoked dope once to a prying teacher – of course I've done it a lot more than once, at least I'm not completely stupid. My mother goes up to the school and insists that the headmaster puts in writing that I've smoked hash once, and that's why he's expelling me. He doesn't want to do that so I'm allowed to stay.

One morning a sixth-former comes into our English class-room. I'm sixteen and taking my O levels soon. I love English, Mr Hazdell's such a great teacher, he looks like Biggles with a huge handlebar moustache, and is full of enthusiasm for Shakespeare – he interprets the plays, brings them to life, makes me love the language. The sixth-former says something to Mr Hazdell and he looks up at me: 'Viviane, the headmaster wants to see you in his office.' Everyone swivels round to look at me. I'm scared. *Has somebody died?* I feel important as I walk to the door. *Not Mum. God wouldn't take Mum. That would be too much.*

I go to the office. My sister's waiting there, we knock. 'Come in.' Mr Lowe looks at us kindly, he's quite a nice man. 'Your father's here. He's in the office next door and wants to see you very much.'

I'm shocked. We haven't seen Dad for years, barely ever think of him – he's written a couple of silly long letters over the past few years, long-winded, emotional, boring – why has he come to school? We don't want to see him; we'd be betraying Mum, espe-cially here, without her permission or a discussion. Not that I need to discuss it, I know what Mum's feelings are on the matter: we're a unit of three now, struggling along together, negotiating life with no money and he's no part of it. There's no way we're going to see him. I don't even ask my sister, I speak for her: we don't want to see our father. Mr Lowe tries to persuade us. 'He's very upset, he only wants to see you for a few minutes, he says your mother won't let him see you.' I tell him it isn't our mother, we don't want to see him. Mr Lowe's got no idea what she's been through, what she sacrifices to bring us up on her own. I won't have anyone judging my mum, saying she's bad, blaming her.

Mr Lowe leaves the room. My sister and I sit in silence, there's nothing to say. I'm resentful that Dad's on my turf, that he's interrupted my lessons and I've been singled out. It's too much for me, this awkwardness, this grown-up pain, this fucked-up relationshipbetween Mum and Dad.

The headmaster comes back. 'Your father's in tears – are you sure you won't see him? Please have another think about it.' Don't make me say it again, I may look sure and hard but this is agony. We know those French crocodile tears, after a strapping, after a shouting, after he's gone back on a promise. We know more than you know, Mr Lowe. There's nothing more he can do. He sends our father away.

13 WOODCRAFT FOLK

1967–1970

The Woodcraft Folk is a youth organisation, a bit like Brownies or Scouts but it mixes boys and girls together and has an arty, bohemian vibe. It's nothing to do with making things from wood, more about living in the open air, close to nature. It's a relief to go to Woodcraft, I feel more at home in this world, mixing with these interesting, open-minded people. The uniform is a thick, forest-green cotton shirt, which we wear oversized and untucked, with a mini skirt or jeans. We call the adults in charge 'leaders' and address them by their Christian names – this is the first time I'm allowed to call an adult by their first name. At Woodcraft children are treated like people, not half-formed irrelevant creatures, we are consulted on every decision that's made. We are divided into 'Elfins' for the young members, 'Pioneers' for the middle age group and 'Venturers' for the older ones.

Every summer there's a big meeting of all the different Woodcraft groups from across London, like a conference. Robin Chaphekar – a handsome boy from the Highgate group – has an electric guitar with him, and spelled out on the case in red and yellow tape is *Safe as Milk*. I keep thinking about it, such an odd phrase, what does it mean? Does it mean his guitar is as safe as milk in a milk bottle, tucked up in the fridge? Or like the free milk you get at junior school? Surely not: that's not very rock 'n' roll. I ask a few people if they know what the slogan means but nobody does. I'm too shy to ask Robin. About a month later I'm in a record shop in Crouch End and see the record, *Safe as Milk* by Captain Beefheart, in the racks. I buy it and as soon as I get home I put it on. I love the way Beefheart plays with his voice, he lets go and messes around with it in such an unselfconscious way. The music is experimental but accessible – my favourite combination – it sounds like pop music, all the songs are short with strong choruses and melodies but they're undermined by Beefheart's deranged singing. He shouts and squawks about 'Electricity', 'The Zig Zag Wanderer' and 'Abba Zaba'.

Woodcraft teaches us survival skills, how to make a campfire, hiking, how to save a life, is educational about global poverty, conflict and the peace movement – but for me, what it's really all about is snogging boys. Meeting boys like Robin Chaphekar is the real reason I go to a school hall and prance about country dancing every Friday night. Most of the boys are gorgeous, they have long hair and are a bit wild and lots of them play guitar. We go camping on weekends, in a field in the middle of a traffic roundabout in South Mimms. We all sit round the campfire at night, someone plays guitar – *one guy who did this was Mike Rosen, later the famous children's author* – and we sing protest songs about the Vietnam war, immigration and other social problems closer to home. My favourite songs are Ewan MacColl's 'Dirty Old Town', Buffy Sainte-Marie's 'Welcome, Welcome Emigrante' and a folk song about the atom bomb, 'I Come and Stand at Every Door'.

After 'lights out', we sneak into each other's tents for a snog and to feel each other up until a leader or Venturer comes round with a torch and sends the interloper back to their own tent. In the morning we're punished with a job like emptying the 'lats' (latrines) – buckets of shit and piss – into the cesspit.

Before I went to the Muswell Hill branch of Woodcraft, I went to the Hampstead branch for a couple of sessions because there weren't any free spaces in Muswell Hill. I dyed an old white shirt apple-green for the occasion and wore a tiny green mini skirt. I felt very out of my depth when I walked into the hall. I'd never seen such cool-looking kids before. I realised Hampstead kids were way cooler than Muswell Hill kids, I felt overdressed, like I'd made too much effort. I stood on the edge of the room and watched them run about. Both the girls and the boys had long tangled dirty hair and wore Levi's and scruffy Converse trainers. They raced around the room shouting and laughing. Only one girl spoke to me, Clio. She had waist-length blonde hair and was very beautiful. Then it was as if the seas parted, everyone seemed to scatter as this boy walked into the hall. He was taller than everyone else and carried himself with a poise and dignity I'd never seen on a young person before, shoulders back, chin up but relaxed, not arrogant. He radiated confidence. He had longish brown hair just below his ears, a strong nose, he was the most handsome boy I'd ever seen. He looked like a young Greek god amongst mere mortals. I stood transfixed and a voice came into my head, *That's the kind of boy I want to marry.* His name was Ben Barson, the most popular boy in Woodcraft and a self-taught virtuoso piano player (*brother of Mikey Barson, later in the group Madness*).

Ben

The boy I most fancy after Ben Barson is Nic Boatman, the naughtiest and cutest boy at Woodcraft. Once when me and Nic were kissing and touching each other on a bed in someone's house, he put his hand inside my knickers and I orgasmed immediately just from the newness of the experience. Well, I think it was an orgasm, it felt like a big twitch and then I wasn't interested in being touched any more.

Paul, Nic (age fourteen), me (age thirteen) and Maggie in a tent on a Woodcraft camping trip to Yugoslavia, 1968

14 MUSIC MUSIC MUSIC

1967–1972

The music I was exposed to when I was growing up was revolutionary and because I grew up with music that was trying to change the world, that's what I still expect from it.

I heard most new music through friends and whenever I went out I'd have a record under my arm – not mine, usually I was returning it. The record you carried let everyone know what type of person you were. If it was a rare record, cool people would stop you in the street to talk to you about it. One good thing about not having a phone was that it was difficult for people to remind you to give them their records back, they had to trek round to your house and hope you were in if they wanted it that badly-and then you could always not answer the door. (Mum taught us never to answer the door, the minute the doorbell rang we all froze. If you were near a window, you had to duck under the sill and try not to disturb the curtains. We all knew the drill: wait motionless until the ringing stops and the person goes away. She was worried it would be a social worker. They kept coming round after the divorce.)

Music brought the war in Vietnam right into our bedrooms. Songs we heard from America made us interested in politics; they were history lessons in a palatable, exciting form. We demonstrated against the Vietnam and Korean wars, discussed sexual liberation, censorship and pornography and read books by Timothy Leary, Hubert Selby Jr (*Last Exit to Brooklyn*) and Marshall McLuhan because we'd heard all these people referred to in songs or interviews with musicians. My pin-ups were the political activist and 'Yippie' Abbie Hoffman and Che Guevara. Music, politics, literature, art all crossed over and fed into each other. There were some great magazines around too, the sex magazine *Forum*, *International Times*, *Spare Rib*, *Oz*, *Rave* and *Nova*. Even though we couldn't afford to travel, we felt connected to other countries because ideas and events from those places reached us through music and magazines.

The first band I ever saw live was the Edgar Broughton Band at the Hampstead Country Club, behind Belsize Park tube station. I sat in the front row on a little wooden chair with a couple of older boys I'd met. I'd never heard live music before and I couldn't get my ears around it. I didn't know how to listen to it. Up until then everything I'd heard had been produced, was on a record. There was a speaker right next to my head and all the sounds meshed together, I couldn't differentiate between them. The band thrashed at their instruments and screamed, '*Out demons out!*' It was deafening.

WhenI was fourteen I heard there was going to be an anti-war demonstration with famous people giving speeches in Trafalgar Square. It was the thing to go to, as exciting as a rock concert. I hoped there'd be lots of handsome boys there. I spent all Saturday morning before the demo tie-dyeing a white T-shirt black, stirring it round and round with an old wooden spoon in a large aluminium pot on the stove. Mum said, 'Hurry up, you'll miss it! Just wear any old thing, it doesn't matter.' But I had to look right. The T-shirt came out great, dark grey rather than black, with a white tie-dyed circle in the middle, a bit like the CND peace sign. I sewed black fringes down the sides of my black cord jeans and washed my hair by kneeling over the bath, drying it in front of the open oven with my head upside down so it would look full and wild. Then off me and my friend Judie went to the demo, chanting, 'Hey hey, LBJ, how many kids have you killed today?' at the top of our voices. We got off the bus and ran down Haymarket towards Trafalgar Square. When we got there it was completely deserted. The paving stones were covered in litter, empty bottles rolled around, leaflets were blowing in the wind. No people, just pigeons. We'd been so long messing around with our clothes that we'd missed the whole thing. We were only disappointed for a minute, then we jumped in one of the fountains and chased each other around. A policeman told us off, said if we didn't stop he'd arrest us and tell our parents. We were scared of going to prison, so we ran off to the bus stop. Sitting on the top deck of the bus, the fringes on my jeans all straggly, my hair damp and flat and the dye from my wet T-shirt leaving grey streaks across my arms, I thought, *What a great day!*

One of the strangest bands I saw around this time was Third Ear Band at the Queen Elizabeth Hall. I found out about them through listening to John Peel on the radio, he was always mentioning them. He played on their record *Alchemy*. The music was over my head, really difficult, but I understood the ideas – experimentation, pushing boundaries and not conforming to musical clichés. I stared at the stage, I couldn't tell if one of the players in the band was male or female, the tall skinny one with long black hair; I stared and stared at this one hoping and hoping that they were female. I left without knowing as she or he had their head down the whole time.

Me and my friend Zaza went to see Third Ear Band again (even though they were very experimental, they played all over the place and had a big following) in July 1969 when I was fifteen. They opened for the Rolling Stones at the 'Stones in the Park' free concert in 'the cockpit' – the big dip in the grass in Hyde Park. King Crimson were on too.

Zaza was a year older than me and insane about music. She was strikingly beautiful, natural, never wore makeup (nor did I), long shiny black hair, always wore clean jeans and a cool T-shirt, never *ever* a skirt. For the concert I wore a long, pale lemon lace dress from the 1930s, it fitted like it was made for me. It was completely see-through and I wore a short mauve slip under it. I loved that the hem trailed in the dirt so it was muddy and frayed. As usual I had bare feet. Zaza and I couldn't get near the stage, so we sat down on the grass towards the back. The atmosphere was laden with sadness because Brian Jones, the Stones' guitarist, had died in a swimming pool two days before. He'd recently been chucked out of the Stones and replaced by Mick Taylor – it felt like they replaced god: how could they do that? Me and Zaza thought Brian probably committed suicide because he was so upset. We wondered how the Stones were going to handle the whole thing, if they'd ignore it or if they even cared that he was dead. Everyone around us was talking about it: *Do the rest of the Stones feel guilty? How does Mick Taylor feel? Will he appear?*

Mick Jagger drifted onto the stage wearing a diaphanous white dress with floaty bell sleeves over white flared trousers. The dress said it all. *We are the Stones. We're shocking but we're also caring and gentle. We will honour and acknowledge Brian's life and death, but in our own way. Black mourning clothes are for straights.* Mick read a poem and then released thousands of white butterflies over the crowd, they fluttered over our heads into the park. We were part of a big moment in history and we knew it. It was like we were at Brian Jones's funeral; the Stones shared this moment with us. During one song, Jagger strutted to the front of the stage and the girls in the front row reached out to touch him. He grabbed Mick Taylor and pulled him to the front, making Taylor sit down beside him on the edge of the stage, and gestured to the girls to touch the guitarist too. Taylor looked mortified, he hung his head down and just kept playing. I felt a terrible pain on the top of my foot, in between my toes. Someone was stubbing a cigarette out on it, we were so tightly packed together he didn't realise. It didn't matter. When the show was finished, me and Zaza walked back through the park, trying to avoid squashing the dying butterflies under our feet. There were so many of them.

Another great free concert was when Fleetwood Mac played an all-nighter on Parliament Hill Fields. My friend Hilary and I climbed out of the bedroom window of her mum's flat in Highgate at 10 p.m. and walked along Southwood Lane then up Highgate Hill, across the fields, towards the corrugated-iron bandstand. Loads of like-minded people were walking along the roads even though it was so late. We felt special that it was happening in our area; we knew Highgate and the Heath back to front. More and more people arrived, hundreds of us. We got talking to two nice boys and hung out with them all evening. Fleetwood Mac came on at midnight. They played *Albatross*; it was like being in an open-air church, the sad guitar crying out over the black trees . . . we lay on our backs and stared up at the sky, transported away from North London by this haunting, elevating music. It was the most magical experience I'd ever had.

Fleetwood Mac only played a couple of songs before the atmosphere was ruined by skinheads running down the hill and throwing things. The concert was stopped, so we went home. The two nice boys walked with us. Me and Hilary played knock down ginger, ringing the doorbells of the fancy white houses and then running away. The boys, who were a bit older than us, weren't so keen. As we all charged down the hill, 'my one' held his hair down as he ran. Completely turned me off. Couldn't wait to get rid of him after that.

Marc Bolan was the most important man in my life for a year. I think what appealed to me most was his prettiness. He was sexual – pouting and licking and throwing his hips forwards – but he wasn't at all threatening to young girls. It was a new thing for men to be so delicate and pretty and overtly sexual at the same time. Marc was almost a girl. He wore girls' tap shoes from the dance shop Anello and Davide in pretty colours, had long ringletty hair, glitter around his eyes and a cupid's bow mouth: you could almost be him. He wasn't scary to fantasise about, you could be dominant or dominate him, he wasn't the kind of guy who would jump on you or hurt you. Fantasising about Marc Bolan (or any pop star) was a great way to discover your sexuality, a safe way in.

Listening to T. Rex was one of the first times I actually noticed guitar playing (apart from Peter Green and George Harrison). Bolan's riffs were so catchy and cartoony – combined with a very distinctive guitar sound – that I would find myself singing the parts. Girls didn't usually listen out for guitar solos and riffs, that was a male thing – *wow that was so fast, wow that was a really obscure scale, wow the way he bends the notes*. I used to listen to the lyrics and the melody of songs, not dissect the instruments. I couldn't bear Hendrix's playing at the time, it was so in your face and he was so overtly sexual, it was intimidating. I remember saying to my cousin Richard, 'The only words I can make out in this song are "'Scuse me while I kiss the sky."' He said, 'I don't even know that many.' He was a huge Hendrix fan and he didn't know one word of any of his songs.

I followed T. Rex around London with Zaza. We used to go to every gig. We couldn't actually go to the concerts – we only saw

Bolan play twice because we were broke – but we used to stand outside the stage door and try to talk to him or June Child, his wife. We were fascinated by June – I changed my name to Viv Child for a while. I saw pictures in *Melody Maker* of a mad hatters' tea party her and Marc had in their garden – I was so jealous – they were in top hats and beautiful clothes, they'd set up tables and chairs under the trees, it was a different world. June was much more interesting to me than other rock girlfriends because she wasn't druggy and she worked in a record company. Me and Zaza talked to her once outside the Lyceum, she stopped and had a few words with us, but she didn't like it when we talked to Marc, she'd call him away – 'Marc! Come on. We have to go in now.'

I remember John Peel playing 'Ride a White Swan' on his radio show late one night. The next morning I was going away on a Woodcraft camp to Yugoslavia (we usually went to communist countries) for a couple of weeks, and I said to Mum, 'That song is going to be a hit.' I thought it was great, I liked it better than his old folky fairy stuff, it was catchier, more of a pop song. When I got back from Yugoslavia two weeks later it had entered the charts and ten weeks later it was at number two. It was January

1971 and I was seventeen years old. Lots of my male friends were appalled that I liked T. Rex and pop music, but I love a good song. Whatever its genre, a good song is a good song.

David Bowie's album *Hunky Dory* was full of good songs,I played it to lots of people at school. One Turkish boy said, 'Viv, his voice really turns me on. I think I might be gay.'

I'd made a friend called Alan Drake, from Southgate, he was very pretty with long straight dark brown hair and sensual lips: we discovered Bowie together. We saw him loads of times in little college halls. The best time was in the Great Hall (not very big) at Imperial College in South Kensington on 12 February 1972. Bowie was wearing tight white silk trousers and a patterned silk bomber jacket open to his waist, showing his bony hairless chest. Mick Ronson, the guitarist, looked uncomfortable in his flamboyant clothes, like a docker dressed up; he was too masculine, couldn't carry off the androgyny. I didn't know he was a brilliant guitarist, I just thought he couldn't pull off the look.

Halfway through the show, Bowie climbed into the audience. I don't know where he picked that up from, no one else I'd seen did that. None of us got it though, we didn't realise you were supposed to lift him up and carry him along, everyone parted politely, thought he was off to the bog or something, and he fell on the floor, it was embarrassing. The gig wasn't very crowded, so there weren't enough people to do it anyway. He got up and walked around a bit. I leaned against the stage, trying to see where he'd gone, but the lights were in my eyes. Then I felt a hand grip my shoulder and Bowie heaved himself up on me. I nearly buckled – I wasn't expecting it, I didn't know what was happening. He climbed over me to get back on stage, kneeing me in the chest and treading on my head with his silk boxing boot – he didn't care – he just had to get back up. He's not as dainty as he looks.

Zaza and I went to loads of Hawkwind gigs too. She liked them more than me, and she'd chat to Dave Brock, the guitarist and synth player, before a show. I was too shy and just hung back behind her but he was very kind and friendly. There was a pretty girl with them called Stacia who danced completely naked whilst they played; she'd paint her body and light projections would swirl over her skin. We chatted to her a few times and she was very friendly too. Hawkwind got to recognise me and Zaza and often gave us a lift back into central London in the back of their van. They never made a move on us or said anything sexual, they were very gentlemanly. Only once did one of them ask for my phone number, he was the new bass player, but I didn't have a phone so he gave me his. I never called. I met him years later when the Slits filmed a video at his recording studio in Wales. His name was Thomas Crimble and he was married to a girl called Nutkin. I reminded him (when Nutkin wasn't around) of that drive in the van, he thought for a minute then said, 'Yes, yes, I remember!' It was obvious he didn't though.

Once me and Zaza were so bored that we decided to hitch-hike across London, anywhere it took us. We ended up at the Hard Rock Café in Marble Arch. It hadn't been open long and we wanted to have a look at it. We went in and looked at the menu but the burgers were so expensive – they were ten times the price of a Wimpy – we pretended we were just looking around and didn't want to eat there. We hung around outside, sticking our thumbs out, trying to get a lift back home. A bunch of guys came out of the cafe and said they were going to get their van and they'd give us a lift a bit further into town. They were in a band called America. Funny-looking lot, checked shirts, denim flares, a bit country bumpkin-ish; very sweet though. They were going to a party and asked us if we wanted to come. We said, 'No thanks, just drop us here in Shaftesbury Avenue at this cafe, the Lucky Horseshoe.' We often went there, sometimes they gave us free soup. We sat down and watched the van drive away. Then we looked at each other. *Are we mad? What were we thinking? We've got nothing in the world to do, nowhere to go, no money and we've turned down a party with an American group who have a hit with 'Horse with no Name'.* It took us months to get over that missed opportunity.

RAINBOW THEATRE
FINSBURY PARK
presents
KING CRIMSON
Chrysalis IN CONCERT
EVENING 7-30
FRIDAY, OCT. 26th, 1973
CIRCLE
75p incl. VAT
R53
TO BE RETAINED FOR ...TIONS OF SALE SEE OVER

I felt so near to and yet so far from music. I thought that actually *being* a musician was something you were born to, a gift you either had or didn't have. A few of my girlfriends had parents or sisters that were classical musicians: I saw them practising five hours a day and knew I wasn't the sort of person to work that hard at anything. It looked like drudgery, plodding up and down scales for hours on end. As for people I knew who played electric guitar, I thought it was something you had to have a willy to do, or at least be a genius like Joni Mitchell or worthy like Joan Baez – and preferably American of course. I liked the look of Liquorice and Rose, the two girls in the Incredible String Band, but the whole set-up seemed a bit cliquey. No way in there. Melanie was fun, but eccentric, with her wobbly voice and clever lyrics. Sandie Shaw was more ordinary; she worked in an office before she was discovered and had a working-class London accent – but she was a singer and didn't play an instrument.

To keep my mind occupied, I fantasised about musicians. There was nothing else to think about. We had no TV, and there was nothing on it anyway, I wasn't missing much. (We eventually got a second-hand black-and-white set but the living room was so cold that we had to sit under a pile of old army coats, blankets and sleeping bags to watch it. It just wasn't worth the effort.) A children's feature film came out in the cinema once a year at Christmas, not many people had telephones (landlines), there was nowhere to go: youth clubs were a joke and I wasn't interested in lessons, except art and English. Music and guys in bands were a way to let your imagination loose. I'd fantasise that Donovan or John Lennon was my brother, or that I'd bump into Scott Walker and he'd fall in love with me; cooking up an interesting world in my head.

I studied record covers for the names of girlfriends and wives. That's how I connected girls to the world I wanted to be in. I scanned the *thank you*s and the lyrics, looking for girls' names. Especially if I fancied the musician. What are these girls like who go out with poets and singers? What have they got that I haven't?

I read the book *Groupie* by Jenny Fabian and I'm ashamed to say I thought it sounded OK, being a groupie. But I knew I wasn't witty, worldly or beautiful enough to even be that. The only other way left for a girl to get into rock and roll was to be a backing singer and I couldn't sing.

Every cell in my body was steeped in music, but it never occurred to me that I could be in a band, not in a million years – why would it? Who'd done it before me? There was no one I could identify with. No girls played electric guitar. Especially not ordinary girls like me.

15 HELLO, I LOVE YOU

1970

There I went again, building up a glamorous picture of a man
who would love me passionately the minute he met me, and
all out of a few prosy nothings.

Sylvia Plath, *The Bell Jar*

I've given up on becoming a pop singer since Dad told me I wasn't
chic enough and I haven't managed to find a way to meet those
beautiful people that I see floating along Kensington High Street
every Saturday – the leggy girls with long blonde hair and astrakhan
boots holding hands with pretty boys in tapestry bell-bottoms and
plum-coloured velvet jackets – but I still daydream about falling in
love and escaping these dreary doldrums I'm stuck in.

I'm sixteen, sitting in Crouch End public library, wearing a
dress I bought from Kensington Market; it's a dark purple cotton
maxi dress with bell sleeves and a tight laced bodice. I've got no
shoes on my dirty feet.

A shadow falls across the page of the book I'm reading – *I Start
Counting*, by Audrey Erskine Lindop – I look up to see a handsome boy standing in front of me. He's a few years older than I
am, wearing a dark blue velvet jacket and a flowery shirt. He looks
at me sadly with his beautiful blue eyes. I can't believe it: this is
what I've always hoped and believed would happen – a handsome
guy looks at me and knows instantly that I'm his soul mate. I gaze
back at him. The boy doesn't speak; this is so intense I think I
might explode. Gradually I become aware he's holding something
in front of his chest. I wrench my gaze from his beautiful face and

look down. It's a newspaper. The words swim, I can't focus . . . I feel sick, it's all too much, the excitement, the romance. I look back up at him and smile, there's a slight change in his expression, a little cooler; I look down again. The headline on the paper is *Jimi Hendrix Dead.* When he sees I've registered the enormity of the occasion, the boy walks away. I'm devastated, not because Jimi Hendrix is dead, but because the messenger isn't my true love.

Sixteen years old, peroxide hair, Ravel shoes. Tan and bracelet from Greece. Blue knitted elephant, 'Ellie', just seen on bed. Not as grown up as I think. 1970

16 AMSTERDAM

1970

Me and Zaza run down Clarendon Road in Turnpike Lane, away from my tiny two-up two-down red-brick council house, past the iron gasworks and abandoned cars, towards freedom and adventure. It's the summer holidays and we're going to Amsterdam, on our own. Our rucksacks – with just a spare T-shirt and a packet of crisps at the bottom (we've forgotten to pack toothbrushes) – bounce up and down against our backs. We own one pair of jeans each – straight-legged Levi's – which we're wearing. I'm sixteen, she's seventeen. We get to the corner and look up and down the high street, wondering which way to go.

Me: 'What country's Amsterdam in?'

Zaza: 'Not sure, Belgium, I think. Or Holland.'

Me: 'Hang on, I'll ask Mum.'

I run back to the house and knock on the door.

Me: 'What country's Amsterdam in?'

Mum: 'Holland.'

I run back to Zaza, shouting, 'Holland!' We turn onto the high street, with its boarded-up shops and piles of rubbish stacked around the lamp posts, in search of a bus, a train, anything that will take us to Holland.

The journey takes two days longer than it should because we keep getting on the wrong trains and buses and have to sleep on station benches, but here we are at last, on Koningsstraat, in the middle of Amsterdam, bleary-eyed, greasy-haired and not a clue what to do next. We have enough money to buy one sandwich a day each, for a week.

We sit on a wall and watch the people go by. A girl passes, she looks a couple of years older than us, has long wavy black hair and bright blue eyes. Zaza runs after her and asks if she knows somewhere we can stay. I cringe with embarrassment but Zaza has no fear, she can make friends with anyone. The black-haired girl looks suspicious at first but Zaza soon works her charm and I see the girl's expression soften. She tells us her name's Bridey, she's Irish and she lives in a street of squats on Korte Koningsstraat: we can probably stay there.

Like two innocent children in a Grimms' fairy tale, we follow Bridey down cobbled streets, across a little humpback bridge and along a canal, whilst thousands of bicycles fly past us – and stop in front of a row of tall thin brick houses with roofs shaped like funny old hats. It all looks so foreign, funny and sweet, like a story book, not like boring old London.

The front door of one of the houses is open and we wander in. The room is dark, there are blankets pinned over the windows: I wait for my eyes to adjust. Looking down at my feet I notice the floors are bare wood and I can just make out rough scribbles and writing on the walls.

Out of the gloom, a double mattress begins to materialise and lounging on it, languishing behind a veil of smoke from a joint, like the caterpillar in *Alice in Wonderland*, is an angelic boy with long golden ringlets curling down onto his shoulders. He looks us over and smiles. 'This is Kieran,' says Bridey. Another boy is leaning against the wall, he's tall and delicate, with long dark brown hair falling into his eyes. He looks at us suspiciously through his long black lashes. His name is Maurice. Maurice wants to know who we are, and listens intently as Bridey explains that she found us on the street and we have nowhere to stay. Me and Zaza stand side by side, clasping our rucksacks to our chests, listening to Bridey's lilting voice and looking from Kieran to Maurice. One makes me think of white Milky Bar chocolate and the other deep, dark Bournville. I can't decide which I like best. Maurice isn't very friendly and says there are no extra beds.

'Maybe in one of the other houses?' says Kieran. I ask to use the bog and Bridey shows me a cupboard just off the main room. There's no door, the cracked bowl is shielded by an old blanket folded over a piece of string. I can't possibly go, I'm much too self-conscious, everyone will be able to hear. When I emerge from the cupboard, after waiting a decent amount of time, Zaza is perched on the edge of the mattress chatting away to Kieran and Bridey. Bridey rummages in her handbag and pulls out a small clear plastic bag, which she hands to Kieran. She searches again and this time produces a syringe. Zaza and I watch Bridey bustle around the room organising needles, spoons and matches. We know nothing about junkies, but it all seems perfectly normal to us, maybe it's her matter-of-fact manner. Kieran shoots up first followed by moody Maurice; they both put the needle into the crook of their arms, but Bridey does it in her foot. They don't offer us any and we don't want it. Zaza and I watch with fascination, whispering to each other that we're so lucky, falling in with such a nice bunch of people.

It's two in the morning and we're very tired. Kieran and Maurice say we can share their beds if we want to. We're not bothered, they seem harmless enough and we're used to going to parties and snogging boys we don't know. I'm not a virgin – I'm still with Mark, but he won't find out what I'm up to – Zaza is, she's waiting until she gets married, she's Greek. Zaza stays with Kieran, I sleep with Maurice in a squat further up the street. Once we're in bed, Maurice and I kiss and fumble around with each other; he apologises for not being able to get an erection because he's taken heroin, says he'll be better tomorrow when it's worn off. I'm relieved, it's been a long day. Just as I start to drift off I feel a thump on the bed, someone's climbing in with us, one of the other guys from the squat. Maurice tells him to fuck off but he won't go, says he wants a threesome. First he whines and pleads, then he switches to charm and jokes – if Maurice gives in, I'm in trouble. I climb out of the bed but where can I go in the middle of the night in Amsterdam? Zaza's in a house up the road with Kieran – what if they can't hear me knocking and don't open the door? Thank god Maurice sticks to his guns and gets rid of the other bloke. I'm going to stay with him the whole time I'm here, as a survival mechanism, to keep the wolves at bay.

I discover some amazing things in Amsterdam. Firstly, the sandwiches; they're made from the strangest bread, like I've never seen or tasted before – it's brown, but nothing like Hovis. The slices are as thick as carpet, heavy and moist, they're a meal in themselves. Another wonderful thing is that the Dutch are mad about peanut butter, which is fantastic because I am too. They have peanut butter with everything. What a great city, where they think peanut-butter sandwiches are grown-up food and sell them everywhere. My favourite combinations are peanut butter with banana or with crispy iceberg lettuce.

I wander the streets in a daze, I can't believe that such a place exists. Street performers, pavement artists, grown-up girls in pretty dresses sucking lollipops, older people in jeans with long hair, everyone's on a bicycle. It's like a playground. There's even hash for sale in the cafes.

On our last night Maurice says he can get us into a club called the Milky Way. It reminds me of the Roundhouse in Camden Town; upstairs there's a room with scarves draped over the lights, scruffy sofas and armchairs. The smell of incense, patchouli oil and hash is heady and seductive, and even though we don't smoke the joints that are passed around, Zaza and I start to feel woozy. I hear music floating up through the floorboards, I go downstairs and sit on the floor in the main hall to watch the band. They're called Bronco and the lead singer is Jess Roden. He has the most amazing voice I've ever heard, I'm captivated, I can't believe I've had to come all this way to discover him – he's from Kidderminster. When I get back to London I'm going to buy every record he's ever made.

My obsession with Jess Roden lasted years, and it was through following him I discovered Island Records and began to listen to other artists on the label, like Bob Marley, Traffic, J. J. Cale, Jimmy Cliff, Mott the Hoople, Nick Drake and Kevin Ayers. The first album I bought when I got back from Amsterdam was an Island sampler, Nice Enough to Eat. *I only had about four records because they were so expensive, but samplers were much cheaper than a normal LP, only fourteen shillings so lots of people bought them, they were important. I listened very hard to all the tracks, I never skipped songs that weren't immediately appealing to me because I wanted to make the experience of having a new record last as long as possible. This is when I became aware of a label as a stable of artists. I trusted Island's taste.*

I saw Nice Enough to Eat *in an Oxfam shop the other day, it made my heart skip a beat, like I'd unexpectedly come across a very old and dear friend that I hadn't seen for thirty years. Someone I'd told all my secrets to. The blue cover with the jumbled-up sweets spelling the bands' names was so familiar, it meant more to me than seeing a family photograph. I bought the record again of course. Couldn't leave it sitting there.*

On our way back to the squat to pack, Zaza drops a bombshell: she's been keeping a secret from me, she's not going home to London tomorrow, she's going to Istanbul to smuggle some hash back into Amsterdam . . . for five hundred quid. Five hundred quid! My god that's a fortune. She'll be rich forever. She asks me if I want to do it too: Kieran needs another courier. It's very simple, she explains, Kieran has bought us nice smart clothes, Zaza, Bridey and I will fly to Istanbul with false-bottomed suitcases full of clothes. When we get to Istanbul we dump some of the clothes (so the suitcase weighs the same), pick up the hash from a contact and bring it back to Amsterdam. They've done it loads of times, she says, it's perfectly safe, girls never get stopped, it can't go wrong. I don't hesitate: No Way. I'm going back to school to do my exams. And I'm going back because I won't risk hurting my mother by getting arrested and messing up my life. Zaza, though, has made up her mind. That night she tries on the navy suit with gold buttons and cream piping that Kieran's bought her. Bridey sweeps Zaza's hair up into a shiny black French pleat. I've never seen her look so sophisticated and grown-up.

As I doze on the train back to England, I dream of what I would spend five hundred pounds on, and wonder whether I should have gone to Istanbul after all.

I arrive back in Turnpike Lane exhausted: I've hardly slept for three weeks. Still, I've made it back in one piece. I've done some things that Mum and Mark must never know about, but no harm done, they won't find out. I snuggle down under a pile of blankets on my blue wooden childhood bed, glad I'm not on my way to Turkey to smuggle drugs – even if I am going to miss out on the money – I'm warm and safe in the bedroom I share with my little sister. The familiar off-white walls close in on me comfortingly; the rattan peacock chair I bought from Biba stands guard at the window. All is well with the world. I conk out.

Early the next morning, as I slowly come back to consciousness, I feel a little tickle at the top of my bum, right at the bottom of my spine. Something's creeping out of my bum crack and crawling up my back. It's barely perceptible but I'm quick and put my finger on it. *I'll just put whatever it is on my bedside table and squash it.*

Oooh that's annoying, I have to wake up a bit more than I want to and lean on one elbow to crush it under my thumbnail, it's quite tough, taking more effort than I thought. I'll go back to sleep and look at it when I'm awake, probably imagined it, just a piece of fluff.

But something in me knows . . . knows to have a bloody good look at it when I wake up . . . knows I'm putting off something unpleasant. I sleep fretfully for another hour, but I can't fight the unease any longer: I lean over and squint at it. Could it be an insect? Surely not. Not down there. How did it get under the covers? Hunched over my bedside table, dressed in a baggy white T-shirt and old knickers, I examine the little critter. That's funny, it looks like a tiny little . . . crab. What's a tiny little crab doing down there? Oh shit! I've got crabs!

I look into my knickers and see there is a little black dot at the base of a pubic hair. Then I realise with horror there's a little black dot at the base of *every* pubic hair. I try and pick one off. It doesn't come easily, the little bugger. I hold the speck in the palm of my hand. Phew, false alarm, it's just a tiny pale brown scab. The squat was so dirty I must have got scabs from scratching myself all the time. But as I peer at it, the little scab grows legs and scuttles off sideways. I scream. Not an 'Oh help I've seen a spider' scream, but an '*I am the host of living creatures! Evil parasites are burrowing into my flesh and sucking my blood!*' type of scream. A very serious and loud scream. A '*Kill me now, I can't bear to be conscious for one more second*' scream.

Crying hysterically, I throw myself down the stairs and into the kitchen. Mum rushes over to me. Poor innocent Mum. I have to tell her everything. The dirty squat, the boys, the sex. (I leave out the junkies, there's only so much a mother can take.) She remains calm, quietens me down, and we come up with a plan: we spread newspapers all over the kitchen table, then we get two spoons and two pairs of tweezers. Using the tweezers, we pick every crab off, one by one, even the ones in very tender hidden places – ones that I have to bend over the table for Mum to access. My humiliation is overruled by terror. We put every crab we find onto the newspaper and crush it with the back of the spoon. We do this until there are no black dots left. It takes two hours. Then I go to the chemist and get sheep dip.

Me, Mum and my sister are sitting down to tea, must be about six o'clock, when there's a ring at the door, Zaza's parents are on the doorstep, they want to know where she is. Of course they do! It never occurred to me, or Zaza, that they'd notice she hasn't come home.

'She stayed on a few extra days,' I say.

'Is she all right?'

'Yes, she's fine.'

'When will she be back?'

'The weekend,' I lie.

'If she's not back by the weekend, we're calling the police.'

And they go away, thank god.

Bloody Zaza landing me in it.

The next day, Mum sends me to the clap clinic in Praed Street, Paddington. ('It only takes a minute at the Praed Street clinic', 'Rabies (from the Dogs of Love)', the 101ers.) A nice nurse gives me a blue cotton gown and shows me where to hang my clothes, then she tells me to lie on the bed, which has a piece of white paper stretched over it. I lie down and look at the polystyrene tiles on the ceiling, daydreaming. The nurse explains patiently that I must slide my bum down the bed and put my feet through the stirrups. I start to do it, but realise this means I'll be lying on my back with my knees bent up to my chest and my legs wide open. I look at her for reassurance, *Is this really what I'm supposed to do?* She nods. I wriggle my feet through the stirrups and rest my ankles on the black nylon-webbing straps. The soles of my feet are filthy, luckily they face away from the nurse. My legs are held really wide open by the stirrups, my vagina is pointing to the door. I feel as if I'm strapped to a raft on a linoleum ocean, my ankles tied to the sides. 'Here comes the doctor,' says the nurse as the door opens. I feel so exposed, it's unbearable, I'm horrified, ashamed. I've never had my legs so wide open before, not even during sex. I've never been looked at down there before, never shown anyone, never even looked at it myself. The doctor appears. A man. He's young and handsome. Why is a young handsome man a gynaecologist? He must be a pervert. I want to die. This is the most humiliating and terrible thing that has ever happened to me (*ever happened to you so far*). I burst into tears.

I visit my boyfriend Mark a couple of times over the next few weeks. One morning I wake up at home feeling really sexy. I stretch out in my bed, feel my warm body touch the cool sheets and think, *I'm going to go to the phone box and call Mark and say I want to come over for him to draw me. I just want to lie on his bed naked, and have him look at me – not touch me – and study me and draw me. That will be so sexy.* I get dressed and go to the phone box on the corner and call him, but Mark doesn't sound very friendly or pleased to hear from me, which is odd because he loves me. I tell him my plan but he cuts me off mid-sentence and says, 'I've got crabs. You better go to the clinic. I got them from you.' Oh shit. It hadn't occurred to me that I could pass them on to Mark. I thought once I was on the medication, I was all right. Now he knows what I've been up to too.

Zaza makes it back home. It isn't until I see her in the corridor at school that I realise how scared I was about her not coming back. We go to the dining hall and she tells me that at the airport in Turkey, as she went through customs with her false-bottomed suitcase stuffed full of hash, the customs official pulled her over and said he believed she was carrying drugs and he was going to tear her suitcase apart. *She talked her way out of it.* Can you believe that? *She talked and joked her way out of going to prison in Turkey.* In the end, the official let her go and said, 'Good luck at the other end.' She has the nerve of the devil. She says she has to go to a bar in Piccadilly Circus tonight to meet Kieran and give him his share of the money. I tell her to keep it, she deserves it, but she's scared he'll come after her for it, he's got lots of dodgy mates. She asks me to go with her. We turn up, it's some sort of seedy fake cowboy bar with half swing doors onto the street. We hang around outside for ages before Kieran shows up. Zaza gets talking to a sweet Geordie boy called Steve. When he leaves she turns to me and says, 'I'm going to marry him.'

Somehow Zaza finds out where Steve lives in Sunderland and we hitch-hike up there one weekend. We go to his address, his mum answers the door and says Steve's not in town, but invites us in for a cup of tea. Zaza nips into Steve's bedroom and rifles through his drawers to see if there's any evidence of a girlfriend but she doesn't find anything interesting. We wander the streets until we see a nice-looking boy with long hair and ask him if he knows anywhere we can stay, just like we did in Amsterdam. He takes us to a house, where we meet some lovely people, stay a couple of nights then hitch-hike home. Zaza tracks Steve down again in Piccadilly Circus: he doesn't stand a chance.

Reader, she married him.

17 ART SCHOOL

1972

Hornsey School of Art must be what heaven looks like. It's full of good-looking, interesting people saying unexpected things, dressed in paint-splattered jumble-sale clothes. I'm still following in the footsteps of the Kinks, who went to Hornsey, and of my heroes John Lennon and David Bowie, who also went to art school. It's just what you do if you're into music, you go to art school. There's no thought of making money or a career out of art, it's a rite of passage.

I have to concentrate to keep up with the other students. Most of them are better educated and more articulate than me. I'm a very small fish in a big pond. I thought I was good at art when I was at school, but not compared to this lot. I'm shit compared to them. I don't finish things properly, have no discipline and don't follow ideas through. I'm embarrassed by my lack of ability in every area, technically, intellectually and creatively. It's OK to be poor here though, as long as you act confident. I stay quiet and observe a lot, especially the girls.

Nina Canal is in my year (*she later formed the experimental New York band Ut*). She's tall and willowy with olive skin, short black hair, and moves like a gazelle; she's languid and self-assured, the most elegant girl I've ever seen. Nina hangs out with an equally stunning girl called Perry – such a cool name – who has long messy blonde hair, is outspoken and interesting; she lights up any room she's in. (*She was the great love of Ben Barson, the Greek god from Woodcraft Folk. And worth it.*) Nina and Perry don't wear makeup, their hands and clothes are covered in splodges of paint, their fingers rough and gnarled, ringed with plasters covering cuts from scalpels and Stanley knives. Working hands, creative hands, the hands of girls who do stuff, who have ideas. Sexy hands. They smoke roll-ups. These two girls eclipse Marianne Faithfull, Anita Pallenberg, Suzi Quatro and June Child (not Yoko though) as role models for me – they're real girls, my age, that I can copy. Although they come from a more privileged background than me, which gives them a confidence I don't have, I think if I watch them and listen to them for a couple of months, I can get there. This is the kind of girl I want to be: natural, passionate about work, articulate, intelligent, equal.

The boys at Hornsey aren't as interesting as the girls. They're fun and a good laugh to hang out with, but it's the girls I'm looking to for the first time in my life. There are a couple of interesting guys, like 'Groovy Graham', the social sec (*Graham Lewis, who later formed the band Wire*). He puts on loads of bands, Dr Feelgood, Kilburn and the High Roads, Brett Marvin and the Thunderbolts . . . he tried to get Pink Floyd once but it fell through. Graham wears very tight trousers that show every bump – we call him 'The Bulge' – and he dances like Mick Jagger, strutting around the hall jabbing his finger in the air with the other hand on his skinny hip, he's full of life and enthusiasm. There's a sweet shy guy called Stuart in the year below me (*Stuart Goddard, he will later transform himself into Adam of Adam and the Ants*), he's pretty and serious, works hard, doesn't say much.

My favourite tutor is Peter Webb. Once a week he gives a lecture on erotic art in the main hall. He's so passionate and captivating about his subject that he sparks an interest in sex and erotica in me that never goes away. He wears a purple suit and is convinced he's Theo, the reincarnated brother of Vincent van Gogh. He's so clever and charismatic that we all believe it too.

One lunchtime, as I'm walking down a corridor to Peter Webb's lecture, I hear very accomplished, live improvised jazz piano music floating out of a room. I slip in and watch the back of the person playing. She has shoulder-length, poker-straight, silky light brown hair and moves sensuously as she plays. Her back muscles ripple as she moves, emphasised by her tight blue-and-white striped T-shirt. I'm entranced, but I have to leave before she stops playing to go to the lecture. Later in the day I see her in the canteen, from the back. I watch her, I want to know what her face is like. She turns. She's a boy. His name is Jan, Jan Hart. Wow. I go after him even though I find out he has a girlfriend, Sue, who is at art school in Bournemouth. I don't usually do that. (*She's forgiven me, she's very cool, I still know her.*) He introduces me to jazz – Mingus, Coltrane, and also Loudon Wainwright III. He lives in a shared house with a bunch of older, bearded guys. They're middle-class, very political and earnest, no sense of humour. They think I'm stupid because I'm not very confident or articulate.

Jan, who turned out to be a boy

One weekend Jan takes me to Bournemouth, his hometown, to meet his family and friends. We visit Robert Fripp, the guitarist from King Crimson. I'm excited to meet him because I have seen him live and have his record *In the Court of the Crimson King*, and this will be the first time I've met a real musician in his home, as someone's friend. Jan and I walk into the front room, to find Fripp surrounded by a group of young people. He looks up and, without smiling, asks Jan, 'Where's Sue?' Then he looks straight at me and says, 'You shouldn't have broken up with Sue, Sue was great, much better.' He doesn't speak to me, or look at me again.

I'm broke, so to supplement my grant I get a job working behind the bar at the Sundown, a massive music venue in Edmonton. During the week there are underage discos, the kids fuck on the floor with a huge crowd around them egging them on. It's animalistic. At the weekend, live bands play. All the bar staff are excited because Rod Stewart and the Faces are playing next week.

We're not allowed to serve people from the side of the bar, that bit's for the glass collectors to put the empty glasses on. Whilst the Faces are playing, this sleazy-looking older guy keeps calling out to me and bugging me to serve him from there, so he can push ahead of the queue. I tell him I can't serve him from there, and he says, 'Don't you know who I am?' 'I don't give a fuck who you are,' I answer. He storms off and gets the manager of the Sundown. Turns out he is a big cheese from the Faces' entourage. Wants me sacked. The Sundown manager suggests I make myself scarce for the rest of the evening. 'Go and watch the show and come back tomorrow night,' he says. So I hang out backstage with my friend Mac who does the lighting. Mac says I can stay in his little lighting room with his friend, a guy called Liam, whilst he sorts something out. The minute Mac leaves, Liam starts trying to touch me. He pushes himself up against me, he knows I can't leave the room, he's heard the whole story. I'm always being touched by boys, in the street, in clubs and pubs, even though I haven't invited them to touch me or hardly know them, that's just the way it is, but this time I feel trapped, no one will hear me if it gets out of hand when I tell him to fuck off. I know it's a bit risky but I reckon it's the lesser of two evils, so I open the door and run off.

I walk up a few flights of stone stairs and open a door. I poke my head into the room, looking around for Mac. It's the green room, full of people drinking and talking. The Faces' Big Cheese turns round, whisky in hand, and clocks me. 'Get her!' He charges at me with a couple of bouncers in his wake. I slam the door shut. I have a split second to decide what to do; I can either run upstairs or run downstairs. I think, *The most obvious thing to do is run downstairs, that's what everyone would do*, so I run upstairs. I hear the Big Cheese and the bouncers go thundering down the stairs as I hotfoot it up. I feel quite clever until the stairs run out and I'm facing the door to the roof. I rattle the door handle, it's locked. I hear a man shout, 'She must have gone up!' They're baying for blood now, excited by the chase. I hear them charging up the stairs puffing and snorting like a herd of buffalo. There's nowhere for me to go. I stand quivering in the corner, a trapped wildebeest awaiting my fate. They're rough, they grab hold of me and pull and push me down the stairs. I've not been handled like this before, I'm frightened. I think they're probably going to beat me up. Something wet is running down my legs. I've pissed myself. Now I know you can piss yourself with fear. Another life experience clocked up.

The men, their hands all over me, drag me to the back door of the venue, they'll probably beat me up outside. One of them pushes down the safety bar and I'm ejected with force, into the yard. A gaggle of waiting Faces fans lift up their autograph books hopefully, then freeze, pens in mid-air as I'm tossed into their midst. The door slams shut behind me. Well, at least they didn't kill me. It's Christmas Eve by the way. I'm on the streets of Edmonton, no money, no coat, piss dripping down my legs, on Christmas Eve. I start to walk. I start to cry. Then I hear shouting and cursing in the distance, a gang of skinheads is bearing down on me. *Oh no. I'm dead. Raped and then dead.* The skinheads catch sight of me and start whooping with delight. Bait! I stand still and let them come. The two at the front of the posse lunge forwards and push their faces into mine. 'Hang on a minute,' says one of them. He flaps his hand to shush the rest of them. 'She's crying.'

The gang go quiet and gather round me. They want to know what's happened. I tell them. They say they're going to go to the Sundown and kill the Big Cheese. I dissuade them from doing that. Then one of them suggests taking me to the nearby police station. I'm escorted by a gang of skinheads to the police station. The policeman on duty looks at them suspiciously. 'Are they bothering you, love?' 'No, no, they've been very helpful.' I thank them and they swagger off, shouting, 'Merry Christmas, darlin'!' The policeman drives me home.

I often dress in flares or platform boots, the glam-rock style of dressing, as a bit of a joke at Hornsey. Glam rock is much more knowing and ironic now. I also wear clothes that reference the skinhead movement, which is the opposite of what art school is about. I like to provoke a reaction. Some days I'll wear a two-tone mohair tonic coat and opaque white tights, black patent brogues and a grey mini skirt because everyone else is dressed hippyish. I wouldn't ever wear the mullety hairstyle that girl skinheads have though; I still like to have pretty hair.

I finish my foundation course, then I do a year of a graphic design degree, then I drop out. I didn't have the courage to apply for the fine art course, which is what I really wanted to do. I chose graphic design because I thought it would suit my style of drawing – quite cartoony and stylised – but the course is all about typesetting, not creasing the paper and not getting smudges on anything. It's the worst place in the world for a messy person like me. I ask the college if I can take a sabbatical year, get my

67

portfolio together and then reapply for a different course. They agree and assign me a mentor, a nice bloke who works in admin at the college. I get a bar job at Dingwalls in Camden Town to see me through the year: I want to immerse myself in music and it's the best small venue in London.

When I try to get back into Hornsey, I fail. I decide to apply for the fashion and textiles degree because I'm getting more and more into fashion and music and I've made some interesting clothes whilst I've been at Dingwalls. I'm accompanied to the interview by the nice man from admin. The tutors on the selection panel take against me the minute I walk in the door. They seem pissed off, annoyed about something. There's tension between them and the suit, who's nothing to do with me, I was assigned him randomly. This has never happened to me before, I've never come across people who dislike me, or won't give me a chance, without a reason. I don't know how to stand up for myself, how to fight my corner. They trash me and my work viciously. I know there's something weird going on, but it doesn't really matter because it's obvious I've got no hope of getting onto the course. I start to cry with frustration. They look alarmed and ask me why I'm so upset, but I can't speak, there's nothing to say, I know the result of this interview is a foregone conclusion. This is the first time I've failed at something I want. I've failed loads of times before, at maths, on sports day, but those things didn't matter to me. I leave the interview room choking and hiccupping. Standing in the drizzle on the pavement outside the college, I see my whole life collapsing in front of me. I've got no future. I'm just a barmaid at Dingwalls.

18 DINGWALLS

1973

I love your hat.
Captain Beefheart

It's not so bad being a barmaid at Dingwalls. I sleep most of the day and start work at 6 p.m. I like the club best when it's empty: lights on, chairs on the tables, the smell of stale beer, and I can see the red-painted iron pillars and the little stage, which is usually obscured by a crowd of people.

Lots of great bands play here, like Kilburn and the High Roads, Chilli Willi and the Red Hot Peppers, Dr Feelgood with their frenetic guitarist Wilko Johnson, some Northern Soul bands – but the band that makes the biggest impression on me is Kokomo. There are ten of them all crowded onto the stage, they aren't rock, more like funk or soul, but what really grabs my attention is the girl on percussion. There are two girl vocalists in the band, but this other girl plays congas and other sorts of percussion instruments. I've never seen a young girl playing an instrument in a band before. I want to be her. I want so badly, for the first time ever, to be a girl I've seen on stage. I want to look like her and be in that band and wear her clothes and have her boyfriend and live her life. It's the first time I've ever thought of being a musician. And the reason I can make that leap is because someone behind the bar said to me, 'Her name's Jody Linscott, she couldn't play before she joined Kokomo, she learnt as she went along.' That's what's allowed me to dream for a moment, that phrase: 'She couldn't play.'

One of my best friends here is Brandi Alexander, a petite American girl a bit older than me, pretty with straight shiny blonde hair. Brandi usually wears a black waistcoat with nothing underneath and you can see the side of her boob as she moves. I couldn't believe it when she told me she liked girls. Because she's a lesbian, she's not interested in impressing guys on any level. This attitude makes her appear hard: she isn't though, she's very kind and generous. It's just unusual for a girl not to use her sexuality when interacting with a man. I'm the youngest person on the staff and often feel out of my depth amongst all the worldly types who work here, so Brandi's friendship gives me confidence. Neither of us take drugs – well, not hard drugs like some of this lot do – so we're a bit left out. I've noticed that people who take heroin are very cliquey, you feel a bit of a loser if you don't partake. At Dingwalls, a group of them are always disappearing off together, whispering in corners. It's a passive pressure; nothing's said, you're just treated as if you don't quite exist. Apart from Brandi, the person I hang out with most is a blond, tousle-haired boy with black eyebrows called Rory Johnston. He's sweet-natured, and has a half-American, half-Scottish accent. He likes me even though I haven't got much going on at the moment: Rory sees something in me. When he isn't working at Dingwalls, he's a barman at the Portobello Hotel, where lots of musicians drink. He's also an art student at Hammersmith College of Art and Building and the unofficial, unpaid assistant to a guy called Malcolm McLaren who owns a clothes shop. Rory's a very motivated person. He often takes me to the Portobello Hotel and I sit at the little bar whilst he works. It's a tiny basement room, not very impressive, just a bit of wicker furniture and a couple of tropical plants dotted around. I like going there because I get to see people like Mick Ronson and the other Spiders from Mars and Ian Hunter from Mott the Hoople, drinking and hanging out.

Dingwalls is full of characters, like the two girls Robyn and Shawn Slovo: their parents were world-famous anti-apartheid activists, their mother was assassinated because of it. Shawn and Robyn are very creative, they're writers and are very confident when they speak. No one intimidates those two. I'd like to be like that. The other person who stands out for me is a waitress called Rose. She doesn't take any shit. Once Captain Beefheart came in for a burger and called Rose over to tell her he liked the way she walked. It's interesting he noticed that about her: she has a very specific walk, a cross between a swaggering docker and a ballerina, with feet turned out, very purposeful, not traditionally feminine, not trying to be all slinky and seductive. He liked her walk for being strong and militant. I'm very jealous that Beefheart noticed her. It was the talk of the club for the rest of the evening.

I had my own 'Beefheart Moment' a couple of years later. I was in a cafe in Portobello Road and noticed Captain Beefheart was sitting across the room. When he left, he passed my table and to my astonishment stopped and said, 'I love your hat.' I was wearing a giant shocking pink silk beret with white polka dots on it that my mum had made for me. It had a fat pink stalk sticking out of the top. I looked back at him with a very serious expression and said, 'I love your music.' He looked surprised, he wasn't a very well-known musician, not the sort who got recognised. He nodded and left.

The bosses at Dingwalls aren't like normal bosses. One's called Dave 'Boss' Goodman, he's a big cuddly guy who used to look after the group the Pink Fairies. Russell Hunter, who was their drummer, runs the bar. They're both cheeky and irreverent most of the time but occasionally they take their jobs seriously and get strict with us, which is quite funny. I've got a crush on Russell – I like his soft voice – but he's not interested in me. Once he asked me to go upstairs with him to the little flat above Dingwalls to collect some empty crates. Everyone jeered as we walked out because the flat is known as a bit of a shag pad. When we got up there he pulled me down onto the waterbed, and started to kiss me. I was so overwhelmed when he put his hand between my legs that I started to tremble. He stopped and said we should go back downstairs. We didn't collect the crates, and he never made another move.

A strange twisted little man who collects the glasses at Dingwalls – he isn't paid, he just comes early and they let him stay because he works for nothing – has developed an obsession with me. It was annoying at first but now it's got out of hand. He calls me 'Tresses' because of my long wavy hair – which is actually a perm I had done at Molton Brown in South Molton Street, copying Maria Schneider in *Last Tango in Paris*. He has long black oily hair and

Growing out my 'Maria Schneider' perm. Muslin top from Kensington Market. Waistcoat homemade by me. Boots, Terry de Havilland. 1973

bulging eyes and talks like Uriah Heep, all long-drawn-out vowels and whiny intonation, whilst rubbing his hands together. He wears tight black trousers and red scarves tied to his wrist, a cross between Max Wall and a demonic Morris dancer. He starts coming to my flat when I'm not working and waiting outside the front door all day. I don't want to be intimidated by him, but I don't fancy going out whilst he's there. He pushes notes under the door, written in this flowery, mediaeval script. The other day he dropped some scented soap through the letter-box with a note saying, 'Dear Tresses, Every time you use this, you will be rubbing me all over your body.' I chucked it in the bin. I ignore him. I never look at him or speak to him and change my phone number. It's the only way to deal with an obsessive.

Working at night brings you into contact with some strange people and puts you in some scary situations. One night I was walking over the little bridge in Chalk Farm Road, just before the left turn into Dingwalls, when I thought I caught a flicker of something 'not quite right' out of the corner of my eye. Foolishly, I ignored it. As soon as I turned into the cobbled yard behind Dingwalls, I found myself on the ground. It happened that quickly. Two boys were on top of me clawing and scrabbling at my crotch, trying to tear my tights off. I screamed and fought back but I wasn't strong enough to fight two of them. Then luckily for me, a big white car turned into the yard; it was Russell, the bar manager. I shouted out to him, he stopped and the two boys ran off. Russell told me later he nearly didn't stop, he thought it was just a bunch of kids mucking about. He called the police and they came and interviewed me. One of them said, 'Well what do you expect, going round dressed like that?' I was wearing a denim skirt, denim jacket and stripy Biba tights. They didn't follow it up.

The longer I work at Dingwalls, the harder it is to get the energy to do it. At first I was very keen and interested and wanted to make a good impression, but after six months of night work, I'm tired all the time and stroppy to the customers. I'm taking speed every night and missing out on life by sleeping all day. I'm getting nothing done except kissing lots of boys. One night when I arrive for work, the bosses call me into the office and sack me. They sack nearly everyone that night, even Rose who's a brilliant waitress. Not only have I been sacked, I've got nowhere to live. I've fallen out with the girls I share a flat with in Bounds Green. It happened when the bog broke. I asked them to chuck a bucket of water down it after they'd been, especially if they'd thrown a tampon in there. I'm not that fastidious about cleanliness but it was beginning to stink. They were furious with me for suggesting such a thing, accused me of not being a feminist and being revolted by natural womanly functions. (It's become quite difficult nowadays to disagree with other women without being called anti-feminist.) Anyway, it's all turned nasty so I'm going to move out.

Now I'm homeless, with no future, and not even a barmaid at Dingwalls.

19 22 DAVIS ROAD

1973

Everyone knows how to get a squat: you go along to an empty house at night, break in, change the locks and it's yours. Sue, who used to work with me behind the bar at Dingwalls, tells me there's a house next door to hers in Acton with an empty flat upstairs. Me and Alan Drake (my friend from Southgate who I went to the Bowie gigs with) set off one night armed with a screwdriver, torch, hammer, candles and new lock, in a plastic bag. Mum says, 'Be careful, dear,' as she waves us off. Alan breaks the front door open, I unscrew the old lock and put the new one in and that's it. We go up the wooden stairs, no carpet – that's good – and look around. The walls are painted olive green, the main room has flowery William Morris-style wallpaper. We spend the night tucked up in our sleeping bags, chatting away excitedly. Later we'll get someone to jam the electricity meter with a pin so we have free electricity. Everyone does that.

Two little old ladies live in the flat below us. Very sweet old ladies. We hear them calling out, 'Hello? Hello? Who's there?' in their wobbly voices. They must be terrified, hearing people break in and clump about upstairs late at night. Even though we have separate front doors, it must be disconcerting. We're surprised they don't call the police. Alan and I go down and talk to them, we explain that we're moving in upstairs and everything's fine. The old ladies look at us with dread, like they're in our hands and if they're going to die tonight, so be it.

We make an absolute racket in that flat. We play music all day and night. The scariest-looking people come and go at all hours.

One night Long John Baldry, an old blues singer who's had a few hits, smashes the front door down because he's fallen for Alan. Another time someone throws a brick through my bedroom window – luckily no one is in the room – we think it must be a disgruntled cabbie because we often get black cabs home from gigs, ask them to stop in the street parallel to ours, jump out, then leg it down a tiny alleyway into our road. We've heard that cabbies aren't allowed to leave their cabs, they have their money in there, so they can't follow us. Obviously one of them's hunted us down and found out where we live. It won't have been difficult, we stand out a mile.

For most meals, Alan and I eat Kellogg's cornflakes with the occasional KitKat or Mars Bar thrown in for a treat. We never eat proper food. I'm perfectly happy with a bowl of cereal for every meal (*still am*). We're thin and spotty with pale grey skin.

I have a little bit of money because I've got a grant to go to Hammersmith College of Art in Lime Grove, to study fashion and textiles. Same college Rory goes to, he told me to apply there, said it would be easy to get in, and it was. When the grant is paid, I have loads of money for two weeks then I have nothing for three months until the next instalment. Alan doesn't have a job, he's on the dole and nicks food from the local corner shop. They really like us in that shop, they're the only people in the area who treat us like human beings. When they catch Alan nicking from them they're very upset. We're banned from the shop now and have to walk miles to get provisions. I feel really bad about letting them down and I'm upset with Alan because I have certain principles that I adhere to, like no stealing (except bog paper from pubs).

Our neighbour, Sue, now regrets ever mentioning the flat. When she told me about it at Dingwalls, I was a ringlet-haired, flowery-topped girly girl. When I turned up at Davis Road with a hammer and screwdriver, I was a shaggy-haired scruff. She asks us to move out, says we've disrupted the whole street.

20 PEACOCK

1974

I'm getting worried. Hammersmith College *looks* like an art college – paintings on the wall, big windows, easels – but this lot don't look like art students. I thought I'd meet interesting people here. The only person I've met so far who has any sense of style is Jane Ashley, daughter of the owners of the Laura Ashley clothes shop. At break, Jane and I wander down the corridor towards the canteen – we're in no rush, we've been told that going to the canteen is an ordeal because the art school shares it with a building college that trains boys to be plasterers, electricians and plumbers and they all sit at the back of the room heckling the art students. Whilst Jane and I are queuing up amongst the builders, trying to ignore their sarcastic comments about our clothes, I see a flash of movement and colour – a blur of dark hair, high-heeled shoes, fluttering chiffon scarves and the longest, thinnest legs I've ever seen. And then it's gone, disappeared into the men's loo. 'Was that a *guy*?' I ask Jane. I keep staring at the door and eventually the creature re-emerges and I get a better look. Yes, it's a guy. He's stick thin with tight red-and-white checked trousers, black high-heeled slingback shoes, a girl's fitted jacket that's too tight, all topped off with fluffy, backcombed hair. The building students erupt at this spectacle, shouting and cat-calling, but he ignores them and struts confidently to the middle of the canteen queue, pushing in to join his mate.

I just know this boy's going to be my friend; even though my look isn't as extreme as his, I like his bravery and style, he's my kind of person. I make eye contact with him and burst out laughing. I laugh with a mixture of recognition and relief because I know our friendship is inevitable, we're obviously like-minded people so we may as well get straight to it and dispense with the slow polite phase of getting to know each other. But I've offended him and my laughter is met with a wounded expression.

So I say, 'Hello, I'm Viv.'

In a soft, shy voice with a South London accent, the boy replies: 'Mick Jones.'

Mick Jones, about seventeen years old. He'll kill me for showing this but I think he's cute

21 HORSES

1975

Every week I buy the *NME*. I find it difficult to read because the writers use such long words, but it's not a chore because I'm interested in what they're saying. One day I read a small piece about a singer called Patti Smith. There's a picture. It's the cover of *Horses*, her forthcoming album, a black-and-white photograph taken by Robert Mapplethorpe.

I have never seen a girl who looks like this. She is my soul made visible, all the things I hide deep inside myself that can't come out. She looks natural, confident, sexy and an individual. I don't want to dress like her or copy her style; she gives me the confidence to express myself in my own way.

On the day the album's released – I half dread it in case the music doesn't live up to the promise of that bold cover – I don't go into college, I get the bus to HMV Records in Oxford Street instead. I'm so excited I feel sick. When I arrive, I see Mick Jones loitering outside the record shop.

'What are you doing here?' I ask.

'Getting the Patti Smith record.'

I rush home and put the record on. It hurls through stream of consciousness, careers into poetry and dissolves into sex. The structure of the songs is unique to her, not copies of old song structures, they're a mixture of improvisation, landscapes, grooves, verses and choruses. She's a private person who dares to let go in front of everyone, puts herself out there and risks falling flat on her face. Up until now girls have been so controlled and restrained.

Patti Smith is abandoned. Her record translates into sound, parts of myself that I could not access, could not verbalise, could not visualise, until this moment.

Listening to *Horses* unlocks an idea for me – girls' sexuality can be on their own terms, for their own pleasure or creative work, not just for exploitation or to get a man. I've never heard a girl breathing heavily, or making noises like she's fucking in music before (except '*Je t'aime*' by Jane Birkin, and that record didn't resonate with me). Hearing Patti Smith be sexual, building to an orgasmic crescendo, whilst leading a band, is so exciting. It's emancipating. If I can take a quarter or even an eighth of what she has and not give a shit about making a fool of myself, maybe I still can do something with my life.

22 FIRST LOVE

1975

There are all kinds of love in this world but never
the same love twice.

F. Scott Fitzgerald

There's only one public payphone in college and it's in the entrance
hall. Whenever I go in or out of the building, Mick Jones is on
that payphone. Every time I go to use the phone, Mick is hogging
it. Mick is in the hall, on the phone for hours and hours every day.
What the hell is he doing? Maybe he's having relationship problems, probably breaking up with someone. Next time I see him in
the canteen, I ask what he's up to.

'I'm putting a band together,' he says.

Mick is that person in a band – and there's always one – who
does all the organising, who takes the pain and the losses of the
band to heart, who lives, breathes and would die for the band.

Mick's eyes shine and he waves his hands around excitedly whenever he talks about music. He tells me that he plays guitar and is
trying to get some musicians together to rehearse. There's a pretty
boy with long blond hair called Kelvin who's a good singer, and a
couple of others, but none of them take him or his guitar playing
seriously. They treat him as a bit of a joke. They only come to a
rehearsal – that he's spent a week arranging – if they have nothing
better to do. He laughs it off. He's self-effacing and philosophical
about it. He wants to be in a band so badly that he'll never give up.
If no one turns up to a rehearsal he's organised he arranges another

one. If the bass player leaves, he hustles around to find someone else. Often he gets chucked out of his own band and has to start all over again. Calling, calling, endlessly calling. Shovelling coins into that payphone.

I see bands a couple of times a week, have done since I was thirteen, but this level of fervour – I've never seen anything like it. I've never met anyone my age so committed to something before. Mick is willing to put his ego and his pride aside and pour every ounce of his energy and time into fulfilling his dream. I'm jealous of his passion.

Mick and I sit around in the college library discussing the bands we like, then I start rambling on about some boy I've slept with. 'God, Mick, he's so handsome. He's got really long blond hair. I'm a bit worried though, 'cos my period is late. I think I might be pregnant. When we were lying in bed he said my back is like a boy's. Is that a good thing? He said it turned him on. Do you think he might be gay?' Mick listens patiently but doesn't offer any advice. Eventually, when I've run out of steam, he asks me if I want to go and see a film with him tonight. It's called *The Battle of Algiers*. Well, I don't like the sound of that, but I love hanging out with him, he's so funny and I can talk to him like he's a girlfriend, so I say yes.

Mick and I meet outside the cinema, a very cool arthouse place called the Electric, on Portobello Road. It begins to dawn on me that he is not only much cleverer than me, he's also much more sophisticated. The film is spellbinding and emotionally captivating, the intensity of the experience amplified by Ennio Morricone's pounding, percussive soundtrack.

We emerge from the warmth of the foyer onto the dark cold street. The lamp posts give off a golden glow, people hustle by, the smell of fish and chips is in the air, white dragon breath puffs from our mouths as we bundle along together talking excitedly about the film. Then we bump into Rory. I'm embarrassed that he's caught me with Mick.

'Hey, what are you two doing out together? Something going on?' he laughs.

I'm mortified. How could he possibly think there's anything going on between me and this flamboyant-looking beanpole? I'm about to protest that we're just friends, I look up at Mick, he looks down at me . . .

. . . Fucking Hell. I've only gone and fallen in love.

An outtake of me and Mick modelling for Laura Ashley at the Clash's rehearsal studios, Chalk Farm. 1976

23 THE LEAP

1975

Leap and the net will appear.
John Burroughs

'Malcolm's new band is playing at Chelsea School of Art tonight, want to come?' says Rory.

'Yes,' I say.

'No,' says Mick.

Mick already knows about the Sex Pistols and even though he's friends with the bass player, Glen Matlock, they are his rivals. He says he's going to rehearse with his own group tonight, not watch someone else's. He tries to put me off but I'm going anyway. They sound interesting.

The Pistols are playing in the school hall. It looks like every other school hall, bare wooden floor, stage at one end with tattered green silk curtains pulled to one side, vaulted ceiling with metal struts and grey plastic chairs stacked high along the walls. Smells like floor polish. Not many people in the audience, just a few clusters, clumped and dotted around the edge of the room. An impish-looking guy dressed in a powder-blue drape jacket, with pale orange curls falling onto his forehead, heads over to us.

'Here's Malcolm,' says Rory.

Malcolm McLaren looks older than everyone else and is better dressed, like he's got a bit of money. Rory introduces us. Malcolm's friendly and charming but not flirty, he seems pleased to see another person at the gig. I can imagine him thinking, *Good.*

There were ten people last time and now there are eleven. He has a very open, non-judgemental expression and a look of amusement in his eye. There's no up-and-down look to check out my clothes, which I would've expected from someone who owns a boutique. As Malcolm touches my hand, I think, *I'm wearing the wrong clothes, in the wrong colour, in the wrong place.* The thought just comes to me in that second as we touch. I'm wearing a tight, kid's-size brown leather bomber jacket, like something Marc Bolan would have worn, handmade baby-blue leather boots and jeans. My hair's been cut and coloured by Keith at Smile in Knightsbridge, very blonde on top and very dark underneath. I just know it's all wrong. I'm mortified. I was quite cool at Dingwalls. I'm very cool at Hammersmith. I'm not cool here. I look around to see what other people are wearing. Black.

The Sex Pistols come on.

They're loud and raucous but not bad musicians. I've seen bands that have this anarchic quality before: the Pink Fairies, the Pretty Things, the Edgar Broughton Band. It's the singer who stands out. Johnny Rotten slouches at the front of the stage, propped up on the mike stand. He's leaning so far forward he looks as if he might topple into the empty space in front of the audience. His face is pale and his body is twisted into such an awkward ugly shape he looks deformed. No dancing about, trying to entertain or attempting to make us like him. He looks ordinary, about the same age as us, the kind of boy I was at comprehensive school with. He's not a flashy star like Marc Bolan or David Bowie, all dressed up in exotic costumes, he's not a virtuoso musician like Eric Clapton or Peter Green, he's not even a macho rock-and-roll pub-band singer – he's just a bloke from Finsbury Park, London, England, who's pissed off. Johnny sneers at us in his ordinary North London accent, his voice isn't trained and tuneful, it's a whiny cynical drawl, every song delivered unemotionally. There's no fake American twang either.

All the things I'm so embarrassed about, John's made into virtues. He's unapologetic about who he is and where he comes from. Proud of it even. He's not taking the world's lack of interest as confirmation that he's wrong and worthless. I look up at him twisting and yowling and realise it's everyone else who's wrong, not him. How did he make that mental leap from musically untrained, state-school-educated, council-estate boy, to standing on stage in front of a band? I think he's brave. A revolutionary. He's sending a very powerful message, the most powerful message anyone can ever transmit. Be yourself.

I've always thought that my particular set of circumstances – poor, North London, comprehensive school, council flat, *girl* – haven't equipped me for success. As I watch the Sex Pistols I realise that this is the first time I've seen a band and felt there are no barriers between me and them. Ideas that have been in the back of my mind for years rush to the front of my brain . . .

. . . *John Lennon, Yoko Ono, the Kinks, the possible female in Third Ear Band, the untrained female drummer in Kokomo, Sandie Shaw, Suzi Quatro, Emma Peel, the two girls in the Incredible String Band, Patti Smith, Mick Jones, Johnny Rotten, my love of music* . . .

. . . This is it. At last I see not only that other universe I've always wanted to be part of, but the bridge to it.

24 VIV AND MICK

1975

The day after the Sex Pistols' gig, Mick comes to my studio at college. He hovers in the doorway until he catches my eye. We lean against the wall in the fluorescent-lit corridor. He's sought me out to ask what I thought of the band. I'm exultant. Inspired. I tell him, 'I can't even remember what they sounded like, what I got from them was, *I can do this too*. Not, this is easy and I can do it too, but this is GREAT and I can do it too. And I'm going to do it.'

Mick listens to me eulogising with a sulky expression – he was obviously hoping I'd say they were rubbish. He seems to think that me liking the Pistols is a criticism of him and his music.

Mick's getting yet another band together – he's found a bass player, a handsome guy called Paul Simonon. He can't play bass yet, but Mick says it doesn't matter, he looks good. He's also found a singer, who's not handsome but has a lot of charisma: Joe Strummer. Joe was in a band called the 101ers. I really liked their single, 'Keys to Your Heart'. The rest of the 101ers are upset that Joe's leaving them, they're a very relaxed bunch of guys and think Joe's selling out by joining a band managed by Mick's dodgy friend, Bernie Rhodes. Bernie puts a lot of pressure on Joe to join Mick's band, he keeps meeting up with him and saying that the 101ers are out of date and this new band are the future. Bernie eventually convinces Joe, and he joins up. They all try and come up with a name, the favourite at the moment is the Young Colts. I try it out by carving it into the wooden counter at the Acton dole office.

Even though he is aware of coolness, Mick would never change himself to be cool. If he likes something or someone, he sticks to his guns – that's one of the best things about him. He's the only one of us who doesn't take drugs, won't touch them, he's adamant, just drinks lukewarm tea. He's an independent thinker and won't drop mates because they don't look or behave right, like lots of people do. He's loyal to the bands he loved when he was growing up too – no hiding LPs for him, like I've done, shoving Donovan and Sparks records in drawers when someone's coming round, or taking them down the Record and Tape Exchange – Mick's kept all his old records. He's turned me on to a lot of good music too: Velvet Underground, the 13th Floor Elevators, the New York Dolls, MC5, Mott the Hoople. He doesn't just play the records, he explains what's good about them, points out nice harmonies or guitar riffs. He half-heartedly tried to teach me a few chords a couple of times, but once you've shagged a bloke he can't really be bothered to teach you anything, he's got what he wants.

I'm not going to let Mick Jones know I've fallen for him, not yet; I've got to get used to the idea myself first. I've never felt proper love before, I've just fancied a boy because he looks nice. Mick's a whole different thing: he's interesting, the smartest, funniest person I've ever met. But I still try to hide my relationship with him from other people. 'I'm independent, we should only see each other when we feel like it, we don't own each other,' I tell him. It's a constant battle between us, because he wants to be with me in a traditional, openly affectionate relationship. He's a passionate, possessive person; it must be hell for him.

I'm meeting new and interesting guys every day. There aren't many girls on the scene, so I get loads of attention. Mick's always having to ward boys off. I don't have sex with other boys but I do spend a lot of time with them. I'm not very reassuring either, I never say anything like, 'Oh Mick, don't worry, darling, I'm only here for you.' More like, 'I'm off. See you later!'

25 THE CLASH

1975

Paul Simonon, Mick's bass player, hasn't got anywhere to live so he's moved into my squat. Paul is as handsome as a film star, like Paul Newman and James Dean rolled together, and he's nice to girls, not chauvinistic. He's a bit tongue-tied and bashful but he can afford to be, his looks do all the talking. It's Paul who comes up with the new band name, the Clash, from a newspaper headline. Paul and I really like each other and he respects me, which always goes down well.

With Paul Simonon, 1976

Because Paul now lives with me and Alan at Davis Road, the Clash have their band meetings here. Mick lives with his grandmother in Royal Oak, so they don't want to go there, and Joe still lives with the 101ers. I wouldn't mind the Clash all filling up the place but they close the door of the kitchen and have this very self-important air about them. I don't take their meetings seriously, but Bernie does: you'd think he was planning World War Three. Bernie's always the last one to arrive. I open the front door and he pushes past me, knocking me out of the way, and stomps upstairs to the kitchen, slamming the door behind him. Not a word spoken. I can't stand him. He's a vegetarian – not that that makes him horrible – he told me once he was brought up a vegetarian, and when he's feeling rebellious he goes out and buys a burger.

The one thing Bernie and I have in common is what we think the Clash's songs should be about. We both think it would be better if they stopped writing soppy love songs and wrote material that reflects their everyday lives. We bang on to Mick and Joe about it, they take it in and turn 'I'm So Bored with You' into 'I'm So Bored with the USA', and write more political stuff like 'White Riot', about confrontations with the police during the Notting Hill Carnival, and 'Career Opportunities', which refers to the time Mick worked at the dole office and had to open suspicious-looking letters that could have been letter bombs – the senior staff wouldn't touch them.

Funny though, now my favourite Clash songs are the love songs: 'Stay Free', 'Train in Vain' and 'Should I Stay or Should I Go'. Mick is a great love-song writer.

26 FIRST GUITAR

1976

There's no such thing as a wrong note.
Art Tatum

I care what people think about me to the point of despair, am over-sensitive to criticism and lacking in self-confidence but I don't let my negative feelings stop me from doing stuff.

My Swiss grandmother, Freda, dies. She leaves me two hundred quid in her will; it takes a huge amount of self-control not to dip into it and fritter it away. I'm sure I'll never have that much money again. I've been mulling over what to do with it for weeks – there's no way I'm going to save it, but what to spend it on? I was thinking of buying an old Norton motorbike, but since seeing the Sex Pistols, I've decided to buy a guitar.

Walking along Shepherd's Bush High Street with Mick, on the way home from college, I say, 'I'm going to buy a guitar. An electric guitar.'

The words come out a bit too aggressively because I'm secretly dreading him laughing at me – when I think about it, this is quite a ridiculous thing for me to say. I'm a twenty-two-year-old girl who's never had a music lesson and never touched a guitar. Everyone I've heard of who plays electric guitar is male and has paid their dues by starting out on an acoustic, which I can't be bothered to do. And electric guitars are very expensive, not something to mess around on, not a toy or a fad. But times have changed. Just for a second, the impenetrable iron door that is convention has been pushed open a tiny crack, and if I'm very quick and very bold, I might just be able to dart through to the other side before it slams shut again.

I steel myself for an onslaught of hilarity and derision from Mick – but after a pause he says:

'Yeah! I've got a girlfriend who plays guitar!'

It has to be the guitar. The look, the size, the shape, it's all recognisable to me – like when you meet someone for the first time but you feel like you've known them your whole life. I like the way the guitar weaves and chops through the other instruments. I know that I'm not grounded and steady enough to play bass, not outgoing and confident enough to be a singer. I need an instrument to direct my emotions through. A little distance. The size of the strings and neck suit my fingers and the frequency of the notes is familiar, near to the pitch of my own voice. The guitar resonates with how I talk. It's all and none of these things really. It just feels right. No question. It couldn't be any other instrument.

Mick and I go to Denmark Street to choose a guitar. I've got no idea what to look for. I might as well be going to buy a semi-automatic weapon. The shop assistant is a bit sneery towards Mick, I can see he thinks it's pathetic that this boy keeps asking his girlfriend which guitar she likes. When he realises the guitar is for me and I can't play a note, he becomes very impatient. He watches with a smirk on his face as Mick tests guitars for me. We ignore him, we know a change is coming and we're part of it. After he's strummed away on it for a while, Mick hands me a little red guitar called a Rickenbacker. I hold it awkwardly.

'John Lennon used to play one,' he tells me.

I've never held a guitar before. I look at it, the assistant looks at me, I can't even hold down a chord. I'm beginning to feel a fool, I'm not sure I can keep up this veneer of confidence any longer but Mick isn't embarrassed, so we keep going. Eventually I buy a single-cutaway sunburst 1969 Les Paul Junior. I love its simplicity, the two gold knobs, the single pick-up, the curves, like it's got a cute bum. I think Mick did well there. He's no idea what kind of guitarist I will turn out to be. He's helped me choose a guitar the right size, shape and weight for me. It's simple and classy. It's a serious guitar. Mick has taken me seriously.

With my Gibson Les Paul Junior at the Stowaway club, June 1978

My new guitar costs £250. I can't afford a proper case so they find a grey cardboard one out the back, it's got an embossed snakeskin print stamped into it, and an ivory-coloured plastic handle. I carry my guitar through the streets of central London, prop it against the bus stop in St Martin's Lane – without taking my hand off it in case someone tries to nick it – heave it onto the bus and sit with the case wedged between my knees, thinking to myself, 'Nobody knows I can't play it. At this moment in time, I look like a guitarist.'

I head down Davis Road to the squat, changing hands every few steps to give my arms a rest. For the first time in my life, I feel like myself.

27 THE ROXY

1976–1977

My insistence on Mick and I not merging into a couple is not just to do with being free to hang out with other guys, it's also about wanting to be seen as a separate entity, rather than 'Mick's girlfriend'. Mick can play guitar, he's been in bands before. He's a bloke. He doesn't have to prove himself like I do. I'm trying to be a musician in front of all these new people, a very bold move as I can't play guitar and haven't written any songs. Sometimes I think I might as well say, 'I want to be an astronaut.' I don't even know if I can do it myself, why should anyone else have faith in me?

Mick still believes in love and romance whereas I'm questioning all my old beliefs and habits. He wants emotional stability. He was brought up by his grandmother, Stella, in a council flat in Royal Oak. I think he's done well. I know lots of people who had a much more auspicious start in life who aren't half the person Mick Jones is.

Every night of the week that it's open, I go to the Roxy club. I've never got any money so I jump the turnstiles at Shepherd's Bush tube station and jump them again at Covent Garden when I get off, then I blag my way into the club for free – the owners, Andrew Czezowski and Susan Carrington, are very sweet about us all doing this night after night – and we don't buy any drinks either. I come here a lot because it's the only place to go but sometimes it gets boring, talking to the same people all the time, just wasting a few hours then trying to get home again.

I hang around downstairs mostly, where Don Letts DJs. I first met Don when he worked at the clothes shop Acme Attractions on the King's Road. He used to buy me a sandwich or give me my bus fare because I never had any money. My flatmate Alan and our friend Keith Levene (Keith lived across the road from Alan in Southgate. I've known Keith since he was fourteen) disappear into the bogs a lot to take drugs. Don plays reggae, lovers' rock and dub. I stand by the DJ booth and try to dance. I feel self-conscious because I don't know how to move. I haven't seen many people dance to reggae, there's no one to copy. It's not the same as skinheads dancing to ska. Don's friend Leo (later the bass player in Dreadzone) tells me to listen to the bass. Before he said that I was trying to dance to the rhythm of the guitar, which is double-time and off-beat. If Wobble's here (when he became a bass player he added 'Jah'), I watch him dance. I don't know how he knows what to do but he's very elegant and light on his feet and has a good sense of rhythm.

With Don Letts and my Hagstrom guitar

By the time the Roxy closes for the night, the tubes have stopped running and I'm stranded. I haven't got any money for a cab and there's no way I can go on a night bus dressed in black rubber stockings, a string vest and a leather jacket. Night buses are dangerous: full of skinheads and drunks, no girls travel on them alone. Also, it's a long walk from the bus stop at the other end to my squat. I know this'll be a problem every time I leave the house but it never stops me going out, I just hope things'll work out. And there's always Mick. He's never sure if I'm going to go home with him or not but he waits until the end of the night when everyone else has faded away, then offers me a lift in a taxi back to his grandmother's flat. He's always looking out for me.

28 MICK AND VIV

1976

We're taking a short cut through the car park behind the Hammersmith Odeon. It's dark. Slinking out from between the cars come the skinheads. They surround us.

Skinheads don't like 'punks' but they don't hate us as much as teds do.

Coming across me and Mick tottering through the car park on high heels, dressed in pink and black leather with our blonde and black spiky hair, is good luck for them and bad luck for us. We must look like two exotic insects wafted into their territory on a rogue breeze. I think, *Oh no, Mick's going to be absolutely useless, why did I pick such a weedy bloke to go out with?*

One of the skinheads swears at us, the rest gather behind him, a sea of bobbing baldies. Mick stays calm. He's used to this kind of thing. The swearer gets more aggressive, taking the piss out of Mick's clothes. Then he turns to me and hisses, 'Next time I see you, I'm gonna *fuck* you.' Without any communication between us, Mick and I take this as an invitation to leave. We walk away together. My back is burning. I tell my legs to stop shaking and my feet to hit the ground steadily. *Walk with confidence, Viv.* I pray they won't come after us. As we get further and further away and there's no thundering of Dr Martens on gravel, I dare to believe they've let us go. Every day something like this happens, or is likely to happen. We're always on edge, always on our guard. It's exhausting.

Danger comes in all sorts of guises and I'm often in trouble because of my own stupidity. On Friday nights we all go to the dances at the Royal College of Art. Tonight, Steve Jones, the Sex Pistols' guitarist, is flirting with me, even though he knows I'm with Mick. I'm fascinated by Steve, not just because he's attractive in his own way, but because he's so different, a 'bit of rough'. Callous and very sexual but with a vulnerability underneath the bravado. John Rotten calls him the Coalman, because he looks like a labourer. Steve and I wander outside together, and he says, 'Come down here.' He leads me down some stone steps into the basement of a big white Kensington house. I don't know why I go with him, I know it's wrong. Then he says, 'Go down on me.' No nice flirty chat. I shake my head. He keeps on at me to go down on him, I keep saying no. He tries another tack. 'I'll go down on you then.' *God no. What was I thinking coming down into this dark hole with him?* I suppose I thought we might kiss, but Steve is the most sexual person in our group, he's always shagging, of course he's not going to want to kiss. I'm getting scared, I'm out of my depth and can't see a way out of this. I've got a feeling that if I run off it might get worse, might excite him.

'Viviane!'

I look up from the basement and see Mick's head poking over the top of the black wrought-iron railings. He must have followed us out, he's always watching me. I know I'm in trouble, but I don't care, I'm so relieved and happy to see him. I race up the stairs. When I get to the top, Mick looks at me and says, 'It's over.' And stalks off.

As I watch Mick walk away from me across Exhibition Road, I realise I don't want to lose him. I'm worried that if I let him out of my sight, I'll never get him back. I run after him and try to explain that I wasn't going to do anything. I beg and plead for his forgiveness, but nothing I say moves him. He hails a cab and I scramble in after him before he has time to slam the door. He doesn't speak to me or look at me all night but I follow him everywhere like a devoted puppy. I jump out of the cab and chase him into the lift of his grandmother's block of flats, stick close to him at the front door so he can't shut me out and sit on the floor of his bedroom amongst the piles of records whilst he gets ready for bed. I lie, fully clothed, next to him on the bed as he pretends to sleep. About ten in the morning, Mick forgives me. He says I've shown how sorry I am and how much I care for him. I think he's surprised how much I want him. What an idiot I am. Nearly lost the guy I love.

After 'The Steve Jones Incident', I accept that Mick and I are serious boyfriend and girlfriend. Our relationship is very volatile, we have huge rows, but we love each other and it's a relief that he doesn't mind my fiery temper. Most guys can't stand it. It's the reason I get chucked usually. But Mick sees it for what it is, a quick flare-up. I can be myself with him and am loved for it, not in spite of it.

With Gibson Les Paul Junior, now sprayed metallic black (sacrilege)

29 SOMETHING IN THE AIR

1976

> Lock up the streets and houses
> Because there's something in the air.
> Thunderclap Newman

There's music and band-forming in the air, and I know I've got to learn how to play my Gibson or I'll just be a 'poseur' – the worst insult any of us can call each other (apart from 'careerist') – just a fake pretending to be something I'm not. Keith Levene was a bit too young to hang out with us a couple of years ago but he's very intelligent and plays guitar brilliantly, so he's caught up and comes over to Davis Road a lot to help me with my guitar playing. I don't find it intimidating to play in front of Keith because I've known him so long. We meet a couple of times a week in my bedroom, which is the large double room at the front of the house, and Keith says, 'We're not going to bother with chords and scales and all that shit, Viv. I'm going to teach you how *not* to play guitar.' But I want to learn chords! How am I going to be able to write a song if I don't know any chords? Keith only has three rules: always start with the guitar in tune (he has to tune it for me), always have clean hands, and never go more than three days without playing. When I'm alone with the guitar, I experiment and try to recreate the sounds of animals and other noises. This is how I build my guitar style from scratch, from a starting point of no chords, no twelve-bar blues chord progressions, and no scales.

I have a Marshall stack in my bedroom, a white amp and huge

speaker, big enough for a concert hall (I bought them from Steve Jones – god knows who he nicked them from). I twang away every day, trying to find my way around the guitar, to understand what pick-ups do, what settings to put my amp on, trying desperately to *hear*. I want to develop a distinct personality with both my guitar playing and my guitar sound. I need to be sure that I am conveying the right message with my instrument. I decide I want a thin buzzsaw-ish/mosquito type of sound. That's what I'm aiming for. 'Why?' says Keith. 'I like that it sounds annoying and dangerous and it's industrial,' I reply. I keep twiddling the knobs on the amp and my guitar to try and find the right combination that will lead me to THE SOUND. It's hard to get it right. Sometimes it's too extreme, too much treble and you can't hear any notes, sometimes it's like a boring old distorted rock guitar. I don't understand why it sounds different when I'm sure I used exactly the same settings yesterday. Every day the task seems hopeless and I feel like giving up. I lie on my bed a lot, just holding the guitar, feeling like a fraud.

There's a lot of tension between Mick Jones and Keith Levene because of how friendly Keith and I are. (*I was chatting to Keith recently and said to him, 'Remember that time back in the seventies when we were lying on my bed and you stroked my back for hours?' He laughed and said, 'It wasn't your back, Viv, it was your front!'*) Joe Strummer shows me how to tap my foot and play along at the same time. He says it's crucial I do this or I'll go out of time and have no rhythm. I find it really difficult to do those two things at once and I think it's unfeminine to stomp your foot so I'm a bit resistant to it. Joe keeps pestering me to go to bed with him, I say no. I can't believe he would do that to Mick.

My neighbour, Sue, comes round. She very politely begs me to stop playing. She says she's been sent by the rest of her flatmates to tell me that I can't play guitar, it's been months now and it's

Walking down Davis Road with Keith Levene and Mick Jones, 1975

obviously not happening, I have no talent for it. 'Please, for your own sake, Viv, as well as everyone else's, stop it and find something that you *can* do. I'm sure there are lots of things you're good at.' She's absolutely right and I know it. I'm not progressing, I have no natural musical talent, I'm making a terrible noise. But I'm not going to stop. I don't know why. Maybe because there's nothing else in the world I want to do.

Luckily I have Keith to bolster me. He talks me round from my constant 'Guitar Depressions' (Keith's term, he says he has them all the time, it happens when you stall in your learning). I play him riffs I've made up, humming, buzzing and fizzing like a wasp trapped in a jam jar. He says he wishes he could write things like that; he feels confined by his knowledge. Keith was very influenced by the guitarist Steve Howe from the prog-rock band Yes. He used to roadie for them when he was very young and idolised Steve. In a way Steve's playing is being passed on to me through Keith, but it's like that game, Chinese Whispers: by the time I get hold of it, the information has mutated and, in my hands, becomes even more mangled and distorted.

Expressing myself through the guitar is a very difficult concept to grasp. I don't want to copy any male guitarists, I wouldn't be true to myself if I did that. I can't copy Lita Ford from the Runaways or the guitarist from Fanny: they don't sound like women, they sound like men. I keep thinking, 'What would I sound like if I was a guitar sound?' It's so abstract. As I experiment, I find that I like the sound of a string open, ringing away whilst I play a melody on the string next to it. It sounds like bagpipe music or Indian or Chinese, oriental and elemental. I try to play like John Cale in the Velvets, I don't realise for ages that he's playing violin and viola, not guitar. I want my guitar to sound like that. I like hypnotic repetition, I like the same riff played over and over again for ages. I like nursery rhymes. I love the top three trebly strings, the higher up the neck the better, and I turn the treble knob on the guitar and on the amp up full.

Then I start thinking about structure.

I don't want to use the same old twelve-bar blues chord progressions that all rock is based on. I can't anyway, I don't know the formulas. (Reminds me of when I was at school and refused to learn to type, I didn't want to rely on it. Like Buddy Holly said to his mother when she suggested he finish his exams so he'd have something to fall back on: 'Ma, I ain't fallin' back.')

Slowly I start shaping a guitar style, twisting strands together, layering then undoing and starting again, until I start to sound like me. I just wish I loved playing guitar. I thought you were supposed to love playing music, that it's a release and a comfort, that's what other musicians always say. For me it's agony.

I've got to form a band soon, whether I can play or not. There's Paul, sitting in the next room, trying to learn the bass, and he's already in a band. If he can do it, then so can I.

The next step is to tell Mum I'm leaving college to make music and hopefully to join a band. We're on the 31 bus together (sometimes I get the 31 from Camden Town to Notting Hill just for fun, it's such a great route), chatting away on the top deck in the front seats, I've got my guitar between my legs. I tell her about the Pistols and the Clash and all the people I've met, she's nodding and smiling, she knows I've always been mad about music, and is proud I'm learning an instrument. I think this is a good time to tell her my plans, I'm so enthusiastic about life: 'Mum, I'm going to leave college and form a band!' She bursts into tears. I hustle her off the bus and into the Chippenham pub, where I borrow some money off her and buy us half a shandy each. I bring the drinks to the table. Mum's worked so hard to get me into college, I'm the first child to go into further education out of our whole family, she's done cleaning jobs in the evenings after work to pay for extra books and clothes so I don't look poor, always believed in me and my ideas, and now I'm dropping out. I can't even play guitar yet and I'm throwing away my chance of a degree. I've got to convince her I know what I'm doing. 'Look, Mum, look how I'm dressed: I look different to everyone else, I'm not like everyone else. You know how I am about music.' She nods and manages a weak smile. Well, I've got to do it now, haven't I – the last person in the world I want to hurt or let down is Mum.

30 TWIST OF FATE

1976

It's a boiling hot Saturday afternoon, Mick and I are walking down Portobello Road, coming towards us is John Rotten, with another guy. I drop Mick's hand immediately – don't want to look like a drip – and we stop to have a chat. John's hair is blond and spiky and his friend's is black and spiky. They're both tall and thin, they look like a couple of handsome book-ends. During the conversation, I mention I've bought a guitar and am going to start a band. To my amazement John's friend says, 'I'll be in a band with you.'

This is an extraordinary thing for a guy to say because there are hardly any boys and girls in bands together. Mick looks uncomfortable: he likes me having a guitar but he hadn't envisaged anything like this. If I form a band with this bloke, I'll be in the enemy camp. The idea of us two playing together makes even the Pistols seem a bit old-fashioned. A group made up of boys and girls playing instruments is something new. I ask John's friend what he plays. He says, 'Saxophone.' I arrange to meet him at Davis Road tomorrow.

As we walk away I ask Mick, 'Who was that?'

'Sid.'

'What's he like?'

'Mate of John's. You don't want to get mixed up with him.'

In five minutes everything's changed. I'm in a band with someone who looks great. I wonder why Sid wants to be in a band with me – maybe he wants to shag me, but I didn't get that impression from him. Sid saw an opportunity and went for it. And then the rest of us thought, 'Of course, why not?'

Sid acting thick

Before Sid arrives at Davis Road the next day, I put my Biba peacock chair out onto the street. We sit around the pine table in the olive-green kitchen talking about our band. For once it's me having a band meeting – not Mick and Paul – and with someone really interesting too. Sid's quite awkward and talks in spurts like he thinks it's stupid to have a point of view, but he's got to communicate, so he forces the words out. I can see it's not that he's unsure of his opinions, he just thinks it's pathetic to have a strong opinion on any subject; to be intelligent means being able to see all sides. Sid likes the idea of the whole band being girls. I say I know a girl called Sarah Hall who plays a bit of bass, and Joe Strummer's girlfriend, a Spanish girl called Paloma, who plays drums. (Paul Simonon can't say her name so he says 'Palmolive' and everyone calls her that now. Paul's not being nasty: none of us are used to foreign names, we have quite a limited existence, we're not very worldly. Everyone we know is a Paul, Mick, Steve, John or Sue. The most exotic it gets is when someone middle-class comes along, like a Caroline or a Sebastian, or a Greek or Turkish mate at school.)

Me, Sid, Palmolive and Sarah all live in squats on different sides of London, and no one has a telephone. Sid lives with John in a council flat on the New End council estate in Hampstead, Sarah lives in Ladbroke Grove, I'm in Shepherd's Bush, and Palmolive's in Joe's squat in Orsett Terrace, Westbourne Grove. The day after Sid and me have our band meeting, I get on tubes and buses and go to each person's place to ask them if they want to be in our group. If they're not in, I hang around for a couple of hours and keep going back and trying again. A whole day is taken up just doing that. One day for each person. I can't get hold of Sarah so I leave her a note and just hope she'll turn up.

Joe Strummer says we can rehearse in the basement of his squat, and all arrangements from now on are made in person at each rehearsal. There's no way of letting anyone know if you can't make it; that makes us turn up. No one misses a rehearsal. We're all determined to make it happen. Not because we're desperate to be rich and famous – well I'm not anyway – it's just something good to do and we don't want to let the others down.

Joe's basement, where he used to rehearse with the 101ers, is set up with a drum kit and amps. On the first day we stand in a circle and look at each other, faces as pale and grey as mushrooms poking up out of the dirt. We decide to start with some Ramones songs: 'Blitzkrieg Bop' and '53rd and 3rd'. Sid helps me find the chords on the guitar, he's got a good ear, but none of us can play very well and we can't get through a song without it all falling apart. Sid's brought a saxophone which he toots on. His hands are on the saxophone, his elbows tucked close to his body, feet and knees together, legs straight as he jumps up and down like a matchstick pinging out of a catapult. (*This catches on when he does it at gigs and is later called the Pogo.*)

31 SHOCK

1976

It's discouraging to think how many people are
shocked by honesty and how few by deceit.
Noël Coward, *Blithe Spirit*

The course I was on at art school, Fashion and Textiles, was run by
a sensitive, serious man and some very nice women who knitted.
At the end of the first term we were set a holiday project with
the brief 'An everyday object'. I did my project about tampons.
I made drawings of bloodied, used tampons swimming about in
pale yellow piss down the bog. I also did life drawings of my friend
Sarah Hall (bass player in my and Sid's new band) naked in lots
of different positions, with the little blue tampon string dangling
from her vagina. I thought the blue string subverted the whole
prurient, porn thing by showing the reality of female bodily functions, which of course you never see in sex magazines. This blatant
reminder of menstruation took away the titillating aspect.

I did the project at Jane Ashley's family cottage in Wales. I was
so consumed by the work that I wouldn't go out to the pub in
the evenings with the others, I stayed behind and drew. After the
holiday, I went back to college with all my drawings. The tutors
were horrified. They refused to put my work – or anybody else's
work – on the wall. For the first time in the history of the course,
they said, 'Nobody's project is going up this year.' The whole class
thought the teachers' response was hilarious.

Another project I was working on was copying a photograph of a pile of dead bodies from a concentration camp and printing it onto T-shirts. I coloured the sky bright blue and the ground bright yellow, like sand. The image was supposed to be like a postcard, a postcard from Belsen, a camp, but not a holiday camp. (This was about the same time as Sid wrote the lyrics to 'Belsen Was a Gas'.) I wanted to draw attention to images that had become stale and make people see them with fresh eyes. The good thing about shocking is that it clears the brain of preconceptions for a moment, and in that moment the work has a chance to cut through all the habits and learnt behaviour of the viewer and make a fresh impact, before all the conditioning crowds in again. To older people, like my mum and the parents of Jewish friends, the T-shirt was irreverent and insulting. I didn't finish the project because I found it upsetting myself.

Sid is into subverting signs and people's expectations too, which is why he wears a leather jacket with a swastika marked out in studs. He isn't so stupid as to think that persecuting Jewish people is a good idea, but he does want to upset and enrage everyone and question what they're reacting to: the symbol, or the deed? Once we hailed a cab and the driver said he wouldn't take us because he was Jewish and offended by the swastika on Sid's jacket. As the cabbie drove away, Sid said to me, 'The cunt should've taken us and overcharged, that would've been a cleverer thing to do.'

My attraction to shocking goes back to the sixties: hippies and Yippies used it a lot, comic artists like Robert Crumb, the underground magazine *Oz*, Lenny Bruce, Andy Warhol. I also studied history of art at school, and learnt how Surrealists and Dadaists used shock and irrational juxtaposition. All this influences my work and I try to shock in all areas of my life, especially in my drawings and clothes. Referencing sex is an easy way to shock. I walk around in little girls' party dresses, hems slashed and ragged, armholes torn open to make them bigger, the waistline up under

111

my chest. My bleached blonde hair is not seductive and smooth, but matted and wild, my eyes smudged with black eyeliner. I finish it all off with fishnet tights and shocking pink patent boots from the shop Sex. I've crossed the line from 'sexy wild girl just fallen out of bed' to 'unpredictable, dangerous, unstable girl'. Not so appealing. Pippi Longstocking meets Barbarella meets juvenile delinquent. Men look at me and they are confused, they don't know whether they want to fuck me or kill me. This sartorial ensemble really messes with their heads. Good.

Tits T-shirt from Sex; studded belt, The London Leatherman; white PVC skirt, homemade; white ballet tights, Freed of London; white patent calf-length boots (unseen), made to order at a shoemaker's in Camden Town; spotty hair ribbon, Berwick Street Market. All the different places you had to go to put a look together

32 BLOW JOB

1976

I've only ever been in love with a beer bottle and a mirror.
Sid Vicious

I've moved out of Davis Road into a huge artist's studio in Fulham. I have the downstairs studio and Jane Ashley has the upstairs one. It's only £10 a week rent because it's subsidised for artists. It's as big as a bus garage with a double-height ceiling, huge doors onto a courtyard and no windows or furniture, except my mattress – which I found in a skip – up on the little mezzanine.

I'm lying on the mattress now, with Johnny Rotten. We've ended up in bed together a couple of times, but usually we're with loads of other people because we've all missed the last tube home and there are no night buses to the other side of town. It's not very private up here; John Grey, Rotten's mate from Finsbury Park (Johnny never goes anywhere without a mate) is downstairs. Iggy Pop's *The Idiot* is playing on the record player.

I've always found Rotten attractive, I like his paleness and androgyny and we get along well, but there's never been any hint of us getting together. I'm with Mick anyway, or should be. Am I with Mick now? I can't remember, we split up and get together again so often, I lose track. Hopefully we're on a break. Anyway here I am, and here John is, on my mattress with all our clothes on. We gossip about Sid for a bit and when we run out of conversation, John asks me to go down on him.

I've never given anyone a blow job before – really, I haven't. I suppose I should've done by now; I'm twenty-two. I've snuffled around down there enough times, but I haven't actually tried to make a guy come by sucking him off. I think the main reason I haven't given anyone a blow job is that I've never seen porn. Nor have my girlfriends. We reckon it degrades and objectifies women. Where's the turn-on in that? Anyway, I've never looked at my own vagina and I'm not interested in looking at anyone else's.

You can only get to see porn films at special cinemas in Soho, and I wouldn't waste the money just to have a laugh, I'd rather go round someone's flat and play records. I've learnt a bit about sex from watching films like *Last Tango in Paris*, Andy Warhol's *Trash* and *Heat*, and a Dennis Potter series on TV (I didn't bother with *Deep Throat* or *Emmanuelle*, they sounded dull), but I know these aren't average people in everyday situations, so I just watch them like I'm watching a nature programme, not sure what's acceptable or not. (Butter up the arse?) When I was at school, a boy would sometimes bring in a magazine he'd found under his dad's bed and flash pictures at the girls – I acted all snooty, like I didn't have those bits on my body. It was the only way I could deal with the embarrassment. Things have changed over the last six months: all of a sudden, every guy you know is trying to get you to go down on him, in the toilets of a club, in an alleyway, in the bathroom of a squat. It's not exactly presented in an appealing way, to make you want to do it, more like something to get *out* of doing. Blow jobs and hand jobs are considered acceptable because no emotional involvement or eye contact is needed. Full-on sex isn't so popular, anti-emotion is the prevailing doctrine.

John has no idea how inexperienced I am, or that it's my first time giving a blow job. From the outside I look very confident and sexually experienced. I think to myself, *I'll give it a go. I've just got to lick it and suck it. How difficult can it be?*

I slide down to his crotch. He gets his willy out. He smells of stale piss. So do I. We all do. I like it – it's familiar. That smell is nice and cosy to me. None of us wash before or after sex. It doesn't occur to us. It's not very spontaneous to hustle off to the bathroom and then present yourself smelling of Wright's Coal Tar soap (Cussons Imperial Leather if you really want to impress). I'm not squeamish about bodily smells, I've grown up with them. I expect it to smell different down there and to be dark and hairy. Maybe even a bit crispy if you haven't been home for a few days. That's the whole point: it's mixed up with, and close to, all your most basic functions. I may not have given a blow job before, but I know what smegma is. I've known that word since I was thirteen. I've seen it on almost every knob I've ever encountered.

I tentatively start sucking.

After a little while of licking away, I hear an imperious voice from on high, like Kenneth Williams mixed with the Artful Dodger – you know, that nasal North London whine – 'Stop it, Viv.' I look up. *What's he want? I'm busy down here.* 'Stop it, Viv,' he says. 'You're trying too hard.'

I laugh, but I'm mortified. I wipe my mouth on the back of my hand and sit up. John zips it away and we go downstairs to join John Grey – did he hear everything? It could have been worse I suppose, he could have said, 'Stop it, Viv, you're useless.'

I make us all a cup of tea; John and John drink it and leave. I cringe inside, imagining them laughing at me as they walk to the tube station.

I'm still cringing now.

Making tea at my Fulham studio. Rubber stockings and pink patent boots from Sex, Sid's leather jacket, rest from jumble sales. 1976

33 CHAINED

1976

At our first band meeting, Sid told me that his name is John Beverley but everyone calls him Sid Vicious because he's got into a few fights. He tried spelling his name with a y (copying Syd Barrett) for a bit, but nobody took any notice and now he just writes it as 'Sid'.

Sid's demeanour is sheepish and bashful; he stands with his shoulders hunched – like people who are embarrassed about their height, as if he wants to minimise his presence in a room. He talks like that too – although he has a deep masculine voice, he mumbles shyly, he's almost coquettish. He acts the clown, the village idiot, like Ollie in Laurel and Hardy: he's no fool so he must want people to underestimate him. Maybe he thinks it gives him an advantage. Sid's whole persona is a mask, which is weird because he despises fakery and bullshit. He makes me think of that Jamaican expression, 'Play fool, get wise.' He's watching everything and listening to everyone, but tries not to let on how clever he is.

Sid swears a lot and spits all the time. Once when we were waiting for the night bus in Trafalgar Square we were bored so he tried to teach me how to spit. Not propelling the spit through the gap in your front teeth like skinheads spit, but coughing it up from the back of your throat, curling your tongue into a channel and blowing. It only looks good if you get a nice clean ball of spit and project it a long way. If any of it dribbles down your chin you've failed of course. I think it's called flobbing. I was useless. Couldn't do it. It made Sid smile to see me try. He never laughs out loud, just smiles or smirks. He doesn't give away much about himself and he's never completely relaxed; consequently I don't feel relaxed when I'm with him, even though he's always very polite to me. We go everywhere together but it's a bit strained between us, overly respectful, and I always have a little knot of tension and anxiety in my chest. The conversation between us doesn't flow, he isn't a flowy sort of guy, he's stilted and monosyllabic and seems to relish the awkward atmosphere. There's a physical attraction between us but we never talk about it or act on it.

With Sid in a pub

One day we're bored and Sid has the idea that we should hand-cuff ourselves together. 'For a laugh,' he says. Everything is 'for a laugh'. It's the only reasonable justification for doing anything. Any other reason is pretentious. It's a good idea but I feel sick at the thought of it. I can't be seen to be scared of anything, or worse still, embarrassed, so I agree. Now we have a mission, something to occupy us for the day. We travel to the depths of South London, to Queenstown Road, where there's a hardcore gay sex shop called the London Leatherman. (There are rumours that this is where the Cambridge rapist bought his leather face mask.) We stand outside on the busy main road, lorries thundering past, honking their horns at us because we're dressed in black leather with studs with spiky hair. Sid raps on the heavy wooden door. It looks like the door to a castle or a dungeon. It's a door to keep people out. A little hatch slides open and a guy looks at us. He flicks his eyes up and down, giving us the once-over, then slides the hatch shut and unbolts the door. The guys in the shop look puzzled. They're not very friendly but they tolerate us because we're obviously outsiders too.

We buy a set of handcuffs. Sid can't wait to get outside so we can chain ourselves together. There's a bit of a tussle between us on the pavement about who gets to hold the key. I insist it's me but as he's stronger, he wins the fight; he's very smug about that. Once we're chained together, we realise we haven't got anything to do, nowhere to go, so we just get on and off buses, pulling each other up and down the stairs to the top deck, ignoring people who stare at us. We decide to go round Barry's house (Barry Black, big record collector and runs the Roxy club) and sit there for a while listening to records. Sid drinks tea. I refuse the tea, I haven't eaten or drunk anything all day because I'm very shy about bodily functions and would rather die than go to the bathroom in front of Sid, which is of course what he's hoping for and smirking about. He loves to make people feel uncomfortable. He yanks me off to the bog and pisses in front of me. I stand half out of the room and don't watch, I think he gets off on doing it, he doesn't wash his hands afterwards. I'm so happy when the day is over. Life is a series of excruciating tests for me, and Sid enjoys putting me through them.

Getting a minicab to the Speakeasy club in Soho one night, we are just about to leave my place when Sid goes, 'Can I wear your jeans?' My heart sinks; those jeans have an old period stain that I

119

can't get out, I didn't wash them soon enough after it happened. I can't possibly let Sid see that, he'll never let me forget it. 'You look good as you are. Anyway, they'll be too short for you,' I say. 'Yeah,' he says. Phew. We get into the cab but just as the driver is pulling away Sid says, 'I've forgotten something.' He nips out and runs back into the house. He comes out a minute later, grinning all over his face, wearing my jeans. I could kill him. Now he knows why I didn't want him to wear them. I stare out of the window for the whole car journey. He chats away, knowing he's winding me up. He doesn't tease me about the blood stain, that's left unsaid.

Sid hasn't got many clothes, none of us have much that is acceptable to be seen in, no shops sell what we like except Sex, and it's so expensive we only have one or two things from there. Sid has two pairs of trousers: holey, faded jeans and a pair of red pegs – they're wool and have a little silver thread running through them, zoot-suitish, pleated at the waist, wide-legged, tapering in quite narrow at the bottom. He wears them with brothel creepers, a bit David Bowie and a bit 1950s. Some of the boys still have this look, Malcolm McLaren and John Rotten wear it sometimes too – it's left over from Too Fast To Live Too Young To Die, the teddy-boy shop Malcolm and Vivienne Westwood had before Sex. I never went there, didn't know about it.

One day Sid turns up in the peg trousers and they're in ribbons. He'd sliced them up with a razor blade because he hated them so much but he couldn't find his jeans so when he wanted to go out he had to stick them back together. He joined the rips with loads of safety pins, all the way down his legs, hundreds of them. That's how the 'loads of safety pins' thing started amongst people in clubs: they copied it, but he only did it because he couldn't be bothered to sew his trousers up.

A while later Sid came round to Davis Road in a new pair of black bondage trousers, said he'd gone into Sex and Vivienne told him she couldn't bear looking at him in those disgusting trousers a minute longer, she made him take them off, gave him a pair of bondage trousers for free and threw the red ones away. I'm really jealous, Vivienne must really like him to do that. She doesn't usually give stuff away.

Whenever Sid gets his dole money he treats me to a Wimpy burger and chips. He never has anything to do and wants to tag along to art school with me, but I say no because I know he'll embarrass me. I love Wimpy burgers and I'm always hungry so when he says, 'I'll buy you Wimpy and chips on the way in, if you let me come with you,' I can't resist. It's such a treat and we can't usually afford it – everyone has their price I suppose. So we get burger and chips for breakfast and then he lumbers along next to me up Shepherd's Bush Road to art college.

He sits in on the lectures, they're about warp and weft, knitting machines and pattern cutting, things like that. Sid slouches so low in the chair he almost slides off, long arms dangling by his sides, skinny legs stretched way out in front of him, foot shaking like he's on speed. Not a discreet presence at all. Then he picks his nose and farts and burps loudly all through the talk. After this happens a couple of times, he's banned from the college and I'm told by the head of year not to bring him in any more. This is actually a relief for me. Not that Sid will take no for an answer – I have to be very firm with him to make sure he doesn't come to college again. Whenever we're together, even if I'm a bit fed up with him and ask him to give me a bit of space, he won't go away. He doesn't care, he's not hurt, he just does what he wants. He thinks it's funny.

I never see Sid with a girl. There's a very young girl we call Wiggy, she wears a grey shaggy wig and has a sweet face, looks about fourteen years old and I think they fiddle about together sometimes. I think Soo Catwoman and him had a tryst, and that's it. No flirting, no talking about girls, no interest shown. I think he's shy and inexperienced: unless a girl grabs hold of him, he never makes a move.

Often when Sid turns up at my place he rushes past me at the front door, races upstairs to the bathroom and looks for stray pubic hairs. I know it's childish and shouldn't matter, but it makes me want to die if he finds one in the bath or on the loo seat. If he does, he laughs hysterically and teases me about it for hours. That's what it's like with him: find a weak point in someone, then pull them to pieces. To help me stay cool and cope with the embarrassment I imagine it's Alan's pube, I act like it couldn't possibly be mine and I don't know what he's talking about. There are times when the doorbell rings and I think with dread about the bathroom and sometimes I even run in there to check it before opening the front door. You never know who's going to be at the door – if someone comes over it's spontaneous, because we don't have a telephone.

The worst situation Sid ever gets me into is when we go to meet some aristocrat he's come across somewhere. Sid thinks it's amusing that this toff wants to hang out with us and buy us drinks at his private club in Kensington Church Street. We often get invited to things like this, as if we're a couple of freaks to be paraded around.

We meet Posh Boy and his posh mate at a pub on Kensington Church Street and I don't know how it happens, but an argument starts. I've got a feeling I started it because I feel safe with Sid here; if I were on my own I'd be more cautious. I say something provocative to Posh Boy, he threatens me with violence, and the next thing I know, Sid's whipped off his studded belt, wrapped it around his fist and smashed Posh Boy over the head with the buckle end. Splits his head open. (*Sid taught me this move: wrap the tongue of the belt round your hand, use the buckle as the weapon, it's important to lock your arm straight whilst you wield the belt, and do the worst thing you can think of first. That's the only chance you've got.*) We all leap up from the table, Sid legs it up the road and I'm left with Posh Boy, blood pouring out of his face.

Posh Boy grabs me by the hair – a clump of it in his fist, like I'm an animal – and drags me up the road looking for Sid, to kill him. I'm a hostage. I am so humiliated: I've never been treated like such a piece of dirt before. No doubt Posh Boy feels the same after being smashed across the head by Sid.

The three of us – Posh Boy fuming and covered in blood, holding me by my hair, me bent over and hobbling along in a subservient position next to him, and Posh Boy's mate, scurrying to keep up – go raging up and down Kensington Church Street. No sign of Sid. Posh Boy lets go of my hair for a second and I dash into a boutique and ask the shop assistants to protect me. They aren't too happy about it, but I refuse to go back outside. I hide at the back of the shop for ages until the posh boys go away.

When I poke my head out into the street to check the coast is clear, there's Sid, looking for me. I'm quite touched because most of the time he has no code of conduct. I apologise to him for putting him in a situation where he felt he had to defend me. I've learnt my lesson; from now on I'll keep my mouth shut and not invite trouble. Things can get out of hand so quickly, especially with Sid around. I also decide never to wear heels again when I'm out with him. I go to Holt's in Camden Town and buy a pair of black Dr Martens. (You can get them in black, brown or maroon, the skinhead boys at school used to buy the brown ones and polish them with Kiwi Oxblood shoe polish – this gives them a deep reddish brown colour, much subtler than the flat red of the originals. They also kept them pristinely clean and polished at all times.) I wear my new boots with everything – dresses, tutus – it's a great feeling to be able to run again. No other girls wear DMs with dresses, so I get a lot of funny looks. (Skinhead girls only wear DMs with Sta-Prest trousers. With their boring grey skirts, they wear plain white or holey ecru tights and black patent brogues.) But as I wear them all the time to clubs and pubs, it eventually catches on with other girls and I don't look so odd.

Sid always says he isn't a violent person, that he's a useless fighter, he'd rather run away from a fight than confront someone, violence is a last resort. But 'Sid Vicious' is becoming a persona he can't shake off, and he lets the myth build, plays up to it. After a while, because of his name and reputation, he's getting attacked everywhere he goes: guys want to take him on. He doesn't care. Everything he does he takes as far as he can. He detaches himself from fear, remorse, caring about his safety or his looks and just becomes a vessel for other people's fantasies about him, like Paul Newman in *Cool Hand Luke*. His attitude is, *Let's see how far this thing goes. Test it to destruction.*

34 THE SHOP

1976–1977

We are going to inherit the earth; there
is not the slightest doubt about that.
Buenaventura Durruti

I've got so used to my life being challenging and fraught with
danger that I don't question it any more. Whether I'm knocking
on the door of a hardcore sex shop, walking through suburban
streets being verbally abused and spat on, or being threatened on
the tube, I don't give in. I don't dress normally to have an easy life.
The pilgrimage down the King's Road to get to the Shop (Sex:
everyone calls it 'the Shop'), the place I want to hang out and buy
stuff, is one of the scariest things I do – running the gauntlet of
teds who want to kill people like me – but nothing will stop me
looking the way I want. It's a commitment.

I usually go with Sid or Rory, they know everyone in there,
which makes it easier. We walk all the way down the King's Road
from Sloane Square tube station, but as we get closer to the Shop,
Rory gets a bit agitated and says things like, 'Do your bag up, Viv,
there's stuff spilling out of it. Looks messy.' That's from someone
who hangs out with Malcolm a lot, he still gets nervous. If we
make it without seeing any teds, we're lucky, otherwise we have
to dodge in and out of the shops all along the King's Road and it
takes ages to get to the World's End, which is what the end of the
King's Road is called and feels like.

As soon as you round the bend and see the word 'SEX' in

giant pink plastic letters, you know you're safe.

I push open the door and am hit by the cloying, sickly-sweet smell of latex; it's funny how you never smell it anywhere but here. The long thin shop floor is empty except for the assistants, Debbie and Jordan. Jordan is a work of art. Her look is so extreme and yet she isn't scary or threatening at all. She has a soft voice, gentle manner and is calm and centred. Sometimes Jordan doesn't wear a skirt, just fishnet tights or stockings, high-waisted satin knickers, a leather or rubber bodice and bondage shoes. She paints two black slashes across her eyelids, looks like a robber's mask, a cross between Zorro and Catwoman, her face is dusted with white face powder and her lips are pillar-box red. Her hair is piled high, ash blonde and sculpted into a huge wave dipping down over one eye. Jordan travels on the train from Sussex all the way into London dressed like this. Every day. She doesn't go into the loos at Charing Cross Station and change her clothes once she's arrived. Her attitude filters through to all of us. You have to live it.

Now I'm inside, I can't wait to look at the clothes, there aren't many, not much to choose from, but that just makes everything more special. High up on the shelves are rows of white, pink or black patent ankle boots, scallop-topped, stiletto-heeled. I wish I could buy a pair in every colour, they're like something out of a Frederick's of Hollywood catalogue (fetish underwear makers in LA), which I think has influenced Vivienne Westwood.

Vivienne's scary, for the reason any truthful, plain-talking person is scary – she exposes you. If you haven't been honest with yourself, this makes you feel extremely uncomfortable, and if you are a con merchant the game is up. She's uncompromising in every way: what she says, what she stands for, what she expects from you and how she dresses. She's direct and judgemental with a strong northern accent that accentuates her sincerity. She has a confidence I haven't seen in any other woman. She's strong, opinionated and very smart. She can't bear complacency. She's the most inspiring person I've ever met. Sid told me, 'Vivienne says you're talented but lazy.' I've worked at everything twice as hard since he said that.

I'm very influenced by how Vivienne looks. She gets it just right. Black lines drawn around her eyes, dark lipstick, pale face. Her hair is dyed white blonde, with an inch of dark roots showing and clumpy spikes sticking out in all directions. I've no idea where she got the look from, it doesn't reference anything I'm aware of, no films or art. I think she's very feminine in her own way. I do my version of Vivienne but it comes out a bit different and looks like my own style. I love changing my hair, you can't get hair wrong, I've spent money on it from a young age. I stopped going to hair-dressers after I copied Vivienne though, they didn't get it. Keith Levene hacks at it and dyes it for me now.

Vivienne has a good figure, she can carry off anything, usually she wears a rubber knee-length skirt and calf-length black boots, not sexy boots, they're flat, slightly baggy, or a see-through rubber top with bondage trousers and lots of tartan. She makes everyone else on the street look irrelevant. Although the clothes she wears are daring, there's something about her that's quite puritan and austere. She's also very private. There are rumours that she has a child but I've never seen one or heard her mention it. Vivienne's a vegetarian and very strict about it, she gives anyone who eats meat a hard time. One day Chrissie Hynde – who's also a vegetarian – saw Vivienne backstage at the Roundhouse eating a ham sandwich. Chrissie confronted Vivienne about it and Vivienne replied, 'Well, it's dead now.' (Once when Vivienne asked Chrissie a question, Chrissie replied, 'Oh, I just go with the flow.' Vivienne thought that was unacceptable and wouldn't speak to her again for a year.) We're all very judgemental about everything, including each other, but if you state your position boldly enough, or just don't give a shit, you can do what the hell you want. In some ways to be too passionate or attached to anything is considered weak; you don't stick to things just for the sake of it or on a matter of principle, that's rigid behaviour.

Malcolm isn't in the Shop so often – when he is, he's always friendly and charming, I've never heard him be rude or confrontational to anyone. Although they're often together, you never see Vivienne and Malcolm touch or kiss and I think that's set the tone for how we all behave in relationships. Hardly anyone in Malcolm and Vivienne's circle is in a couple; only Siouxsie Sioux (Siouxsie is part of the Bromley Contingent, followers of the Sex Pistols from the very beginning), who's with Steve Severin, and sometimes Paul Cook has a steady girlfriend. I've heard rumours that some of the girls who hang around the Shop do hand jobs on Park Lane for money, which fits in with the way everyone views sex: as a commodity, no emotional involvement needed. Maybe things go on behind the scenes. Sometimes, when the Roxy or our other haunt, Louise's, closes (Louise's is a lesbian club in Poland Street, with a little hatch in the red door at eye height so the doorman can look you over before deciding to let you in), a group of people start whispering and arranging something, then they all disappear off together. I can't imagine what they do. I wonder if they all go off and have an orgy somewhere. I don't know, I'm not part of it. I don't quite fit into that side of things, I'm a bit too straight, like Mick. I dress in fetish and bondage gear, rubber and studs, and give off sexual signals with my clothes but don't act on them in real life.

LOUISE

61, POLAND ST. LONDON W.1. 01-437 1693

I warrant I am over 18 years of age

Expiry Date 1-10-77

Signed.

3878

Debbie and Jordan always point out something new that's come in or that they think will suit me. There's lots of black, splashes of pink, silver and red; I love all the different textures: rubber, leather (the only other places you can buy anything leather in London are sex shops and motorbike shops), mohair, zips and fraying edges. Vivienne is very aware of texture, she uses it along with cut and text to make statements. She's made me conscious of the signs and signals I'm giving off with my clothes, I've become much more visually aware from going to the Shop, more than from any art-school teaching.

Today I choose a transparent skin-coloured T-shirt, a cowboy T-shirt (two cowboys with their cocks out screen-printed on the front) and black leather jeans (you have to get them taken in every couple of months as they keep stretching and losing their shape. We all go to a guy who has a little alteration booth in the back of the launderette on the King's Road) and go into the changing room, which has floor-to-ceiling pale pink rubber curtains. There's a photo shoot going on. Vivienne, Chrissie Hynde and Jordan are going to paint the word 'SEX' across their bare arses for the picture and Vivienne asks me to be part of it. I'm honoured but say no, not because I'm against it morally or am too prudish but because I'm not confident about my arse. It's the part of myself I hate most. Not that I say this to Vivienne, she'd never accept that as a reason not to do it. She's hard to say no to, so it's quite something for me to hold out and go against her. I feel pathetic and uptight for not joining in.

I'm always trying on the shoes and boots in the shop. One time there was a pair of red ankle boots shaped like buckets, a bit fetishy but too ugly to be sexy, on a shelf. They'd been there for ages and Vivienne was musing out loud about how surprised she was that nobody had bought them because she thought they were beautiful. Then she turned to me and said, 'You should get them, Viviane, they'll look good on you.' I looked at these hideous boots, not convinced at all, but I had to try them on; she insisted. They made my legs look fantastic. I still thought they were too expensive and very odd-looking but I bought them anyway, I couldn't say no to Vivienne twice.

I still wear those boots. They're my favourite item of clothing.

The clothes in Sex are so expensive that most of us own just one or two items, a T-shirt or a pair of shoes, and we wear that treasured piece all the time. I think to be dressed head to toe in brand-new stuff from Sex is risible. You have to be very careful which piece you choose because it defines you. Just because you've bought something from Sex doesn't mean you've bought the right thing. Within that very narrow choice is an even narrower margin. We all care a lot about style; everyone is united on that subject, even if we have different taste (for instance Siouxsie and I buy very different things from Sex). How we look is extremely important and the nuances within the small scene are rigorously observed and judged.

I've recently thrown away all my Biba T-shirts because the necklines are boat-shaped and the shoulders are puffed. I can't wear my beautiful Terry de Havilland boots because they're brown. You can't wear brown. It's the most reviled colour. Not just because it's considered lame, being a mixture of other colours – even a colour has to state its position – but because it's bourgeois, worn by people who live in the countryside. It's too comfortable. Acceptable colours are black, white, red, shocking pink, fluorescent yellow or green (almost impossible to find anything in London in these colours), tartan, anything bold. Pastels are weak, unless you wear them ironically or in a contrasting fabric like rubber; grey is for old people and suits. As for beige, you may as well be dead.

Vivienne and Malcolm use clothes to shock, irritate and provoke a reaction but also to inspire change. Mohair jumpers, knitted on big needles, so loosely that you can see all the way through them, T-shirts slashed and written on by hand, seams and labels on the outside, showing the construction of the piece; these attitudes are reflected in the music we make. It's OK not to be perfect, to show the workings of your life and your mind in your songs and your clothes. And everything you do in life is meaningful on a political level. That's why we're all so merciless about each other's failings and why sloppiness is derided.

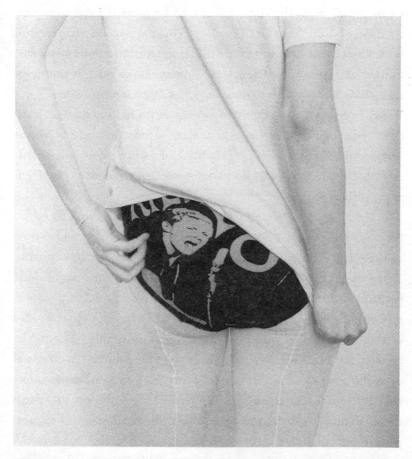

Wearing white seamed ballet tights from Freed of London; tits T-shirt and Jerry Lee Lewis knickers from Sex; white patent boots (unseen). Daytime outfit

35 THE FLOWERS OF ROMANCE

Summer 1976

O Rose, thou art sick.
William Blake

Every day is so hot, I'm glad to be rehearsing in Joe's basement – at least I'm not getting a tan – but it's hard work lugging my guitar backwards and forwards in these high temperatures. We're down here for five or six hours a day, and it's getting a bit uncomfortable, not just because of the heat. We don't have any of our own songs and Sid is so judgemental and difficult to talk to that rehearsals are becoming excruciating; I'm finding the awkwardness unbearable. I try and start discussions to fill up the time, like whether Bob Dylan is a good lyricist or not. I think he is, Sid thinks he isn't. I say, '"Positively Fourth Street" has good lyrics.' 'Like what?' says Sid. 'It's just one big put-down. It's very honest.' He wants me to convince him. He doesn't care what I say, as long as I don't waver. Another time we discuss the concept of 'cool'. Sid says, 'There's no such thing as cool.' I say, 'You're cool.' 'No I'm not,' he replies.

The not knowing how to play or how to structure a rehearsal is wearing us all down. Sid decides he's not going to play sax, he's going to be the singer. He keeps on at me, 'You've got to write a song. We can't meet again until you've written a song.' The pressure. Every night, on my way home from rehearsal, I go into the bakery on Queensway and buy a soft white watercress and egg mayonnaise roll. I look forward to it so much, it's my little treat.

132

I try and ditch Sid at the end of each rehearsal so I don't have to share it with him.

By September, despite the hot summer, we're as pale and spotty as ever, and despite rehearsing every day, we don't have any songs and our playing hasn't improved. We do have a name though: the Flowers of Romance. I think it's the best band name in the world, reminds me of *The Grapes of Wrath*. Rotten thought of it, just came out with it, he's so good with words. I love that the name goes against all the other band names that are fashionable at the moment, all the hard, shocking, aggressive names. Also, it's true: we're the children of the first wave of divorced parents from the 1950s, we've seen the domestic dream break down. It was impossible to live up to. We grew up during the 'peace and love' of the 1960s, only to discover that there are wars everywhere and love and romance is a con.

Some evenings we go to a pub in Notting Hill after rehearsal and slump in the comfortable chairs. Journalists come up to us and ask if we're in a band. We don't have to do anything except look a bit different and we're already being followed around. Sid won't talk to them unless they buy us drinks, then he says, 'Yeah, we're in the Flowers of Romance.' The journalists scribble it down, desperate to have something to write about. They know something's happening but they can't find the bands, can't find the records. There aren't any. *When are you playing?* they ask. 'Soon.'

I don't look forward to rehearsals any more because I know Sid's going to ask me if I've written a song, but every time I try and write something I'm crippled by the thought of him judging it. A song that Sid would like? Impossible. What subject can I write about that he won't find stupid? I'm not going to write about Belsen, torture or S & M.

After a couple of months, Sid decides to chuck Palmolive out of the band because she doesn't look right, too hippyish – but I think it's more to do with her standing up to him and disagreeing with him. Then he boots Sarah out because she can't play. I realise he's ruthlessly ambitious underneath his gawky facade. He gets in a bloke called Steve Walsh, he wants him in the band because he can play guitar. Steve wears a grey suit and his hair is immaculate. He can't write a song either.

Most nights after rehearsals Sid and Steve come back to my place and hang around until it's too late to go home. We sit around smoking, sometimes taking speed, talking and listening to records with Alan and Paul until four in the morning. When I've had enough I say, 'I'm going to bed. There's room for someone else if anyone wants to.' As I walk out of the room I hear a scuffle behind me. I say to myself, *Please let Sid win.* He does. He pushes Steve out of the way and stumbles into my room with a grin on his face.

I take my jeans and T-shirt off and get into bed in my bra and knickers, Sid takes his top and jeans off. We lie facing away from each other. I don't know if he sleeps. I don't. I can't, it's too weird. As the sun comes up, we edge closer and closer to each other in tiny little movements, hoping not to be detected. By the morning we're pressed hard against each other, back to back, stuck together with sweat, making as much physical contact as possible. This is what we do every time we're in bed together, never anything more.

Sometimes I manage to drift off during the night, but I come back to consciousness, revived by a strong smell of Newcastle Brown Ale, a thick treacly brown smell – mixed with ammonia, like a dose of smelling salts.

'Sid! You've wet the bed again!'

He giggles. He doesn't care.

One day Sid says something that really scares me. 'Siouxsie's asked me to be in her band, Siouxsie and the Banshees, and play their first gig at the 100 Club.' My heart sinks. *Oh no, he's going to leave the band. This was bound to happen, he's so interesting, of course someone's going to pinch him.*

So this is it, the first time one of us is going to play live and I'm not part of it. I don't really mind, I don't feel ready to do it. I don't have the guts to do what Mick, John and now Sid and Siouxsie are doing. But Sid's going to try and make his dream a reality, no more talking and posing, he's going to put himself on the line and actually do it. I'm excited and nervous. They've only had one twenty-minute rehearsal. Will it work? This is a huge moment for us. Although we like the idea that anybody can do anything, without any history, talent or technical ability, if you miss the mark, by even a tiny bit, you'll be derided. Sid is the most stringent critic of all, so in a way, he has to get it the most right.

36 THE 100 CLUB

1976

No one talks as we sit around in the half-empty 100 Club on Oxford Street, waiting for Sid and Siouxsie to go on stage. We're all nervous but it's important not to show it. Apart from the Sex Pistols, nobody else playing tonight has performed live before.

Outside, Oxford Street looks Dickensian. Most of the shops are boarded up, there are mountains of rotting rubbish piled along the edge of the pavements because of the dustmen's strike and half the street lamps are off due to electricity rationing.

Inside, the tension is mounting. Siouxsie's on first, she's doing 'The Lord's Prayer' and Sid's drumming (he's never drummed before), Steve Severin, Siouxsie's boyfriend, is on bass and Marco Pirroni (later in Adam and the Ants) plays guitar. They climb up onto the stage and start. Sid is good, no rolls, no fills, no cymbals. He pounds away at the drums, steady as a rock. He looks great and shows no fear. The song goes on for about twenty minutes, it sounds menacing with Siouxsie intoning over the insistent beat. I think she's inspiring, she has such self-possession. I'm relieved when Sid tells me later he's not going to join the band, he doesn't want to sit at the back behind a drum kit, he wants to be the star.

Me and Sid go along to the 100 Club again the next night to hang out. A group called the Damned are playing. I wear a black mesh see-through top with no bra. I saw Siouxsie wear a transparent top with no bra once and thought she looked great; the thing is, she has a much more boyish figure than me, my boobs are bigger and the effect is not the same. I ask for a glass of water at the bar, fighting the urge to cross my arms over my exposed chest whilst the barmen gawp at me. I'll never wear this top again, I don't have the bottle to carry it off. Whilst I'm standing there trying to look nonchalant, I hear shouting and scuffling coming from near the stage. I don't think anything of it, probably people jumping on top of each other whilst the band's playing.

About ten minutes later someone tells me Sid's been arrested and carted off to the police station for throwing a glass – it hit a post and shattered, injuring a girl in the audience. I know Sid didn't do it, he was standing near me when I was at the bar, leaning against a pillar, he was miles away from the stage. I bet it's been pinned on him because of his reputation as a troublemaker.

I talk to Vivienne about the situation: there's no doubt in our minds that Sid didn't do it. She says she'll find out what's happening and let me know.

Two days later, there's a knock at the front door. It's Vivienne. She has a car and says, 'I'm going to visit Sid at Ashford Remand Centre, come on.' I'm horrified. I'm wearing ripped Levi's and a baggy old T-shirt. 'I'll just go and change,' I say, cursing myself for looking so shit. Vivienne's impatient, 'There's no time for that, Sid won't care what you're wearing.' It's not Sid I'm worried about, I'm much more upset that she's seen me dressed so badly.

I run upstairs and change in about ten seconds flat, there's no way I'm going to keep Vivienne waiting. I look around for something to take Sid. I can only think of a book, but I've never seen him read anything. I pick up Dostoyevsky's *Crime and Punishment* but the title is too preachy and will put him off, so instead I take *Helter Skelter*, by Vincent Bugliosi and Curt Gentry, on the Manson Family murders. It's written in a very matter-of-fact, cold style, almost like a list, which I know will appeal to Sid. Vivienne doesn't approve and tells me off in the car. (Sid thought Vivienne left him the book, she would have been furious if she knew.)

When we walk into the visiting room, Sid's already there, slumped at a table. He looks broken, not the Sid I know. When he talks he sounds emotional and grateful that we've come. I've never thought of him as having feelings and I'm glad Vivienne and I are visiting him. Left to my own devices, it would never have occurred to me to see him, that he would have wanted it. He tells us how awful it is in here, that the worst thing is sharing a room with someone else. He's already been moved once because his first cellmate was too violent; his current cellmate sings and whistles all the time but Sid doesn't dare ask him to stop. Another guy tried to kill himself. Sid assures us he's innocent and pleads with us to do all we can to get him out.

A couple of days later I get a letter. I don't know what I'm more surprised about: that Sid wrote to me, that his writing is pretty and girly with little circles over the i's, or that he's so articulate. I can tell that some of what he's written is for the benefit of the prison wardens – he sounds so nice and well balanced and sorry to be there – but some of it shows a softer, more affectionate side of Sid that I've never seen before.

I hear that the young girl who was hit by the thrown glass has lost the sight in one eye. Due to lack of evidence she drops the charges against Sid, so he's let go. This incident changes everything for me. I thought the group of people I've been involved with were so intelligent. Now everything feels tainted, the atmosphere has changed from positive and exciting to negative and violent. Not a scene I feel so good about being associated with.

Sid told me a year later that he did throw the glass.

In replying to this letter, please write on the envelope:—

Number A03293 Name BEVERLEY

H. M. REMAND CENTRE
WOODTHORPE ROAD
ASHFORD,
MIDDLESEX.

Dear Viv,

I don't feel quite as bad as I did before. Suzie and Steve came to visit me to-day, which made me feel a hell of a lot better. They said that it is pretty certain that the girls eye is okay, I certainly hope so. Maybe I'll get out altogether, on Wednesday. What has been happening at your end? Have you started practising with Suzie and Marco yet? And also, do you know whether you will be able to rehearse in your new place, when you get it.

I get so worried and agitated in here that I can't sleep at all. And when I do, I have the most awful nightmares. I feel certain that just a couple of months in a place like this, would drive anyone crazy. I'm in a state of nervous agitation at

No. 243 Dd. 112574 11/73 G & C

Excerpt from the letter Sid wrote to me from Ashford Remand Centre, 1976

37 CHRISTMAS '76

The news reaches us from across the Atlantic Ocean that the Heartbreakers are coming to London and renting a flat. The Heartbreakers are respected because their leader, Johnny Thunders, was in the New York Dolls, a band that influenced both the Pistols and the Clash. Hearing Thunders is on his way to England is like hearing Dracula is on his way to our shores in the hold of a ship – a dark powerful presence, ominous and seductive, creeping closer and closer. We're doomed.

Keith, Mick and Sid can't wait to meet Johnny. Leee Black Childers – the Heartbreakers' manager, who's arrived ahead of the band – says to me, 'You and Johnny are going to love each other, Viv. Johnny's going to go crazy when he sees you.' I'm even more wound up after this comment. Eventually the band arrive, they've arranged a warm-up gig in Plymouth. Some of the London lot travel all the way down there to see them; bit uncool.

And then I meet him.

I'm at Caroline Coon's house on Christmas Day. Caroline – the artist, writer and activist – has invited a bunch of us over for Christmas lunch, which is a very generous thing to do and quite funny because we're all so untraditional. The Heartbreakers are there, so are Sid, John Rotten, Soo Catwoman, Steve Jones and some others. Rotten gives Sid a Christmas present of a doll he's customised to look like Soo and when you pull down her knickers – which Sid does – John's written 'Sid' with an arrow pointing to her vagina.

Johnny Thunders and I sit on opposite sides of Caroline's living room, stealing glances at each other when we each think the other one isn't looking. He looks like he's walked straight out of a Shangri-Las' song: bad but good. He asks me polite questions, like what instrument I play and what I'm doing for the rest of the holidays. He's older and much more confident and charming than English boys. He's handsome and has a worldly, sexual aura about him. He keeps telephoning New York. 'I'd like to place a collect call to New York.' I don't know what a collect call is. Hearing him talk in his New York accent is fascinating. A couple of things aren't quite right about him though: he's wearing a black-and-white spotty shirt, black waistcoat and a shoelace tie, it's all a bit too neat and dapper. He hasn't bought anything from Sex yet and his hair isn't uneven enough, it needs to be messier and chopped about. But he's bewitching; a beautiful, exotic alien from another world.

Things get a bit out of hand at Caroline's. No one eats anything, someone pisses in the pot plants and the turkey is stuffed, arse up, down the toilet. I didn't see who did it, but it was obviously the silly English boys, the Americans would never do anything like that, they're much more respectful.

After the lunch, I walk back to my studio and Mick comes over; he's been at his grandmother's. He's pissed off that he wasn't invited to Caroline's, he thinks it's because people think the Clash aren't cool, he's very sensitive about it.

Johnny Thunders, wearing the skull T-shirt he later gave me. 1976

38 ME AND JOHNNY T

1977

Not long after the Christmas lunch, the Heartbreakers are playing at the Roxy in Covent Garden and I go down to see them.

I stand at the front to soak up the band. I want to see Johnny's fingers on his guitar, watch his face as he sings, check out his moves. He looks over at me from the stage. He doesn't smile. The Heartbreakers launch into their first song, 'Born to Lose': Johnny shakes his head and pouts, he holds his guitar like it's glued to him. He acts like he

Thunders in action, 1977. (Give him a great big kiss)

can barely stand up but his fingers glide up and down the guitar neck as easily as if he's running them through his hair. He fixes his dark brown eyes on me. How great! Johnny Thunders looked at me from the stage! He doesn't look away. He sings the whole song looking into my eyes. This is the sort of daydream I've been having since I was a little girl and Johnny Thunders has made it come true. I smile at him at the end of the song. It's the most romantic thing that's ever happened to me. Johnny Thunders understands romance and big gestures. He likes the Shangri-Las and the Shirelles as well, groups that English boys think are lightweight: he likes girls.

Jerry Nolan hammers away at the drums and they're on to the next song. Johnny doesn't take his eyes off my face, he sings this song to me too. I'm rooted to the spot, I can't believe what's happening. This is the way to win a girl. He sings the whole set to me. Every single song straight into my eyes. He changes the words to 'Can't Keep My Eyes On You' to 'Can't Keep My Eyes Off You'. The rest of the band don't seem to mind, I think they understand romance too. Anyway, Johnny can do what he wants. After the show, he walks over to me – his hair plastered to his forehead with sweat – and asks what I'm doing later. I invite him and Jerry Nolan back to my studio. Whilst I make tea, Johnny plays my guitar and sings 'Baby It's You', 'Walking in the Sand' and lots of other sixties girl-group songs. When we kiss, he breaks off and shouts to Jerry, 'I felt something!' He's amazed, says he hasn't felt anything in a long time. 'I've got to call someone and tell them.' He makes a collect call to New York (I know what it means now).

Johnny: 'I met a girl.'

Pause.

Johnny: 'Viv Albertine.'

Pause.

He turns to me, 'How old are you?'

Why did that fucking New Yorker have to ask that of all

questions? Why didn't he ask what I do or what I look like? 'Twenty-two,' I say (furious inside, sounds so old). 'Twenty-two,' Johnny says into the phone. I'm sure I can hear a bored exhalation of air from New York.

Jerry Nolan falls asleep downstairs. Johnny and I end up on the mattress on the mezzanine. He can't get an erection, it doesn't bother me, we have a lovely time talking and touching. He says he can't show his feelings that way, it doesn't work any more. After a couple of hours I make breakfast for him and Jerry, beans on toast.

Very quickly, me and Johnny Thunders become flirty friends. He's a sweet and sensitive guy but heroin comes first for him and although he often calls me and we chat for ages, eventually he'll ask if Keith (Levene) is there and I realise he's after drugs. Keith has become central to the Heartbreakers crowd now, he's best friends with the Yanks. He's all 'Thunders this' and 'Thunders that'. Me and Johnny still spend a lot of time together at the Heartbreakers' flat in Denbigh Street in Victoria – which I take as a compliment considering I'm not into drugs. The flat is blandly decorated with off-white walls and fitted beige carpets, it has no atmosphere, like a hotel room. When he first moved in Johnny was worried about his image and asked me if Victoria was a cool neighbourhood. I told him it wasn't.

It feels like we're meant to be together. If he wasn't a junkie, I think we would have something very special. I'm as close to falling in love as you can be with a drug addict. I'm going out with Mick off and on throughout all of this, but the chemistry between me and Thunders is overpowering.

One afternoon a whole bunch of us are sitting around at Johnny's place, smoking and talking. I'm wearing a very thin worn-out black T-shirt with a skull and crossbones printed on the front that Johnny's given me as a gift, his favourite T-shirt he said. It's beautiful, ripped and holey with the sleeves cut off. I love it.

144

At some point in the evening I look down and notice my right nipple is poking out of a tiny hole in the T-shirt. I'm not wearing a bra, god knows why, I usually wear a bra. I've been sitting here for hours with my nipple sticking out and no one's said anything. I adjust the T-shirt and take a long drag on my cigarette. Best to act cool and nonchalant about it. I give it about twenty minutes then say I've got to go. All the way home on the bus, I can't stop thinking about my nipple. Why didn't Johnny say anything? The thing is, we all dress so provocatively that he probably didn't know if I'd done it deliberately or not. Or maybe he just thought it was funny. I can't face him again for a couple of weeks.

Wearing Johnny's T-shirt (hole sewn up). Bullet necklace. Hair by Keith Levene. 1977

39 HEROIN

1977

Rock and roll is simply an attitude.
You don't have to play the greatest guitar.
Johnny Thunders

It's three o'clock in the afternoon. I've got to get up, can't lie here any longer, the room's too hot. I can smell the baked beans from last night rotting in the sink. I throw off the bed covers – scraps of leopard-print fabric given to me by Mick, which he bought when Biba closed down – and run downstairs to answer the phone.

A thick New York accent drawls down the line. 'Hey, Viv, what's happenin'?'

It's Thunders. He asks me to come and see him at his friend's flat in Chelsea.

'OK, I'll come over for a couple of hours. I'm meeting Sid at six.'

He says, 'Yeah I know, I saw him last night.'

No time to eat, I'll buy a packet of crisps on the way. I put on a tight black lace dress Sid got me from a jumble sale. It didn't quite fit so he slashed a split in the side – which is now held together with safety pins – then he hacked the bottom off whilst I was wearing it, leaving the hem really short and frayed. I pull on holey black tights and Dr Marten boots; I still never wear heels if I'm seeing Sid.

I post a letter to Rory on the way – he's moved to New York – telling him all about my great band, the Flowers of Romance, and how Sid is a brilliant front man, as good as Johnny Rotten.

As soon as I arrive at his friend's flat, Thunders grabs my hand and leads me across the living room. He pushes aside a heavy curtain and takes me through the French windows, out onto a tiny wrought-iron balcony where we perch like two scruffy crows, jagged hair and torn black clothes, silhouetted against the backs of the grand white stuccoed houses.

I can't imagine what Johnny's going to say or why he's being so secretive. Maybe he wants drugs? But he wouldn't come to me for that. Is he going to talk about love? No, that's impossible, he's got no room for love, his heart is full of heroin.

I ruffle my hair so it falls over my face and press my back into the railings, trying to get a little distance between us. I bet my skin looks terrible in this bright sunlight. I pray that he has bad eyesight.

Johnny tells me that he saw Sid last night and Sid confided in him that when I meet him at six tonight, he's going to chuck me out of the Flowers of Romance.

No. It can't be true.

Not thrown out of the band we formed together. I made my mum cry to be in this band . . . we've been rehearsing all through this unbearable heatwave . . . and *the Flowers of Romance* is such a great name. If I'm not the guitarist in the Flowers of Romance, I've got no identity. Johnny sees my face collapse, I'm too shocked to act like I don't care.

'Viv, I *told* Sid he was wrong. I said what the fuck does it matter how well she plays? She's totally cool and looks great.'

But no one – not even the revered *Johnny Thunders* – has any effect on Sid. I'm out. There's nothing more to say. We step back into the haze of the living room. Has Johnny told them? No one takes any notice of me, so I flop onto a floor cushion.

Thunders, always the leader, takes command of the room.

He announces that it's 'Time to shoot up now,' like a playschool teacher. There's a ripple of excitement. He looks down at me.

'Want some, Viv? It'll make things better.'

I've been offered heroin before. I've never taken it. I've never had any intention of taking it – but today is the perfect day. Today I'm devastated. I want to belong, if not to my band then somewhere else, anywhere, I don't care, I just need to make the world go away.

So I nod. 'Yeah.'

Johnny knows I've never taken smack before and he becomes reverential. He tells me that I can go first as we're all going to share the same needle and he wants it to be cleanest and sharpest for me. I understand – this is an honour. He produces a black-and-red bandana from out of nowhere like a magician. I remember seeing him wear it around his head on stage. He ties the bandana round the top of my arm and taps my veins with two fingers to bring them up. I've seen this ritual *so many times*. It doesn't impress me, it doesn't excite me. I'm numb.

As Johnny sucks the liquid out of the spoon into the syringe, I feel no sense of occasion – no *Oh my god, this is Johnny Thunders from the Heartbreakers, about to turn me on to heroin for the first time in my life.* And I have no fear. I'm detached, just watching it all happening to me. Johnny compliments me on my lovely virgin veins, then slides the needle into the biggest blue one in the crook of my arm and unleashes the smack.

A rush starts in my toes and surges up through my body. Thousands of tiny bubbles of love and happiness are released into my veins. I feel like a shaken-up bottle of Lucozade. Then I vomit. Right there on the carpet. I know I should be embarrassed but I can't quite muster up the feeling. I look at Johnny and he smiles. He strokes my hair and tells me everything is OK, this is completely normal, then he crouches down and injects himself.

A door slams. Someone's shouting. I step off the kerb and fall in slow motion, down into the gutter. Car horns blare. Tyres screech. I'm in the middle of Fulham Road. I think I might die. Black shadows prance on the edge of my vision. Faces loom. A leaf falls. Buildings lean. Everything's happening at once . . .

. . . Cool air blows across my face, I'm in a long dark corridor. Black and white tiles dance away from me, I follow them, they lead me to Sid. He's leaning against my front door. Long skinny legs, huge cartoon feet in thick rubber-soled brothel creepers, bike chain dangling from his waist, padlock around his neck, black currant eyes, spiky hair.

He looks at me nervously. 'Alright?'

What a strange moral code we all have:

Sid, on time for the first time in his life, to chuck me out of the band. Insisting on doing it face to face, because his mum – who's a junkie – has told him to be nice.

Me, out of my head on smack, risking my life to meet Sid, knowing he's going to tear my world apart.

And Johnny Thunders, kind and thoughtful enough to warn me of the impending doom and then shooting me up with heroin.

Sid and I go inside. He mumbles something or other about me not being in the band any more: 'You can't play well enough.' I can barely hear him. I'm far away in another world. It doesn't matter. It doesn't hurt. I don't give a shit.

Sid's a bit put out that I already know what he's going to say and that I'm not in the least bit bothered about it. He can see I'm stoned. He must have seen his mother like this enough times. I get a faint feeling that he disapproves. He asks if I want him to stick around.

'No no, I'm fine,' I mumble and wave at him to leave.

He leaves me sitting on the floor of my flat, chin drooping onto my chest, eyes half closed. Out of my head. And out of the band.

40 SHIFT

1977

Every limit is a beginning as well as an ending.
George Eliot, *Middlemarch*

I hear a phone ringing through the thick fuzzy air. It's Thunders, asking me to join the Heartbreakers. He says to come over to the rehearsal studios right now. I'm scared, but I go anyway. That should be written on my gravestone. *She was scared. But she went anyway.*

When I arrive he says, 'OK, let's figure out some songs you can sing.' He asks if I know the words to 'These Boots Are Made for Walking', by Frank and Nancy Sinatra. I say, 'Yes, most of them.' The rest of the Heartbreakers stand around looking polite but not very keen: *Another one of Johnny's mad ideas.* Johnny plays the intro to the song and the band join in. I don't know what the hell I'm doing. I've never played in a proper band, I can't sing, I haven't used a microphone before. Johnny nods to let me know when to come in. I talk my way through the words in a deadpan voice, my fear slightly cushioned by the heroin that's still trickling through my veins from earlier. At the end of the song, Johnny says it was great and he loves my delivery. We run through it a couple more times, then they move on to another song and I slump into a chair on the edge of the room, steeped in an idiotic stupor.

Johnny must have missed my vein when he injected me, because my arm turns black from my wrist to my armpit. It stays black for three months. I have to hide it from everyone including

150

my mum, which isn't easy, as I am evicted from my studio (for not paying rent and complaints from the neighbours about Sid threatening them with broken milk bottles) and have to move back home. I'm so ashamed of myself. I've been so weak. I almost owe it to Mum more than myself to have some self-respect. I'll never take heroin again.

A couple of weeks later I go to The Camden Music Machine (a club in Kentish Town, now Koko), and bump into Ben Barson (the guy from Woodcraft Folk I was going to marry). Now I'm his equal, I've caught up. Don't you love it when that happens? You meet someone who wasn't interested in you, then a couple of years later you meet again and you've reinvented yourself. Ben fancies me now, dressed in my pink and black fetish gear, Dr Martens and feisty attitude. As we talk, he slides his arm around me, like we're teenagers, but I'm meeting some people backstage so I have to go.

Backstage I'm chatting to Johnny Thunders. He asks me what I'm doing later, do I want to hang out? I glance over at Mick, he glares back at me, furious. Johnny sees Mick's expression, laughs and sings, *'Who's it gonna be? Him or me?'*

Something snaps in me. *What are you doing, Viv? Stop messing around. What do you want out of life?* I realise I don't want to be with either of them, so I walk out, hail a cab and go home. It's time to show people, and myself, what I'm made of. Time to try, and maybe to fail again, but better that than never try at all.

41 SIDNEY'S DREAM

1977

Me and Sid are still mates, I'm not going to be petty about him dropping me from the band. We still hang out together all the time, endlessly listening to the *Ramones* album, it encapsulates what we're trying to do, pushing everything to extremes. Sid takes some speed and says he's going to stay up all night listening to the record. I go to bed. When I get up in the morning he's still in Alan's room, but now he's playing Paul's bass along with the record. He can play every bass line of every song. He's never played bass before but he's worked it all out by ear and made his fingers do it. Those bass lines are really fast and he can play every one perfectly. I'm in awe of him, he's done that in one night, turned himself into a bass player.

Because of what he did that night, Sid's ready when John asks him to replace Glen Matlock as bass player in the Sex Pistols. Talk about a dream come true. We were standing at the back of the Screen on the Green watching the Pistols only last week, saying, 'What's the point of being in a band? If you can't be better than the Pistols then don't bother.' Unbelievably, Sid actually thinks twice about joining them, even though to him they're the best band in the world. He asks me what I think he should do, should he join them or create his own thing? He's not sure about being part of something he hasn't formed. This dilemma only lasts about five seconds; he says yes, of course.

42 THE COLISEUM

1977

The Clash, Buzzcocks and Subway Sect are playing at the Coliseum tonight but I haven't come to see them, I see them all the time. I'm here to see the Slits.

The Slits asked me to join them a couple of months ago, I can't remember how they contacted me, probably through Nora, the young singer's mother, who I hang out with quite a lot. Nora is German, tall, athletic, blonde, sophisticated. She wears vintage suits and heels, she's very feminine compared to the rest of us. I respect her for sticking to her own style. The Slits were looking for a bass player back then. I play guitar, I don't want to play bass, I don't feel bass. Your instrument is not interchangeable. I'm a guitarist: even though I haven't been playing long, I know I'm a guitarist. And anyway, I don't want to be in an all-girl band.

I talked to Chrissie Hynde about it. (I got to know Chrissie when I met Mick at art school. He was trying to get a band together with her, she's still not in a band but she really wants to be in one.) I said, 'It's gimmicky and tokenistic being in an all-girl band, isn't it?' She told me to shut up and get on with it. I read a lot about feminism and I'm a feminist, apply it to everything I think and do, but I don't want to be labelled in any way.

I'm interested in what Palmolive's up to now she's not in the Flowers of Romance any more. I'm not expecting much, I've seen the Slits around town with paint daubed on their faces, wearing black bin liners, and Ari, Nora's fourteen-year-old daughter, is usually charging up and down the room screaming.

The lights dim and four girls tumble onto the stage, all fired up and cocky and excited. Ari's wearing a long dirty beige mac over a leopard-print top, vinyl mini skirt and fishnet tights, her hair is long and tangled, with a comb stuck in it. Palmolive looks great in leopardskin trousers and a black plastic waistcoat. They start playing. A blast of energy, a cacophony of sound, and pumping through it all is Palmolive's insistent drumming, ferocious, wild, a call to arms. Her eyes burn with passion, she's focused and charismatic. I've never heard anyone drum like her; it's primal. Her whole body and spirit are thrown into the performance.

Ari is in her element: suddenly, she makes sense. Too big a personality off stage, on stage she rules. Ari's husky voice and German accent are sensual, she stamps her foot, screams and warbles, she's abandoned and unfettered – prancing around like a demented pony. She flashes her mac open and closed like a parody of a dirty old man; she's so funny. She's completely unselfconscious and like no girl or boy I've ever seen live before. Whenever I watch a lead singer, I think to myself, 'Are they as good as John Rotten?' Me and Sid still compare every band we see to the Pistols and every singer to John. It's unnecessary to add another band to the world if it isn't doing something different or better than bands that already exist. Ari stirs up all sorts of feelings in me, visions, aspirations, possibilities – she inspires me, like Rotten did last year. I get all these feelings and thoughts without understanding a word of the songs, just from her presence.

The next morning I lie awake and think about the Slits, then I get dressed and go to the phone box on Acton High Street and call Nora's house. Ari answers. I don't know why I've called really. I just have to say something, to make contact. I tell her I think the Slits were great last night. We arrange to meet at a squat in Edgware Road where they rehearse. I'm excited. I've made something happen.

43 DAVENTRY STREET

1977

I'm going to play with the Slits. I'm anxious because playing with Sid in the Flowers of Romance was nerve-racking.

The rehearsal room is in a squat on Daventry Street, West London. There are egg boxes stapled to the walls and a smelly damp mattress leaning in a corner – a feeble attempt to dampen the noise – old torn carpet on the floor, two amps and a drum kit. Palmolive's kick drum is weighed down with a couple of bricks on an old towel.

Kate Korus, the Slits' guitarist, isn't here. I didn't ask for her not to be here, but I'm glad, because maybe they're thinking I might be good in their band, and I'm beginning to think I would like to be in their band.

I've no idea how this rehearsal or jam is going to turn out. I've seen the Slits play and I know they aren't musical virtuosos, but it's still daunting as I'm very new to guitar playing. I tell them I'm not very good, I haven't been playing long and I've no idea how to jam, and they chorus back that they can't either and it's fine. I feel a bit better and get my Les Paul Junior out of its cardboard case.

Ari is the only one of us with any musical training; she's reached grade six on piano. She shows me the chords to a song they've written called 'Let's Do the Split'. I can just about hold down the bar chords and we thrash through it a few times. They don't seem horrified with my playing, in fact they get it wrong as often as I do, and I begin to relax.

They ask me if I have a song to show them. All I have is a guitar riff I've made up and some lyrics that came out of a phone conversation I had with Johnny Rotten about Sid a couple of weeks ago. It's called 'So Tough'. I play the riff. They love it. I show them the words written in my little lyric book. They love them. We start working on the song, and that's when things really get good. Me and Ari click creatively. We respect each other's ideas, we take suggestions from each other easily, without any ego, and we have the same sensibility. We like the same sounds, we understand and spark off each other. After the experience with Sid, I know that being able to write comfortably with someone is a rare and precious thing. The song comes together: it sounds good. Just how I'd imagined it, but better.

After the rehearsal I have a warm feeling inside. That feeling you get when you've created something. A cross between doing a job well and stretching yourself. We lounge against the speakers, Palmolive leans forward with her elbows on her snare and we chat and laugh. They tell me that when I called them the other day at Nora's, after Ari put the phone down they all started laughing and saying to each other, 'Oh, so *now* she's interested!'

We move into the cold kitchen and huddle around the stove. I look at the girls as we drink tea out of cracked, stained mugs: Palmolive with her sparkly Spanish eyes, toned brown body and beautiful heart-shaped face, framed by cropped auburn hair; Tessa, skin white as snow, hair black as raven's wings and eyes azure blue, she's like a young Elizabeth Taylor, but dressed as a boy; and Ari, long tousled brown hair, full mouth, large unblinking blue eyes, a smattering of freckles, completely unaware of her beauty – Lolita crossed with Minnie the Minx. Every one of them beautiful and interesting. Why didn't I see it before? They're fantastic.

I want boys to come and see us play and think *I want to be part of that*. Not *They're pretty* or *I want to fuck them* but *I want to be in that gang, in that band*. I want boys to want to *be* us, not have the usual response like that one at the party in Islington the other night, he told me he played guitar.

'I play guitar too,' I said.

'Great! We could do with some crumpet in our band.'

His name was Paul Weller. Mick wanted to have a go at him when I mentioned it but I thought that would make me look weak so I stopped him.

I reckon the Slits' clothes are cool enough, our attitude is rebellious enough and our music so unusual and powerful that we might be able to change that kind of attitude for good.

We're all excited and start to do each other's hair. I backcomb all of them to look more like mine, I don't mean to, it just happens. We gather around a cracked old mirror and stare at our reflection. And that's it. We look like a band.

The Slits – me, Ari, Tessa, Palmolive

44 THE SLITS

1977

It takes a few weeks for me to decide if I definitely want to be in the band. I don't want to hang out with a young girl just out of German boarding school every day if it's not going to be for a very good reason. Ari's a virgin, she's never had a boyfriend, so she doesn't know about passion, sex or love. How can she write songs? She has pictures of ponies on her bedroom wall for god's sake. But there are other differences, like her private education and family money. Ari has no idea about social injustice, poverty or racism. She's totally unenlightened politically, not just because she's so young, but because she's had a sheltered, privileged upbringing in Germany.

I bump into Chrissie Hynde at the Speakeasy and tell her I've changed my mind, I've decided to join the Slits if they ask me again. She says, 'If you didn't go for it, I would have!' If they ask me I'd better say yes before Chrissie moves in on them. But they wouldn't ask Chrissie. No one wants to be in a band with her, she's too good.

I play with the Slits a couple more times and we start to hang out. But no one mentions anything about me being in the band. There's now no doubt in my mind that I want to join. I'm so excited about the songs, we've reworked their old ones and added a couple of my new ones, so why haven't they said anything?

We're waiting for a train at Queensway tube station and Ari is talking non-stop, making babyish comments about the posters on the wall. I feel frustrated so I say to her, 'Ari, just tell me if I'm in the band or not. I need to know.'

She looks shocked and says, 'Yes, of course.'

'What about Kate?'

'We've told her.'

I'm so happy! I'm in a band. I'm in a great band!

From now on we go everywhere together. We march down the street four abreast and people scuttle out of our way, or spit on us or swear at us and it just makes us laugh. We're invincible together. We have no doubt that the Slits are great and are going to change the world. We're on a mission and pity anyone who doesn't get it. We spend hours talking about our look, our stance on all sorts of subjects, from feminism to what is good and bad in music. We play each other our records and point out backing vocals, string sections or guitar riffs we like. We especially love *Dionne Warwick sings Burt Bacharach* and *Low* by David Bowie. We also listen to *The Sound of Music*, the Beatles, the Ramones, MC5 and Iggy and the Stooges.

I'm so excited about the girls that I want to take them round to meet all my friends. First they have to meet Keith Levene: they'll all respond to his sensitivity and Ari will love his musicality – they'll adore each other.

We set off to find Keith and track him down at Barry Black's flat in Elgin Avenue. I introduce everyone and we wander between the kitchen and the living room chatting, when Palmolive says, 'My purse has gone.'

I help her look through her bag but I have a sinking feeling I know where the purse has gone. Keith takes heroin, so do a couple of other guys at the flat. I'm worried because I know that often people who take heroin steal. Anger starts to mount up in my chest. I ask Keith if he knows where the purse is. He says no. I'm furious. I've brought the girls here to meet my friends. They are my band. I'm determined to get the purse back, I scrutinise the room looking for a guilty face. A hammer leaning against the wall catches my eye. I pick it up and in my mind I have a flash, a vision: *I'm going to smash Keith's knees to pieces with the hammer.* I lift the hammer and walk towards Keith, he starts to gibber, 'Viv! Viv! We'll find the purse!' The Slits rush forward and talk me down, they take the hammer off me. The purse reappears.

As we walk back down Elgin Avenue towards the 31 bus stop, the girls look at me differently. No, I'm not the nice, balanced, well-behaved grown-up they thought I was. I'm a nutter.

With Ari

45 ARI UP

As she was German und *quite new to the English language, Ari thought adding 'Up' to her name made it 'Hurry Up', because we all dropped our aitches. And when the Sham 69 song 'Hurry Up Harry' came out, she thought they were singing about her. "Urry up Ari, come on!"*

Ari is wonderful and terrible in equal measure. She's great when we're writing, rehearsing or playing, but the rest of the time I find her difficult to be around. She's loud, boisterous, rude, unstable and desperate for attention every second of the day. She's not an ordinary fifteen-year-old, they discovered that about her at her last two schools; in the end they asked her to leave, they couldn't control her. She makes enemies wherever we go, pissing off soundmen, promoters, potential managers and other bands with her attitude. I know she's young and just beginning to discover the adult world but she's so extreme: at one point she was convinced she was god's mistress reincarnated. It's worrying.

Because Ari's the singer of the band she's our mouthpiece. The trouble is, she doesn't know enough about life yet to be a mouthpiece, and she doesn't know that she doesn't know – that's the worst thing. I'm not very patient with her, I hardly ever let her naïve comments pass without a withering look or a sharp retort. I wouldn't care what she says or does if I wasn't in a band with her, but I am and it's important to me.

Being involved in music is a great outlet for Ari – I can't imagine her finding a place in society otherwise. She's lucky her family has money; plenty of people with her extreme character traits but no money must end up in some sort of institution because their parents can't cope. The combination of money and a bohemian mother who moves in artistic and musical circles means that people are more accepting of Ari's behaviour. I think a lot of Ari's attitude is a rebellion against her mother's cool, blonde beauty. She knows she can't compete with that, so she goes to the opposite extreme.

Difficult as she is, and different as the band are as people, there are core beliefs that we all share and I'm amazed and excited that we've found each other. One of the many things we all agree on is, we hate double standards and false people and all of us are very vocal in our damnation of any hapless person who crosses our path who hasn't thought rigorously about life.

When we were on a TV show in Holland, Mike Oldfield's sister, Sally, was on the same bill. She had a single out at the time ('Mirrors'). Sally was dressed in a peasant gypsy-type dress and warbling away in a breathy little-girl voice. We went up to her afterwards and told her she was shit, that she was compounding stereotypes and doing a disservice to girls, that she should take a good look at what she was doing and how she was projecting herself and be honest about who she was. She burst into tears. We do that sort of thing all the time.

Living in England means Ari has a lot of freedom; her father isn't around, all her family are in Europe and Nora has a free parenting style. Although Ari has to be in bed by about ten thirty, Nora's happy for her to hang out with us – even to miss school sometimes to do shows (it helps that her new school is Holland Park Comprehensive, it's very lax). Ari gets on with us older musicians much better than with the kids at her school, they just don't compare. She doesn't even want to try and fit in with her peer group, she's found something more interesting – so there's no one in England she gives a shit about impressing or disappointing and no real authority figure to rein her in. This translates into her performances: she has no self-consciousness and there's an unpredictable

162

edge to her. I watch her performing with great respect, almost awe.

Ari crosses so many boundaries and is so innovative, with her voice, in her moves – you've never seen a girl move how she moves – she hasn't watched many bands, all her dancing and vocal performance is down to her imagination and her own inventiveness. She reminds me of Kaspar Hauser: like him, she's Bavarian, been closeted away and then let loose on the world.

Ari hides nothing from our audiences: if she's in a bad mood, she shows it, and if we happen to be on stage when she's not happy, she just does a shit gig. There's no *You've paid money to see this so I'm going to give you a good time*, or *I'm not going to let the band down* – she's just grumpy and uncommunicative. This is a good thing in many ways, we're against faking it, we tell it like it is. People in bands are just like the audience: they have good days and bad days, we're not pantomime or theatre, we're no different to anyone else. We don't see ourselves as entertainers, trying to make the audience forget their troubles for forty minutes. We see ourselves as warriors. We'd rather people confronted their anger and dissatisfaction and did something about it. Like Luis Buñuel said, 'I'm not here to entertain you, I'm here to make you feel uncomfortable.'

Ari's greatest strength is that she's a talented and committed musician. She plays classical piano and reads music and brings those melodies and rhythms into the Slits. Her musicality is the only thing she has over the rest of us and boy does she use it. Who wouldn't at fifteen years old? Everyone's older than you, everyone's done everything before you, the one advantage you have is that you can play an instrument and read music, and they can't. Ari pulls us apart musically, haranguing me, Palmolive and Tessa, constantly telling us we're out of tune and out of time. It's become almost crippling. She makes us feel stupid, which is no doubt how we make her feel the rest of the time.

Ari would like to play bass and drums as well as sing in the band if only she had extra arms, so she does the next best thing and helps compose the bass lines and drum rhythms too. (Luckily for me she's not very interested in the guitar so I'm left to my own devices.)

There's another trait that adds to Ari's liberation: *she doesn't care about being attractive to boys.* She's not bothered about looking pretty or moving seductively for them, she only does that for her own pleasure. She doesn't see her body as a vehicle for attracting a mate, and she doesn't squash bits of her personality to avoid overshadowing boys. I realise I'm learning a lot from her, and it would be foolish of me to dismiss her because she's young. Since knowing Ari, I've become more aware of how uptight I am about my body, bodily functions, smells and nudity. Ari moves her body with the unselfconsciousness of a child, and I don't see any reason why I can't reclaim that feeling, even though I'm older. I'm constantly questioning stereotyping through my work but I'm still enslaved by the stereotype of femininity in my mind. (*'It's hard to fight an enemy who has outposts in your head'* – *Sally Kempton*.) Ari has no such hang-ups. When we played the The Music Machine in Mornington Crescent, halfway through the set she was dying for a piss, she didn't want to leave the stage and couldn't bear to be uncomfortable, so she just pulled down her leggings and knickers and pissed on the stage – all over the next band's guitarist's pedals as it happened – I was so impressed. No girl had pissed on stage before, but Ari didn't do it to be a rebel or to shock, it was much more subversive than that: she just needed a piss. In these times when girls are so uptight and secretive about their bodies and desperately trying to be 'feminine', she is a revolutionary.

The Slits get a lot of shit on the streets but even though being in the group is uncomfortable for all of us in different ways, we'd fight to the death for each other. We feel as if we haven't chosen the band, it's chosen us – that's the funny thing about bands, sometimes the chemistry works because it's not all cosy, it's more critical and outspoken, like family. Life's more frightening when I'm travelling around London without the rest of them. Like when I was getting eyeballed by a gang of skinhead girls on the tube, I thought to myself, *I may have to fight for my life here, if they follow me off the train and attack me (and no one would intervene with me dressed like this) . . . I'll have to do what Sid told me, smash one of them over the head with my belt buckle.* The prospect of being attacked is terrifying. It's a very real threat. Chrissie Hynde was attacked by a gang of skinhead girls and stabbed with a stiletto heel.

Ari is the one of us who gets the most hatred channelled through her, she's been stabbed twice, once when we all left a rehearsal studio in Dalston. It was getting dark, the studio was in a very isolated, industrial area, this guy dressed in a leopard-print shirt (*we found out later he was known as Leopard Boy*) ran up to us and stuck a knife in Ari: luckily it didn't go very deep. Palmolive went mad at him and he ran off. Another time we were walking along Islington High Street, on our way to see the film *The Harder They Come* for the fifth time at the Screen on the Green cinema, and we heard a voice behind us say, 'Take that, *Slit.*' We turned round and saw this guy running away, there was blood on Ari's clothes; she'd been stabbed in the arse. Being attacked, spat at, sworn at and laughed at is part of all our lives, but I think Ari's especially brave. Being so young, she is more vulnerable but she never hides away, or adapts her clothes and behaviour to protect herself. They'll never beat Ari into submission.

When her period started a couple of months ago, there was no shouting and fuss. She was excited to be a woman, not horrified and disgusted like I was. Now, whenever she has a period, she talks about it and shows us the blood. Nora tells her not to use sanitary towels (says they have some dangerous absorbent chemicals in them) or tampons, because they cause cancer – I've never heard that before, but I suppose if you think about it, all that blood pooling up near your cervix can't be too good for you – so Ari stuffs her knickers with huge hanks of cotton wool, fat white tufts stick out either side of the gusset. When the cotton wool is saturated with blood, she pulls it out and holds it up for everyone to see, then wraps it in paper and puts it in the bin, replacing it with a new clump. All this whilst she's wearing the shortest mini skirt in the world and you can practically see her knickers. In fact I'm sure people get glimpses of the cotton wool sticking out as she jumps and twirls around the room. I'd rather risk cancer than ever have a boy know I was having my period, let alone actually see the workings of it. You can smell it too.

Anyway, thanks to Ari, I'm becoming more and more relaxed about bodily functions, and sometimes for a laugh I wear a tampon – dipped in reddish-brown paint, so it looks like stale blood – looped over my ear like an earring. Once, I was wearing it at the bus stop in Elgin Avenue when I noticed a middle-aged Jamaican woman staring at me. I took no notice, straight people are always staring at me. I was wearing a pale blue tutu, with opaque baby-blue dance tights, Dr Marten boots, a shrunken cashmere leopard-print jumper, my bleached hair matted and backcombed and loads of black kohl around my eyes. I'd forgotten about the tampon dangling from my left ear.

The woman started to edge towards me hesitantly. I looked away. She sidled right up next to me. I was just about to step away from her when she said, 'Excuse me, dear.'

Her kind tone took me by surprise so I turned back towards her. She had a strange expression on her face. Horror, embarrassment, nervousness; I couldn't quite work it out.

She leaned close to me, I bent down so she could reach my ear.

'Excuse me, dear,' she said again, 'I'm so sorry . . . I don't know what to . . . how to say . . . I don't know how . . .'

What's she on about?

She stepped back and looked pleadingly into my eyes, like she was hoping I would pick up what she was trying to say telepathically, but I just stared back at her blankly, so she took a deep breath and blurted out:

'You've got a . . . it's in your hair . . . must have got caught there when you were, you know . . . dressing.' She waved her arms in the air above her head to demonstrate pulling on a jumper. 'I'm so sorry . . . I didn't know if I should . . . or what to . . . I had to tell you . . . so sorry . . .'

Oh phew, she had me worried for a moment. The 31 bus pulled up and I jumped up onto the platform, calling out to her, 'I know! It's meant to be there!' I smiled and waved as the bus trundled off.

As Ari grows up in front of me, I start to notice something unsettling happening: she's always watching me. Always. She doesn't take her eyes off me. This goes on for over a year. It's terrible. I can't walk across a room, dance to a record, get something out of my bag, talk to a boy, flirt or have a conversation, without her drinking it in. I'm still learning, I'm shy and reinventing myself in front of all these people, my head is full of new thoughts and it's not like I know how to dance – especially to reggae – or talk to a guy, and yet I'm being scrutinised by an unsmiling Ari whilst I do all these things. Dancing is especially agonising with her unblinking blue eyes boring into me until she's absorbed my moves, and I know full well that she thinks most of them are rubbish; it's not like she's looking at me thinking I'm completely wonderful. She's an amazing mimic, learning a new language, different accents, attitudes and moves, all in such a short time-frame. I can see her mentally sifting the bits she will use from the bits she'll dismiss. She's building herself like a machine.

My mum's noticed the way Ari is fixated on me and when she came backstage after a gig recently, she took me aside and said, 'Viv, it's like Anne Baxter and Bette Davis in *All About Eve*. Try

167

and stay away from her as much as possible, she's stealing your soul.' I know what she means. It's chilling. I feel like I'm going mad. She mimics and copies me relentlessly and it doesn't seem flattering or admiring, it feels cold and vampiric.

When we do an interview and I give my opinion on something, Ari repeats what I've just said word for word, straight after I've said it, same intonation and everything. Not like she's reaffirming what I've said, but like she's just thought of it. And it's amazing when you speak with that kind of conviction, how many people, even journalists, are taken in. When the articles come out, the opinions are attributed to Ari. Maybe it makes a better story if these thoughts come from a fifteen-year-old rather than a twenty-two-year-old. It's like *Gaslight*, that Ingrid Bergman film; after a while you don't know if you're insane or they are. I begin to lose my marbles and start thinking, *Well, I'm not going to speak in interviews if she's going to repeat what I say, let's see how she does if I don't say anything.* But I can't keep that up for long; when I disagree with something she says, I pipe up again.

Having my words stolen and all my actions scrutinised makes me want to escape from the band as much as possible. I think of leaving so many times, but I don't because I believe we're greater than the sum of our parts. What we create together and what we put across is more important than the painful day-to-day reality of being together.

Ari's unhealthy attention comes to an end when Rastas and reggae take over from me as fascinations for her to study. It's a bitter-sweet release. At last I'm not under her microscope, but at the same time I'm dismissed. She has more equal relationships now, with people her own age; the same happened to me with my sister. There comes a time when they relish not needing you any more and move on triumphantly, almost disdainfully. It was painful when my sister did it. I really missed her. It's the lot of an elder sister, you get the good and the bad of being first. I'm still glad I'm the eldest though, I like blazing the way.

Another odd thing is that if any bloke looks at Ari in a sexual way, I think he's a pervert. I want to kill him. It's not just because she's young and I see her as still a child, but it seems a bit sick to me. She's an innocent, an *enfant sauvage*, and I think they're taking advantage of her. Maybe I'm just being possessive and territorial. Ari's not interested in sex, although she wears her clothes provocatively – to her it's playful: knickers over trousers, short skirts (tufts of cotton wool on view) with boyish Chelsea boots.

She's dressed like this, in a tiny skirt, sparkly tights and an oversized lurex drape jacket, when, in an attempt to bond, I agree to go along to a reggae night at the 100 Club with her. When Ari listens to reggae on a cassette player, she rocks backwards and forwards manically, sometimes for five or six hours on end. It calms her down, especially on long journeys to gigs. She's obsessive about the bass lines, the drum patterns, the lyrics (I could almost hate reggae for the way she's taken it and made it her own, as if she invented it).

At the 100 Club, Ari takes over the dancefloor, displaying her extraordinary dance style, which is cobbled together and customised from watching young boys at sound systems we go to, like Sir Coxsone and Jah Shaka, or late-night clubs in Dalston, Phoebe's and the Four Aces. We're often the only girls at these all-nighters, and the fact that we are white and dressed so strangely is even more extraordinary, but no one gives us any trouble or is antagonistic towards us. Ari never watches the girls dance, they're too discreet and understated, just shifting from one foot to the other – she watches the athletic boys and copies what they do. She's amalgamated their moves and now has an amazing praying mantis dance style, reminiscent of White Crane kung fu. She bobs up and down on one bent leg, using her arms and hands as claws, or feelers – it's very beautiful, sometimes funny, almost mime, telling little stories to the music. People clear a space round her and she gets lost in the rhythm.

Ari dancing, 1980

When the 100 Club closes, we all spill out onto the pavement, but Ari doesn't want to go home, she's still buzzing from dancing all evening. She starts chatting to two older guys and asks them if there's anything else going on. At first they say no but then they remember there's a party in Peckham. They tell us to wait whilst they go and get their car. I really don't want to go to a party but I don't want to seem a bore so I go along with it.

The guys pull up and we climb in the back. By the time we're on the Mall, heading towards Buckingham Palace, I'm dreading the thought of spending a couple of hours, maybe all night, at a house party in Peckham and, knowing I'm being a drag, I confess to Ari that I don't want to go. She tries to persuade me but I've made up my mind. I tell her she shouldn't go either; it's too far away and she doesn't know these guys – I say she'll just have to let it go and come home with me. But she refuses, she loves the idea of meeting new people and she loves dancing, she can happily dance all night.

I give up trying to persuade Ari and ask the guys to stop the car and let me out. As I say it, I get a tiny little twinge in my chest and realise I'm worried they won't stop. They haven't given me any reason to be suspicious, but I'm relieved when the driver slows down and pulls over. I scoot out quickly and lean into the back seat to have one more try at persuading Ari to come with me. She's adamant she's going to the party, they drive off. I'm so relieved that I'm out of the car and not going to Peckham. I walk back up to Trafalgar Square and get the night bus home.

About six months later, when Ari and I are alone, she tells me what happened after I left her that night. They drove to Peckham and pulled up in front of a big old house. Ari and one of the guys went inside, the other guy went to park the car. When they got inside Ari saw that the house was empty, abandoned, derelict. The guy grabbed her and raped her. He was so violent she begged him not to cut her face. After a few hours he left, saying if she told anyone about it, he'd find her and kill her. This was her first sexual experience. She said she was embarrassed to tell me at the time because she'd been such a fool, said she should have listened to me. It broke my heart in so many ways. She didn't let this experience define her though. After a while she healed and went on to enjoy a normal, healthy sex life and then I knew for sure that she was astronger person than me. I also realised I was right to trust my instincts. No matter how silly you feel or uncool you look, no matter how small that voice inside you is, that voice telling you something isn't right: listen to it.

46 WHITE RIOT

1977

We are not afraid of ruins.
Buenaventura Durruti

Mick and I are back together again and in a week's time the Slits are going on the *White Riot* tour with the Clash. I've got to learn all our songs, I can't even play guitar standing up yet. We haven't played a gig together either, so we go down to the Pindar of Wakefield pub in Islington to see if we can have a quick go on their stage. When we arrive we see that a bunch of boys are churning out some old rock music, we've got our guitars with us but we hold them behind our backs so no one suspects anything. In between songs I go up to the guitarist in the rock band and ask him if we can play a song. He says no, so I pull him off stage and Ari, Tessa and Palmolive pull the other guys off, there's an uproar, a couple of cymbals get kicked over but Palmolive doesn't care, she doesn't use them anyway. We bash through 'Let's Do the Split' before the manager and barmen pull us off. That's our warm-up gig done.

I've only been playing guitar for five months – and now here I am standing in the wings of the Edinburgh Playhouse, looking out at hundreds of people, waiting to go on stage. Mick comes up behind me: 'Sorry you didn't get to soundcheck.' We arrived too late to soundcheck but I'm not bothered, never done one before, wouldn't know what to do anyway. I am bothered about my clothes though. I'm wearing silver rubber stockings and black stiletto patent boots from Sex, a short blue ballet tunic that I've had since I was eleven, and loads of ribbons tied in my matted bleached blonde hair. Just as we're about to go on stage, I look down and see that one of my brand-new rubber stockings has a rip in it, all the way from my knee up to my thigh. It flaps like a gutted fish. How did that happen? I took such care putting them on, used loads of talcum powder so they slid on easily. All my other clothes are back at the hotel. A roadie, seeing my distress, leaps to the rescue and tapes up the slash with a long strip of black gaffer tape. Looks quite cool.

I count in the first song, 'One two three four!' and off we go, careening through 'Let's Do the Split' and 'I'll Shit on It' as fast as we can. (Mick explains to me later in the tour that when you shout 'One two three four' you're setting the speed of the song. I don't know this, I've copied it off the *Ramones* LP, I just think it's a warning to the band that you're starting and it's to be shouted as fast as possible, the quicker, the more exciting.) We all play at different speeds. Ari screams as loud as she can, I thrash at my guitar, Palmolive smashes the drums – the stage is so big and Tessa's so far away, I can't hear what she's doing. I can't differentiate between the instruments. There's roaring and squealing and air rushing and heat, like we've all been hurled into the mouth of a volcano. We all play the song separately, we know we should play together, but we can't. I hope that if I remember my part and the others remember theirs, with a bit of luck we'll all end at the same time. That doesn't happen. During rehearsals, at least one of us usually makes a mistake and plays the chorus twice, or forgets a change into the next section and ends up in a completely different place to the others, but we all keep playing until the end of the song, often a whole verse behind. That's what happens with 'Let's Do the Split': we all finish at different times. Palmolive is the last, still clattering away obliviously, the rest of us glare at her and eventually she looks up, realises we've all finished, gives the side tom a couple more thumps and stops.

'One two three four!' On to 'Shoplifting'. If my guitar's out of tune, I can't tell – sometimes Ari tells me it is, but what can I do about it? No way I can tune it myself. I keep playing. We're only on for fifteen minutes anyway.

A hail of spit rains down on us throughout the set. Great gobs of phlegm land in my hair, my eyes and on my guitar neck, my fingers slide around as I try to hold down the chords. I look over at Ari and see spit land in her mouth as she sings. I don't know if she gobs it back out or swallows it. I have to look down at my hands or I'll lose my place. Someone in the front row tries to pull Ari off stage – we all stop playing and attack them – I hit them with my guitar, Palmolive beats them up, the bouncers haul them off with blood dripping down their faces and we start playing again.

It's all over in a flash. We slam down our instruments and stalk off. A couple of beer cans come flying through the air and clunk onto the empty stage. Mick is waiting in the wings. 'Well done,' he says and kisses me. I'm high on adrenalin. That was great! Can't wait to do it again tomorrow.

Straight after our set, Palmolive, Tessa, Ari and me pile out into the audience to watch Subway Sect. We dance around in front of the stage, people stare at us, they've never seen a band mingle with the audience before.

I remember seeing Subway Sect play at the Coliseum in Harlesden, the same night I saw the Slits for the first time. I was standing right at the front because if I'm interested in a band, I don't act cool and stand at the back or in the VIP area, none of us do, we get down the front and watch like hawks, see what we can learn, read the signs, the attitude of the group. What are they saying? What's their stance? What kind of energy do they have? Rob Symmons, Subway Sect's guitarist, was so intense, he stood with his feet together, rooted to the spot, slightly knock-kneed. He wore his guitar really high, almost tucked under his armpit, and he strummed it so hard that his fingers bled and he dropped his plectrum, he just kept on playing with his fingers and there was blood all over his guitar. I wanted to pick up the plectrum and give it back to him, but I was too shy.

After all the bands have played, we go to the hotel. First time I've stayed in a hotel. I unpack my suitcase and throw my clothes around the room.

The next morning on my way to breakfast, I see Chrissie Hynde come out of Paul Simonon's room. Paul tells us later that last night Chrissie decided she didn't want her tattoo any more (a dolphin I think) so they tried to scratch it off with a pumice stone. Then she read to him from the Bible. Sounds like such a sexy and sophisticated evening to me.

After breakfast, me, Ari, Tessa and Palmolive climb onto the official tour bus for the first time; Norman, the driver, gives us a dirty look. Yeah well, we've all seen that look before, we get it everywhere we go from men. There are just a few boys in the world who get us and they're almost all on this bus. Norman scowls through the rear-view mirror at Ari: her skirt is so short her bum is showing, her hair's backcombed so it looks like she's had an electric shock, and she hugs a huge ghetto blaster under her arm which pumps out dub as she races up and down the aisle deciding who to sit next to.

Norman shouts at Ari to sit down, she takes no notice. Ari takes no notice of anyone, Norman doesn't have a hope. He stomps off and refuses to get back on the bus whilst the Slits are on it. He tells Don – Don Letts has agreed to manage us for the *White Riot* tour – he's not driving the Slits and we'll have to find another way to get to Manchester. Here we go. Eventually it's sorted out. He's bribed to take us but still he has a condition – *The Slits don't leave their seats until Manchester.* This is going to be impossible. Ari's fifteen, she's excited, there's no way she's going to be able to sit still until Manchester! And sure enough, after rocking back and forth to her mix tape for half an hour, she jumps up to dance in the aisle. Norman screeches to a halt.

'The Slits must leave the bus.'

He's bribed again and Ari is locked in the bog to keep her out of harm's way. She doesn't care, as long as she's got her music with her. We're all worried that if Norman discovers her age, he'll tell the police and we'll be kicked off the tour. She should be at school.

We arrive in Manchester. The Slits charge off the bus and explode into the hotel foyer like chickens released from the coop. Whilst Don checks us in, we drape ourselves over the chairs, Ari coughs up some phlegm and spits it onto the carpet. The manager looks up from his desk, clocks us – in a mixture of leather jeans, rubber dresses and knickers on top of our trousers, matted hair and smudged black eye makeup – pulls Don aside, and says, 'They are not staying in this hotel.'

We have to go and find somewhere else to stay. But this hotel manager has called every hotel in Manchester ahead of us and no one wants us. (He got hold of the call sheet and contacted every hotel on the rest of the tour, telling them not to let us stay. So most nights we're in a different hotel to the rest of the bands.) Eventually we find a B & B. Occasionally the Slits are allowed to stay at a nice hotel, if we go straight from the front door into the lift and stay in our rooms until morning. The hotel management don't allow us to stand in the lobby, use the bar or come down to breakfast. No one must see us. We do not exist. Everywhere we go, we're treated like we're a threat to national security.

Don tries to control us but it's impossible. It's all so new, to all of us, no one knows what to do or how to do it. Ari shouldn't even be on the tour, not just because of school, she's too young to even be in the venues; if the promoters get a whiff of it and want to get rid of us, we'll be sent home. Don tries to be sensible, tells Ari to be in bed at a certain time and not to come out of her room, but with all the boys enjoying themselves in the bar and us excluded like little children, it's hopeless. We feel like outsiders so that's how we behave. We race up and down the corridors, banging on doors, pissing in shoes left in the corridor, playing music too loud, shouting, swearing and spitting. We're definitely the most controversial band on the tour and although the Clash support us musically, they also want to have a successful tour; they're not going to jeopardise that, so I'm quite stressed a lot of the time. Ari isn't bothered, she doesn't know that opportunities like this don't come along very often.

I become so nervous that before every show I get a kind of narcolepsy; I can't move my legs or arms, my eyes won't stay open and my brain goes foggy. We leave the dressing room and I drift like a sleepwalker towards the stage. I say to the others in a panicky voice, 'I can't go on, I can't walk, I can't keep awake.' They ignore me, thank goodness, and the second I step out onto the stage, it's gone, I'm full of energy.

Something that doesn't help my nervousness is that Tessa gets pissed before the shows. If the bass player falls apart, it doesn't matter how good the rest of us are, the show is going to be a mess. Palmolive used to drink before shows too, but after a band meeting where me and Ari put the case for them both to wait until afterwards, she's stopped.

Our shows are still great, even though they're not as together as they could be. Most of the audience have never seen girls play music before, let alone with the fuck-off attitude we've got. Lots of people come just to have a look at us and cause trouble. They think 'punk' is an excuse to let their frustrations out in a violent, non-creative way. The hysterical media coverage of the Pistols' swearing on Bill Grundy's *Today* show has added to that.

The Slits are a very tight gang and we believe a hundred per cent in what we're doing. For all our arguments – sometimes there are even scuffles between the other three on stage – we're extremely protective of each other. As soon as we leave the stage the roadies start to dismantle Palmolive's sparkly purple drum kit – bought for her by Nora – and we rush into our dressing room to eat the rider. There are carrot sticks and chocolate bars, Coke, celery, crisps and sandwiches. It's like a children's tea party every night. I'm in heaven. Now all my nerves have gone I can enjoy the rest of the evening.

There's an argument backstage when I say to Palmolive she should wear a bra when she plays, her boobs bounce about because she drums so manically. She says that she's a free person and this is who she is, why should she change? That it's more feminist to not wear a bra than wear one. I argue back that although she's right, the impression she gives off whilst playing doesn't match her ideals. 'We won't be taken seriously if people are looking at your tits. Even I'm looking at your tits when you play. It's not the reason we want people to look at us.' I know she's wild and untamed, it's not a sexual thing, but most people have never seen a girl drum before and instead of watching her play and thinking she's great, they're fascinated by her boobs bouncing up and down. Eventually we reach a compromise and Palmolive agrees to wear a tight body-stocking which sort of straps them down.

Subway Sect are so different to the Slits, very understated, they look like they've been kitted out by one of those old-fashioned boys' and men's outfitters. Hand-knitted, V-neck grey jumpers, black school trousers and brown suede Hush Puppies – they make everyone else look gaudy and overdressed. They're anti-rock in every way. No wide-legged stance and low-slung guitars. No dancing, leaping about, posturing or snarling aggression. The lead singer, Vic Godard, leans nonchalantly on the mike stand; he makes no attempt to be entertaining. His nasal voice, cynical lyrics and dry delivery make him seem slightly superior.

I feel drawn to the guitarist, Rob, who I think is beautiful and mysterious. I watch him during soundchecks, sitting with his knees pressed together, feet turned in; he's so delicate and shy. He has a gentle, unassuming air about him. I smile and say a few words whenever I can and he slowly starts to open up and talk to me. I learn little things about him: how he is not at all streetwise, he went to an all-boys school, he doesn't know many girls, has never slept with a girl, has strong views and opinions on music and film, reads a lot. I think he plays guitar really well but he tells me he only knows two chord shapes. He's not ashamed of being himself. Not trying to be anything he's not.

Rob and I get closer as the tour progresses. It's not too difficult to hide this from Mick; often the support bands stay in cheaper hotels than the Clash – they're not being mean, they're subsidising all of us. Mick says I can stay with him but I say no, I have to be with my band. I don't tell him I also want to hang out with Subway Sect and the Buzzcocks.

Rob and I often spend the night snuggled up together in a single bed in one of Subway Sect's rooms. We don't have sex, we lie facing each other holding hands and I make him promise he will not be the first one to close his eyes and go to sleep. He has the most beautiful green eyes and he looks through his long lashes at me until I fall asleep. He understands. He's intense and serious and romantic, like me. We start spending more and more time together. After we've finished our sets, we meet in the wings of whichever bingo hall, ballroom or Top Rank night club we're playing that night. When the Clash have taken to the stage, we run down the corridor – 'London's Burning' fading into the distance until it's just a dull thump of bass and drums – push open the fire doors and escape out into the night.

Cold air hits me in the face and jolts me out of my romantic little fantasy. Why do I feel like I'm escaping from authority, from my parents or my teachers? It's Mick and the Clash for god's sake. My boyfriend, my friends. I feel guilty; even though there's nothing physical between me and Rob, I know I'm not being fair to Mick, he thinks I'm in the audience watching him. What I'm doing is a betrayal. Not just to him personally, but to the Clash, who invited us on the tour and are paying for us to be here. No wonder Bernie Rhodes hates me.

I shiver. I'm wearing a pale pink short-sleeved T-shirt from Sex, printed with text from a cheesy porn novel and zips over the breasts, black leather jeans and Converse baseball boots. Rob takes off his black Harrington jacket and wraps it round my shoulders. We head off to explore Newcastle. It's like a ghost town, boarded up, closed down – even poorer than London. Litter blows around and catches on lamp posts, weeds grow out of the pavement. We pass the corner shop, the bingo hall and the Co-op. The street lights flick on and off, most of them aren't working. Factory chimneys poke out of the mist on the edge of town. It's a dirty old town, just like Ewan MacColl's song about Salford.

Rob Symmons from Subway Sect, 1977

'I feel like we're in one of those sixties films, *Saturday Night and Sunday Morning* or *A Kind of Loving*,' says Rob.

Yeah, the city is as black and white as those old films, and grey,

grey, grey. It's like nothing has changed here for years, and they don't think it's ever going to change either. They think this is how England is always going to be. Well, not if us lot have anything to do with it.

We walk to the docks and climb over the boats until we find one with the cabin unlocked. We sit huddled together as it rocks on the water, talking until morning, carried away by our mission. *We're pioneers. We're fearless. Above the law.* When it's light we try and find our way back to the hotel. We're hungry and broke, but even though we could easily nick a bottle of milk off a doorstep, there's no way we're going to drink milk. We find a greasy spoon and order a cup of tea and a KitKat between us. Then we head back to the hotel, arriving before anyone is awake. I go to my room and stuff my clothes into my bright pink plastic suitcase. Ari looks up from her pillow sleepily. I'm exhausted, but I can sleep on the coach.

The following night we're all staying in a fancy hotel as a treat, paid for by the Clash. It's so fancy that the Manchester hotel manager hasn't thought to call ahead and warn them we're coming. As soon as we arrive, I dump my suitcase and go to Subway Sect's room. We're all sitting on the beds talking when we hear muffled shouting outside. Mick is stomping down the corridor, he sounds furious. We all know what it's about.

'Where are you?' he bellows. He hammers on the doors, booting them open one by one – getting louder as he gets nearer.

Paul Myers, Subway's bass player, is quaking in his Hush Puppies. 'Sit apart, you two, sit apart!' he says to me and Rob.

'Don't you worry about that Jones,' says Vic. 'He's just a little squirt, we can duff him up.'

Mick reaches our door and kicks it open. He's worked himself up into a right state. Glowering next to him is his mate from school, Robin Banks (Mick wrote 'Stay Free' about him). Unlike Mick, Robin is actually quite scary, he's done time in the nick. Although what they see is a pretty innocent scene – me, Rob and

Paul on one bed, Vic and Mark Laff on the other – Mick is angry and upset. I know I'm wrong and he's right, what he suspects is happening *is* happening, but I pretend he's imagining it all. I tell him to calm down, we're just sitting around chatting. He threatens to get Rob thrown off the tour.

I jump off the bed and go out into the corridor to take the heat off the boys. There's a scuffle between me and Mick. The Slits appear out of their rooms and try to intervene. Robin weighs in. He thumps Palmolive and beats up Rob. Now it really kicks off – a ball of arms, legs and fisticuffs goes rolling down the corridor, like a scene from the Bash Street Kids.

Mick and I break up.

No more smart hotels for us, from now on we're in B & Bs, cracked washbasins in the corners of the rooms, bathrooms down the hall and beds with smelly nylon sheets. I lay my clothes down over the bedclothes and cover the pillow with a T-shirt before I go to sleep, so I don't have to lie on them.

Next gig is the Rainbow in London. I've been going to the Rainbow to see bands like Alice Cooper, Arthur Brown, Rod Stewart and the Faces for years. I'd see anything and everything there, I knew people who worked behind the bar and they'd get me in. Never did I dream that one day I would be on this stage. Even the Beatles and Jimi Hendrix have played here. My mum comes to the show and I'm so happy that the Slits are good tonight.

On the last night of the tour, we play the California Ballroom in Dunstable. All the support bands have made a plan that at the end of Subway Sect's set we're going to go on stage and play the Velvet Underground song 'Sister Ray'. We all steam on, the Slits, Buzzcocks, the Prefects and Subway Sect – singing and playing for ages, we make a terrible racket. Mick's annoyed that he didn't get asked to play.

The Clash come on after us and the crowd goes wild, but something's not right.

During the dub bit of 'Police and Thieves', Mick calls into the mike in a heartbroken voice. 'Where are you? Where are you?' It's so sad, it's terrible to hear. I start to cry. I go out front and listen to the Clash's last set, then go back to my hotel room alone. I don't feel like partying.

In the morning the Slits have to leave before the Clash. We're all going our separate ways. Mick's given instructions that he's not to be disturbed but my guitar is in his room. He has all the guitars in his room overnight for safe keeping, wherever we play.

I find a roadie, and tell him, 'I've got to get my guitar out of Mick's room, we're leaving.' The roadie says there's no way he can let me into the room, he has strict instructions. I smile sweetly. 'I'll just tiptoe in and out, he won't even know I've been there. Anyway, Mick won't mind, we're still good friends.' The roadie unlocks the door.

The room is stuffy and airless and swamped in yellow light from the thick gold curtains. It smells like a stagnant pond. I look over at the bed. I can just make out Mick, and beside him, a girl, fast asleep. I'm jealous. Pain stabs at my heart. But the pain is quickly replaced by fury. I leap onto the end of the bed and jump up and down. They're shaken awake – I keep jumping like a maniac, making the bed bounce violently, Mick and the girl are tossed about like boats on a stormy sea, their heads thumping against the pillows. The roadie runs out of the room. Mick leans over to the bedside table, picks up a water jug and hurls it at me. I duck and it smashes into a mirror. Water and glass shards spray all over the guitar cases.

'Pathetic,' I say as I jump off the bed, pick up my guitar and scoot out of the room.

That's the end of the *White Riot* tour.

A week later I get a call from Mick at my mum's.

Me: 'Hello?'

Mick: 'It's me.'

Me: 'What?'

He tells me that I had better go and get myself checked out as he's got something. He doesn't know how he caught it.

Me, bored voice: 'OK. Thanks.'

Pause.

Mick, hysterical voice: 'You knew, didn't you! You knew and you didn't tell me!'

Yes, I knew.

When I got home from the tour my period started. A couple of days later I went to the bathroom to change my sanitary towel. It was clean and white as I had almost finished. In the middle of the towel was a tiny black dot. I recognised that tiny black dot. I knew immediately what it was. I went straight to the chemist, got some anti-lice lotion and on to the clap clinic to get myself checked for VD. Then I waited to see what Mick would do. The thing is, I knew I hadn't given it to him, because I hadn't slept with anyone else. Somewhere along the line, before we even went on the *White Riot* tour, he must have been unfaithful.

Postcard to me from Mick Jones – when the Clash were touring the States – mentioning a line from 'Ping Pong Affair' ('dreaming on a bus'), the song I wrote about him, and complaining about how we split up

184

47 JUBILEE

1977

Rob and I are going out together now, we still haven't had sex but our relationship is intensely romantic. I'm wary of making a move on him because he's so shy. I know he's a virgin, maybe he wants to wait? Or he's too nervous. I feel a certain responsibility not to mess him up. If I'm the first girl he sleeps with, I want it to be a nice experience. One night we're holding each other and we start touching and although he's trembling we do it and it's beautiful. I would rather have sex with this intense, strangely old-fashioned boy who has no preconceptions, no 'moves', just his imagination and his passion, than some Lothario, any day.

Meanwhile Subway's singer, Vic, has started going out with Nora and for a while Vic and Nora and me and Rob become an odd foursome. We go to places in Nora's car, like a Jean-Luc Godard all-nighter at the Paris Pullman, holding hands and kissing in the back row. We see the Fall at Alexandra Palace, and in June we go to the River Thames for the Queen's Silver Jubilee. Malcolm's hired a boat for the Pistols to play on as they float down the river past the Houses of Parliament. We turn up, but have no hope of getting on, I see Palmolive try and leap across the gang-plank but she's turned away. There are lots of record-company people on board.

Rob says that's it. It's all died for him right now at this moment, tonight. This is the end of the dream. He's really upset. I know what he means, but it was over for me at the 100 Club with the glass-throwing incident. Commercialism and press coverage is what's important now, that's the message coming from Malcolm today.

Nora and Vic aren't bothered, they want to go and watch the boat sail under Tower Bridge, so Nora drives us onto the bridge and parks haphazardly, on a double yellow line. We abandon the car and lean over the railing looking down into the choppy old Thames.

I don't know what gets into Vic, he's usually so restrained, but he picks up a huge piece of hoarding that's lying on the road and chucks it down into the river as the boat is coming towards us. The bridge police arrive and arrest him. Nora tries to get him off the hook in her slinky German accent: 'I made him do it, he did it for me, to be showing off.' But they don't buy it, they take him to Bow Police Station and down into the cells. We spend hours there, sitting on a wooden bench, staring at the shiny green tiled walls. After Vic is charged, we all go back to Nora's. Johnny Rotten turns up later.

The Slits' contribution to the Queen's Jubilee comes when Derek Jarman asks us to be in his new film, *Jubilee*. We're not sure. As usual, we talk about the offer for days, arguing whether it's right for the image we're putting across. We take too long to get back to Derek, the first filming day arrives and we don't feel we can say no. Nora drives us to the location somewhere on the North Circular and Derek shows us a spiral staircase going up to a bridge crossing the motorway. He tells us to run up and down the stairs a few times. After that we go to another location, a street, where we have to smash up a car. We give it a good kicking and then go home. But we're not happy about being portrayed as violent. Although we often get into fights, it's only because we're being attacked; we don't do mindless destruction, so we decide we don't want to be in the rest of the film.

I call Derek and tell him. I feel very grown up, normally we just wouldn't bother turning up again, but because I like Derek I make a huge effort to do this embarrassing thing and let him know. I'm sorry to let him down because I imagine it's very annoying when you've already started filming and then someone drops out. He's very sweet and understanding about it, but he uses the footage he has already shot of us in the final film, even though we asked him not to. Can't blame him really.

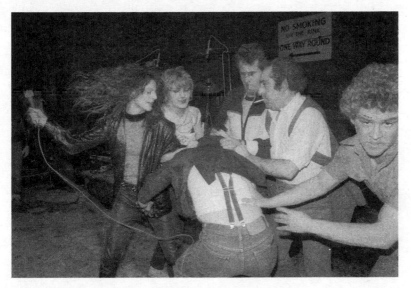

With pick in mouth, pausing mid-show to sort out a common occurrence – a skin-head attacking Ari (note the bouncers: teddy boy haircuts, woolly waistcoat and stitches above right eye). Woolwich, 1979

48 PEEL SESSION

1977

John Peel and his producer, John Walters, come to see the Slits play at the Vortex in Soho. I'm impressed that they seem more interested in us than the Heartbreakers, who we're supporting. We have a laugh with the two Johns before we go on and Palmolive throws a drink over John Walters as a dare – he doesn't seem fazed by it. The club is packed, even Keith Moon is here, dressed in a floor-length fur coat and sunglasses. He sits in the corner with a bunch of cronies. Tonight means a lot to me because it's the first time Johnny Thunders has seen me play and I want to show him I'm in a great band and I've recovered from being chucked out of the Flowers of Romance. There's nothing between me and Johnny any more, we've drifted apart, but I still want to impress him. Shame the club's so hot and sweaty that my hair's gone flat. I'm wearing my blue ballet tunic and Sid's leather jacket. We play a great show, our energy is ferocious, I think we're better than the Heartbreakers by miles. Let's see if they can follow that.

John Walters comes up to us after the show and asks if we'd like to do a John Peel radio session for the BBC. We tell him we'll think about it, we're not sure we want to put our songs out until we can play them better, we're perfectionists. We've turned down offers from labels that just want to get a record out quick whilst there's a bit of interest in 'punk'. We have a different vision, we want to make a record that lasts, that stands the test of time. We have faith in our songs and our message. Eventually we decide, yes, we'll do the radio show, we've never been in a studio before, it'll be good practice and we really like the two Johns, they're the only men we've come across in the music industry who talk to us like we're normal human beings rather than savages.

The recording day comes; Nora drives us to the studios. The main BBC recording studios are booked so we have to use the old Decca studios in Broadhurst Gardens. Decca was the Rolling Stones' label. I remember the blue and white logo in the middle of my singles. We jump out of the car, unload the equipment and barge through the doors into the hallway, heaving the gear backwards and forwards past two grumpy old doormen who look like they've been there since the sixties. One says to the other, 'You can't tell if they're boys or girls.'

'I bet that's exactly what they said when the Stones came through the door!' I say to the other girls as we tumble into the studio.

I can tell immediately by their expressions that the studio engineer and producer are not happy to be doing this session. They keep telling us we can't do this and we can't do that. The same obstructive attitude and closed-mindedness we encounter wherever we go. If we didn't have each other, we would've been crushed by guys like this ages ago.

Our guitars keep going out of tune and these two guys act like they're so superior because they know how to tune them. They think the whole music industry turns on whether you can tune your guitar or not. Well, maybe it has, until now; we've only been playing a couple of months and yet here we are in a studio. Nobody's recording *their* songs, no matter how well tuned their guitars are.

John and John come down to our session, which is rare for them, but they really rate us and are intrigued, wondering how the engineers will cope. They think it's funny that these two old musos have to get their heads around working with people like us. We fight with them to sound how we sound, not to be polished up and smoothed out. It's as if they've never heard a garage band, or never themselves been at that stage musically where they're struggling to voice the sound that's in their heads and the excitement and creative tension that come from that. It's more than hating our lack of technical ability though, there is a real fury, which they attempt to disguise as ridicule and contempt. Resentment hisses out of their pores like steam off a cowpat.

Anyway, we know what we want, we aren't daunted by being in the studio for the first time. We just want to get it right. At last we can hear each other's instruments and all the components of our songs in time with each other. It's fascinating to hear the tracks so clearly and it gives us ideas about backing vocals and different melodies to layer on top. There's not much time though and we don't want to fail on that count: no way we're going to be the one band that didn't get all their four tracks finished ('Vindictive', 'Love und Romance', 'Newtown' and 'Shoplifting').

When we get back to Ari and Nora's house in Bloemfontein Road, we listen to the session over and over again, thrilled to hear our songs captured on tape at last. I'm amazed at the ferocity of the music. We sound like we have enough energy to conquer the world.

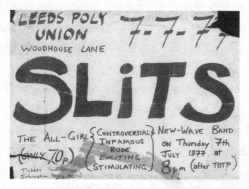

Slits flyer 7/7/77 (note the time – 'after Top of the Pops'*, the only programme anyone watched on TV)*

49 ABORTION

1978

It's a waste of time to think that if you coloured a painting red what might have happened if you painted it black.

Yoko Ono

Anxiously looking for blood. Please come, blood. I forgive you, blood. I will never be so stupid and careless again. I will never be horrible or have a fit about you again, if you will only come.

I'm pregnant. Mick's the father. We got back together after we bumped into each other at the paper shop in Shepherd's Bush. I was looking at the magazines when I heard his lovely soft voice behind me, asking for a paper. I turned round and there he was with Tony James (Generation X's bassist), my heart leapt. I just can't get him out of my system. I'm twenty-four – just the age I always thought I'd be ready to have a baby – and pregnant. But now it's here, I'm not ready at all. I did what my friends said worked for them and always put a contraceptive pessary up myself after sex (although it is supposed to be combined with a Durex). I haven't had a period for a couple of months, which isn't unusual for me, but my breasts are all swollen and painful so Mum bought a pregnancy test. My friend Becca was with me when I did it. She was shocked at how calm I was when we saw the result was positive. The thing is, I knew.

Well I'm not going to keep it. No question. Mum says she'll help me raise it. No way. Yuck. Me and my mum and a baby crammed into the top-floor flat of a council block. Nappies hanging on the clothes airer suspended from the ceiling in the steamed-up kitchen, no money, no heating, the metal lift that smells of piss: the thought of it makes me feel sick. It just can't be, not now, not in this situation. I've been warned so many times not to mess my life up by getting pregnant and now I've gone and done it. I can't keep the baby. Mum suggests adoption, but I think that's crueller than death. That's my opinion. To burden a child with abandonment and rejection right from the start. A living death. All or nothing, that's me. I choose nothing. Nothingness for baby. I think this is a responsible decision. I will not countenance any other option.

I make an appointment at a clinic. You can't just go and have an abortion, you have to prove you're mentally incapable of having a baby or they make you keep it. I don't know how I can think of getting rid of a baby so calmly and yet get so upset when some spotty boy doesn't call.

I go to the clinic and cry. That's what other girls who've been through it told me to do. If you cry, they'll let you have an abortion. I'm sure the doctor would have let me anyway. He sits behind his desk, looking at me sobbing in a short, tight, pink second-hand child's dress, fishnet tights and black Dr Marten boots, blonde hair sticking out all over the place. *Better not let this one have a baby.* In two days' time I'll be over the legal limit and then they'll make me have it. I'm sent to a clinic in Brighton. Mum waves me off at the station. I've got a little overnight bag, it's a duffel bag with pictures of 1970s pop stars printed on it, I bought it at a jumble sale, thought it was funny. I don't feel like I have a baby growing inside me. I don't even think of it. It's just something that needs to be sorted out. Before I leave I tell Mick over the phone that I'm pregnant and I'm off to the hospital to deal with it on my own. He offers to come with me but I don't want him to. I don't want to feel anything. If he's there I might feel something.

I'm given a place at the end of a long row of beds with girls about my age in them. A nurse comes in to give us a talk. 'You will be taken into the operating theatre. You will be given an anaesthetic. The foetus will be removed by suction. You will be wheeled back into this room. When you wake up you will experience cramping in your stomach, it will help relieve the pain if you draw your knees up to your chest and roll onto your side. Then you will be served dinner.'

The other girls are nervous. I'm not. I'm last to go in. I've never been to hospital before. I'm not allowed to walk anywhere, I have to be wheeled in a wheelchair. I don't like it, I'm perfectly healthy. Two orderlies trundle me down the corridor, doors crash open and swing shut behind us. People hover over me fiddling with tubes and charts as we glide along. In the anteroom a doctor says he's going to give me the anaesthetic now, it will feel like I've drunk a large gin and tonic. Just as he puts the needle into a vein on the back of my hand, the plastic casing on the ceiling light above me crashes down and lands on my face. A nurse rushes forward apologising.

I wake up in my bed. The girl next to me is sobbing. My stomach hurts, I draw my knees up to my chest and roll onto my side. The pain subsides. A trolley arrives with our dinner. I'm starving and it's a Sunday roast, my favourite. The girl next to me can't eat, she's too upset. I ask if I can have her roast potatoes.

The next day I get the train back to London. Mum meets me at the station. We go home. I go straight to bed. Tomorrow I'm going to Paris with the Slits. Julien Temple is coming along to film us for Malcolm McLaren.

I can't sleep. I think about the terrifying power that women and mothers have. We don't need to fight in wars. We have nothing to prove. We have the power to kill and lots of us have used it. How many of you boys have ever killed anyone? I have. I've killed a baby. It doesn't get much worse than that. Maybe your mother has secretly used her power to kill in the past and not told you. Maybe she even thought about doing it to you. It's a secret and a burden she carries with her.

I don't tell the Slits what I've been through. I'll look like a bloated milk pudding in Julien's film though (*luckily it was never made*). When I look in the mirror I see a round pale face with two little currants poked into the doughy, uncooked skin. I keep the hospital identity bracelet on my wrist, I think it looks good: no one notices it. Emotionally I'm in a bit of a state. I'm physically weak too.

After the Paris show – in a club called Gibus – along comes a very handsome French boy called Jeannot. He has dark hair, dark eyes and olive skin. He says that my name, Albertine, is considered ugly in France, it's a servant's name, a peasant's name. I laugh it off but inside I'm crushed. I have no confidence. It's been sucked out of me with the baby. Jeannot offers me heroin. I'm tempted. Not because I want to forget what I've done, or because I'm so down, even though both are true, but because I've lost my identity. I haven't a clue who I am. I feel like a nothing. But I know without a doubt, if I take heroin now, I will destroy the tiny morsel of myself that is left, I will be lost forever. (Funny how heroin comes along at times like this. These guys can smell your weakness, like sharks smell blood.) I muster all my strength and say no. Jeannot sneers. He goes off with Tessa and Palmolive. He doesn't speak to me again. Julien follows Ari around with the camera, because she's the one Malcolm's interested in. I sit in my little hotel room and stare out of the window at Paris, watching people walk up and down the street, the heels clacking on the cobbles keeping me awake all night. So this is what I've chosen over a baby: the Slits, gigging, hotel rooms, music, self-expression, loneliness. It was the right decision – wasn't it? I wish I was at home with Mum.

I didn't regret the abortion for twenty years. But eventually I did

194

and I still regret it now. I wish I'd kept the baby, whatever the cost. It's hard to live with. But I still defend a woman's right to choose. To have control over her own body and life. That cannot and must not ever be taken away from us.

50 SID AND NANCY

1977

A groupie from New York has arrived in London, she's been here a couple of days. Well, this is a first: there aren't any proper groupies in 'punk'. Doesn't fit with the ethos. There are girls who sleep around a bit, the usual thing in a group of mates, but nothing official like a groupie. Who will want her? Maybe Steve. She's followed the Heartbreakers over. I suppose groupies are more of an American thing. Her name is Nancy Spungen, not a sexy name like the groupies I've read about: Pamela Des Barres (Miss Pamela), Bebe Buell or Sable Starr. I heard rumours that she was in trouble in NY and had to get out quickly. And she takes heroin. I wonder if she'll be scary and sophisticated, will she be cold towards us other girls? Bet she's beautiful.

Although we hang out there a lot, none of us go to the Roxy to pull. We go there because it's the only place to go. Of all the people who end up pulling at the Roxy, it turns out to be Sid. I think one of the most shocking things he's ever done is get involved with Nancy Spungen.

Like any groupie, Nancy went for the singer first; she tried it on with John Rotten a couple of nights ago – he wasn't interested. Next she tried the guitarist, Steve Jones, and worked her way down through the band. Tonight I see it happen with Sid. It's been a good night, the Heartbreakers are here and it feels a bit more exciting than usual. I see Nancy early on, slinking around, all pouty; I know it's her immediately, she stands out a mile, doesn't look right at all. She has bleached blonde hair, but that old ladies' hair-salon colour, sort of yellowy blonde, all curly in a long wedge shape, boring. Her eyes are nice, big and brown with a bit of a squint, quite cute, like a kitten or the actress Karen Black. She wears loads of leopard print but she looks like a barmaid – more Bet Lynch than Bebe Buell – a slick of red on her lips and a dark triangle of rouge on her cheeks, like a giant hand has grabbed hold of her face and left two bruised fingerprints. Her eye makeup is conventional and her tits are pushed up and out showing loads of cleavage. I'm quite disappointed; she's a cartoon groupie, not an interesting one. She's the embodiment of everything we're against: American for a start, a boring dresser, uncreative, just a follower. And on top of that, she takes smack. I'm not going to bother getting to know her, she's trouble, and not in a good way.

Towards the end of the evening I notice Nancy lurking behind a pillar – it looks like she's hiding from someone; what's she up to? She leans forward out of the shadows, pursing her glossy mouth and batting her eyelashes. With a come-hither look, she does a sexy beckon with her index finger to someone across the room. It's hilarious. I follow her eyeline and see that the person on the receiving end of all this is Sid. I try and catch his eye to laugh with him about it, but to my amazement, he grins shyly and with his long arms dangling by his side, trots over to Nancy like an obedient little puppy. I can't believe it. This cynical, judgemental guy is going against everything he's ever said and falling under Nancy's – very corny – spell.

Sid tells me a couple of days later what happened that night: Nancy gave him heroin – *as far as I know, Sid hadn't taken smack before he met Nancy, certainly not regularly* – and a blow job (I bet she was good too). And that was it. From that moment on they went everywhere together: it was *amour fou*.

In January 1978, before he goes on tour to America with the Pistols, Sid and I meet up and he asks me to spend some time with Nancy at Pindock Mews – the house they're renting in West

London – whilst he's away. He says she's very lonely, no one will have anything to do with her. I say I'll do it (only because he means a lot to me, I'm dreading it). A couple of days after Sid leaves, I call Nancy up; she's really excited to hear from me and invites me over for the evening. We sit on the squishy black sofa drinking Coke. Nancy smokes a lot and drones on and on. 'It's not fair, they all hate me, they'll only be happy when I'm dead,' she whines. 'Malcolm hates me the most. But I'm going to show him, I'm going to cut off my head and send it to him in a jar, I'm going to have it pickled. That's what he wants and that's what he'll get. Then he'll be sorry.' She goes on like this for hours. It's torture.

It's really late, I've got no money to get home and Nancy asks me to stay the night. There's only one bed, it has black satin sheets on it. Nancy doesn't take her makeup off, she undresses and puts on one of Sid's old Sex T-shirts – the cowboy one – with the armholes cut out really wide – 'to remind me of my baby'. I get into bed next to her, fully dressed. Nancy talks for another half-hour and eventually falls asleep on her back, mouth open, snoring loudly.

There's no way I am going to sleep a wink tonight, I'm not good at sleeping in other people's homes even when I know them really well, let alone with this strange and annoying girl next to me. I lie awake, the minutes crawl by, god it's unbearable. *I wonder when the buses will start running again. Then I can leave. Maybe about six o'clock.* The sun comes up slowly, watery and thin through the blinds. I stare at the ceiling. Nancy rolls over towards me and her boob falls out of the armhole of Sid's T-shirt. It rests there next to my shoulder on the black satin sheet, pale and pert, like a perfect little meringue, floating on an oil slick.

When Sid gets back from America I go round to see him. He's really grateful that I visited Nancy and thanks me, says that I'm the only person who came to see her and it meant a lot to her and to him. He's quite moved. I feel a bit guilty because I only went once.

He says Nancy's told him all about our conversations that night, including the one where I said I'd never really had an orgasm. 'I'll give you an orgasm, Viv,' he says. He wants to do something nice for me, as I've been so nice to Nancy. Nancy says, 'Sid's fucking great in bed now. I've taught him what to do.' Sid agrees with her, he's very open about his lack of sexual prowess before he met Nancy. There's no sexual jealousy between them, he says he would just as happily 'lend' Nancy out to someone.

I thank them both for the kind thought, but not at the moment. He says any time I want to, just let him know.

It's so funny because I've only ever known the shy, bashful Sid, not this bragging, sexual Sid, he's got a swagger about him now. I've also never seen him so soft and affectionate, he really loves Nancy, cares about her, he's very protective, almost fatherly towards her. It's quite beautiful to see. She's found someone to love her. Not an easy feat. But everyone deserves love, even Nancy.

Sid: May 1957–February 1979
Nancy: February 1958–October 1978

Sid's signature from the Ashford letter, when he was still spelling his name 'Syd'. 1976

51 PERSONALITY CRISIS

1977–1978

The Slits go through managers very quickly. No one can control us. I don't think a manager should control a band, ideally they should guide and facilitate, but control is what they seem to want to do. Also, when girls have an opinion, and the manager is a man, sexual politics rears its ugly head. They don't hear, *We don't want to play those kinds of venues, we're trying to create a whole new experience, so even the venues we play have to be thought about carefully.* They hear, *I don't want to fuck you.* They try and treat us like malleable objects to mould or fuck or make money out of.

It's me who organises the band and liaises with the manager – if we have one – and it's getting me down. Tessa and Palmolive are happy just to rehearse when they feel like it but I want to make this a great band, I wouldn't bother with it if I didn't see the potential. I'm sure it's a bit of a bore for all of them, the way I've come steaming in full of ideas about clothes and hair and lyrics and image and rehearsals, but annoying as I am, there must be a part of them that wants that too, or they would've chucked me out by now.

Palmolive and Tessa are very close, they muck around together all the time, play-fighting, teasing, calling each other names, rolling around on the floor like a couple of lion cubs. I feel left out and boring. I can't do that physical slapstick type of communicating. I feel stiff and awkward around them. Ari joins in occasionally, she's younger so it's not too difficult for her. Sometimes all three of them are rolling around on the floor and I stand there like a twit trying to laugh, trying to find it endearing and amusing. They must think I'm so uptight.

I get on well with Palmolive; of everyone in the band it's Palmolive that I feel naturally closest to, in age and in thought. I think she's interesting and wild and clever but although we occasionally have a good chat, she prefers to hang out with Tessa. Ari is making new friends of her own now, she inspires great loyalty and devotion and no doubt she feels liberated to be amongst people she hasn't grown up in front of, that she can reinvent herself with.

When we go to Berlin I pick up on the decadence of the city and decide to try a new look on stage: Sid's leather jacket open over a black bra. It's very sexual. I feel brave, not sure if I can carry it off. The rest of the Slits hate it. They think it's not right for the image of the band. I'm into feminist politics, always going on about it, and they don't understand why I'm using such tired old iconography. But I like to use some of the old stuff, to invert it, or even, dare I say it, just to revel in the response. So I wear it anyway. That's how I feel today. I feel sexual. I'm safe on stage to explore that stuff. It isn't safe to do it on the streets of London, but I do it there too.

I've noticed English girls don't show their sexuality, not like French and Italian girls do. We seem to be either ashamed of it or turn it into some sort of jokey, slapstick, seaside-postcard pantomime thing or a porny caricature. European women feel sexy their whole lives. Even older women behave like they're sexually active and attractive. I've seen them do it since I was a child, when I used to visit France with my father. Older French women's attractiveness isn't taken away from them by society. In England we're not supposed to relax into ourselves in any way – to enjoy the power of our sexuality. I remember when I was seventeen and I wore a child's shrunken Mickey Mouse T-shirt to art school that showed my stomach – I was experimenting with crossing the boundaries between childhood and womanhood and also Disney was so unfashionable in this rarefied artistic environment, I thought it was funny and iconoclastic. A middle-aged male lecturer said to me, 'Eugh! Who wants to look at your fat stomach? Put it away.' I was seventeen, skinny. My stomach was as flat as a board. But he managed to make me doubt it. Is my stomach fat? Am I disgusting for showing it? Am I offensive? I never wore the T-shirt again.

I'm so exhausted one Saturday afternoon, I fall asleep on the sofa in Nora's living room. The others have gone out, I'm too tired to go with them. I've become so wary of them all, so estranged, that I think to myself, *I mustn't let them see me like this, so vulnerable, but it'll be OK, I'm a light sleeper, I'll wake up when I hear them come in the front door.* I'm worried they'll see me asleep for fuck's sake. Things have got that bad. I open my eyes and see Ari, Tessa and Nora staring down at me. *Oh no, I didn't hear them.* I sit up quickly. *What horrible things are they going to say?* I brace myself. Ari says, 'You looked so sweet lying there asleep. Your face looked so gentle and lovely.' I can't believe it. She's utterly sincere. Ari is always sincere. She never lies.

The only time I feel I can safely express my vulnerability is when I'm with a boyfriend. Having a boyfriend is very important to me at the moment, it's an emotional escape from the band. With a boy I can be soft and silly and funny. Mick's on tour a lot, we write to each other but I know what he's up to and he knows the same about me. Officially we've split up but we meet again when our mate Sebastian Conran invites a load of people to his parents' house in Albany Street one night. Mick and I haven't seen each other for months. It's raining, I've got my red Vivienne Westwood boots on and I don't want to get them wet. He picks me up and carries me across the road, splashing through the puddles in his blue suede Chelsea boots. It's so romantic. Sebastian says we can stay in his parents' bedroom tonight as they're away. There's a huge white bed, white walls, white carpet and a private bathroom. The next day Mick goes on tour with the Clash. A couple of weeks later I go on tour with the Slits. And that's it, the end of Mick and Viv.

The Slits are on tour when Tessa's father dies. She adored him. I have no idea what it feels like to lose a parent you love, how I would deal with it. Tessa shuts herself in a cubicle in the loos of a Top Rank we're playing and refuses to come out – except to do the gig – or speak to anyone. She doesn't want sympathy, she doesn't want chats – all that sharing and caring nonsense. I realise she's a very strong person in her own way.

Most of the time the Slits see me as bossy (they're right). I wouldn't stay with them if it weren't for Ari; despite being so young, she has an obsessiveness, a drive, I don't know where it comes from, it's more than I ever had at fifteen. But Ari's too young to organise things, I can't expect any help from her in that department, so I have to do it. I book rehearsal rooms, ring around everyone in the band – or beg them to ring me if, like Tessa, they don't have a phone – so I can tell them when the next rehearsal is. Palmolive is always late to rehearsals nowadays, sometimes she doesn't turn up at all. I call her about getting together next week but she's become enamoured with a guy called Tymon Dogg and his music – Tymon's teaching her how to play tablas – compared to him she thinks the Slits are devoid of spirituality, she's lost interest in us. I track Tessa down and tell her about the rehearsal. She can't be bothered to come; it's the last straw. I shut myself away in my tiny bedroom in Mum's council flat in Highgate. I give up.

Ari phones me, Mum answers, I refuse to speak to her. I never want to see any of them again. Ari comes round to my home, no mean feat: I live right across the other side of London and she has no sense of direction, it will have taken her hours and many bus changes to find me. She knocks on the front door.

'Viv, please talk to me.'

I ignore her. She knocks again.

'I'm sorry, Viv. We do want to rehearse. Please open the door.' It's like we're lovers, I'm upset, she's begging forgiveness. Ari stays outside my door for a very long time pleading with me. With every knock my heart hardens. Even Mum takes pity on Ari and tells me to answer the door but I'm mad with grief and self-righteousness. I tell Ari to go away; eventually she does. I hate her. I hate them all. I'm deranged and defeated by their lack of commitment. And I'm ill.

I've been coughing for a year. Deep chesty coughing. I haven't slept through a whole night for ten months. Mum's given up trying to get me to go to the doctor. I have a permanent headache from the racking coughs, I can feel them right down in my diaphragm, right down in my pelvic floor. *For a whole year.*

I spend the night with Phil Rambow – an American singer I met through Rory – at Mick Ronson's flat. Me and Phil don't have sex, he can't get near me, I cough and hack all through the night. In the morning I'm bathed in cold sweat with a red face and puffy eyes. I'm embarrassed. I must have kept everyone awake all night. No one says anything; I'm so grateful and impressed by Mick's politeness as he offers me tea and toast. I see myself through his eyes: pale, spotty, ill, neglectful of my health. Unattractive. I go to the doctor. He says it's serious and sends me to Brompton Chest Hospital. I lie in bed on a ward full of older women. Hospital is clean, white, restful. An oasis. No Sex clothes, just a nightie. No arguments, no goals, no decisions. I'm just a girl again. A week goes by. My face relaxes. After two weeks the colour returns to my cheeks and the coughing has subsided. I'm thinking more clearly. I decide I can't be in the Slits any more, not as things are.

It will be devastating for me to leave them, but I'm not going to saddle myself with this situation any longer. Look where I've ended up for god's sake. What I care about most is the music, but it's not developing. I can't bear the uncertainty every time we go out on stage, I never know if we're going to make it through a song without it collapsing.

At the end of my second week in hospital I feel strong enough to call a meeting – Palmolive doesn't come. Tessa and Ari gather round my bed, I lie propped up on a bank of pillows like a scene from *The Godfather*. I say I won't go on as we are. I want to progress musically: to get tighter, not perfect, but enough to know we can get through a song and convey its meaning. I tell Ari and Tessa I need them to be behind the music and to have a more dedicated attitude to songwriting and rehearsing. If they can't do that, I'm out. And lastly, I say, 'I go, or Palmolive goes.'

Ari and Tessa take me seriously – maybe the surroundings help – I've never said anything like this before. I ask Tessa what she wants. I have no idea what she'll answer, if she'll answer. She says she agrees it's time to buck up and Palmolive should go. Ari says the same.

I concentrate on getting well. My back is pummelled twice a day by physiotherapists, my lungs are drained of mucus every morning by nurses, I take inhalers, I sleep and I eat. The consultant tells me if I don't give up smoking I will be dead within eighteen months. I give up smoking.

In just a few weeks I've started to forget who I used to be. Now I'm in this normal setting, talking to middle-aged women, house-wives, I realise I'm not so different from them after all.

During my last week at the hospital, Mick strides in wearing his black leather jeans and leather jacket. He's holding a bunch of flowers. I didn't tell him I was here, he's annoyed about that, but I don't like people to see me when I'm ill. Ben Barson, who I fell in love with at Woodcraft, also visits me, bringing a pineapple. Two boys; that's more like it. I feel more comfortable with Ben, he has no fear of illness. Mick's squeamish about things like hospitals, germs and diseases.

When I leave hospital I'm very thin. I walk down the road with Ari and Tessa, just the three of us now. It feels weird without Palmolive, they say they've already told her she's out, which I'm grateful for, it shows that they are taking responsibility. Together we hatch a plan – we're going to get a new drummer, we're going to record our album, it's going to be on our favourite label, Island Records (they haven't approached us yet, but we'll convince them they want us) – and it's going to be brilliant, a classic.

With Ari and Tessa at the Tropicana Hotel in LA, wearing a vintage dress and giant paper bow from a bouquet of flowers in my hair

52 SONGWRITING

1977–1979

We love Dionne Warwick's record *Golden Hits Volume 1*, where she sings loads of Bacharach and David songs. We own it collectively; I can't remember how we came across it, probably at the Record and Tape Exchange in Notting Hill. We've pulled the record apart, listened to every instrument, the drum patterns, the backing vocals, the very understated *chk chk chk* guitar sound, which mostly plays on the off beat. *I wonder if reggae was influenced by this sort of music? I heard American 'crooning' was big in Jamaica and influenced lovers' rock, so maybe it was.*

Ari and I try and emulate Bacharach's classic song structures when we write, but the result is warped because it's filtered through our lack of technical ability. Our songs come out in funny time signatures and structures – and we like it. The lyrics are different to David's because we are being honest and specific about our own experiences, which are very different to an American man's experiences (and he is a master of course). We were trying to write great pop songs, but ended up creating something new by accident.

My guitar style is developing into its own sound even more now I know what I'm listening for when I hear a record. I'm moving away from the buzzsaw, industrial whine I was developing with Keith. I still don't have any female guitarists to listen to and be inspired by, and I hate the note-bending, flashy solos, posturing and lip pursing of a lot of male rock guitarists, but I've found some I like. I'm influenced by Steve Cropper (of Booker T and the MGs) at the moment, also the guitarist on the Dionne Warwick record and reggae guitar playing, and I love Carlos Alomar on David Bowie's album *Low*.

Until now, I was just as likely to notice the horns, or a Hammond organ solo, as a guitar part, it just depended on whether the melody of the solo or the rhythm of an instrument stood out. When I listen back to music I liked when I was much younger, I realise none of it has a distorted, rocky guitar sound. I didn't like Led Zeppelin or Hendrix, any heavy rock, it felt masculine and unappealing.

In the past I listened to tracks as a whole, paying most attention to the lyrics. Words were what I knew, what I was familiar with; they worked or didn't work for me. That's how girls listened to songs. Most of the songs I've been exposed to are about romantic love. They're an extension of the fairy tales I read as a little girl – *I'll love you forever. You're the only one. I'll rescue you. You broke my heart. Blah blah* – which is shocking when you think about the effect that obsessive listening and repetitive exposure to songs about idealised love must have had on my brain. I've been brainwashed. The Slits' lyrics are very carefully thought about and scrutinised. No peddling clichés and lies for us. No lazy escapism. Words have to be true to your life. Write what you know. And make people think.

Flyer for one of the sound systems we went to

53 GRAPEVINE

1979

> I heard it through the bass line.
> Ari Up

Nora phones Island Records and sets up a meeting with Chris Blackwell, the head of the label. It's easy, just like we expected. We think we're good. Lots of record companies want us. Why wouldn't Island? At the meeting we tell Chris we love the label and that we want to be on it. He's amused and says yes.

We have a couple more meetings with Chris; he's smiley and friendly and a little bit flirty. Although he likes us, I can tell he doesn't really get the music. He loves reggae, which should bond him to us a bit more, but there's something a bit old-fashioned about him. He's caught up with people his own age, rock-star types, he talks about Mick Jagger and other old farts reverentially. At the moment he's very taken with Marianne Faithfull, who's recording and releasing an album called *Broken English* for him. We don't understand why he's so excited about her. We've seen her around over the past couple of years, hanging around squats, drugged up. She's the past, we're the future.

That was my initial impression of Marianne Faithfull – I now think she is an interesting artist, a survivor and an inspiring role model.

Stage one of our plan is completed. We sign a deal for one album with complete artistic control and an advance of £45,000. It's quite a good deal. Although out of that figure has to come our recording and touring expenses, and wages.

The first thing Island do is assign a photographer/art director to us. His name is Dennis Morris, a young guy, full of himself and his own ideas. He says the record cover should be bright pink plastic with rips and zips in it. For fuck's sake. I say we want something that reflects who we are and the music we make, and pink plastic doesn't do that. He takes offence. His masculine pride is wounded. He turns against me as I'm the spokesperson for the band. From now on, he undermines everything I say and do. We do a photo session with him, he wants to use a wind machine, for the pictures to be sexy. I say no, and we want to vet the photos before they're released: he's beginning to hate me. Luckily, as we have artistic control, there's nothing he can do about it. We want to stay friendly with Island, so I'm loath to go against the first person they've put us together with and appear all stroppy and difficult, but we've waited so long and been so careful about our output and our image, we can't just let it be taken over by people who don't understand what we're trying to do and say.

The first recording we do is at Island's Basing Street Studios to lay down a cover version of Marvin Gaye's 'I Heard It Through the Grapevine'. We don't have a drummer so we use a guy called Max, 'Maxie', 'Feelgood' Edwards; Island recommended him to us. Maxie's a proper reggae drummer from Jamaica and has played with Dennis Brown, Tapper Zukie and Big Youth and he's recorded at King Tubby's studio with Scientist and Prince Jammy; we can't believe our luck. I'm worried we won't be up to the job of playing with an experienced drummer. We've never played with anyone except Palmolive before. What if we can't keep in time with him? Or he thinks we're terrible and unprofessional?

We go into the room – only our second time in a proper recording studio – and play the track live as a whole band. Ari is so pumped up about playing with Maxie, she gives the first take everything she's got. Me and Tessa rise to the occasion and play in time. Maxie is open-minded and relaxed with us, no attitude or sneering. Such a relief. The song sizzles with life and attitude, it flies off the tape when we go into the control room to hear it played back. We do a couple more takes for luck. Chris Blackwell pops in to see how things are going. He says he thinks the first take is great but can we do a couple more, try and get a different vocal performance out of Ari? He sends me into the recording studio to try and explain to her what he wants. I try reverse psychology, telling her we don't need any more takes, just chuck something out, and everything else I can think of, but nothing she does matches that first take. Ari tries so hard, but she looks a bit bewildered, we all know that take was the one. We waste a couple of hours, just to please Chris, before we give up.

We sing the original horn parts because we can't afford horns: 'Dah dah dah dah!' like you do when you sing along to a record. We add our own bridge, chanting 'Grapevine, grapevine' over and over again. We make sure we do it in our real voices, not little-girl voices the way so many girls sing. As we come towards the end of the bridge, Ari counts Maxie in, so he knows where to change. And out of respect to the original, we don't change the gender of the song, we can't stand it when people do that.

Island have sent along Dennis Brown to mix. Dennis Brown! 'Money in My Pocket' is one of our favourite songs ever. Our track's got to be finished in one day. We want to prove ourselves, that we're reliable, not just a bunch of crazy girls. A big star like Dennis Brown turning up is stressful and exciting at the same time. We want to impress him, but as we watch him in the control room, it starts to dawn on us: he doesn't know what he's doing. He's not getting anything done. At midnight we call in the Jamaican tape op from the studio next door who we've really bonded with; her name is Rima. Rima is sensitive and confident, she understands what we want and starts to mix the track. She really saves the day. (Dennis Brown doesn't seem bothered and leaves with his gangster-type mate.) This is a bold step, to get rid of a big name and use a tape op. But we are bold. Island haven't got a clue what we've done.

Whilst all this stress is going on, Dennis Morris rings up the studio and tells me he's developed the photos from our shoot and he has to choose which ones to use tonight because the prints have to be at Island first thing in the morning. Funny that. I decide to leave the mixing of the record with Ari and Rima and get a cab to Dennis's flat to approve the photos. He's well pissed off. We spend hours going through the contact sheets. Doesn't he realise how important these first official images are to us? I leave his place about four in the morning. I call Ari at Nora's and she says the track is mixed and it's great.

Island suggest Dennis Bovell produces our album. He has a very broad knowledge and love of music, has just mixed an experimental band called the Pop Group for instance, but also runs his own reggae sound system and is in a reggae band (Matumbi) as well as mixing lots of reggae artists. Sounds perfect. We meet Dennis and like him immediately. He tells us he wouldn't have considered the project if he didn't like the songs. A couple of weeks' recording is booked at Ridge Farm Studios somewhere out in the sticks. Island are worried that we're untogether and Dennis is so busy he can't be pinned down – this way they'll have us all captive.

After our final scheduling meeting at Island, Dennis takes me aside and says, 'I just want to warn you, Dennis Morris is trying to get you thrown out of the band. He's gone to the bosses and told them you're disruptive and they'd be better off without you, they've had a meeting about getting rid of you.'

I feel sick. I'm terrified. My body feels like it's going to implode, my mouth dries out, I can't focus . . . we're on the verge of recording the album. All the work I've done to get us to this place . . . to be chucked out now, disposed of, just because I care so much. Dennis's mouth is still moving, I focus back in on his words: '. . . don't worry, Viv, I argued your case, told them that's the most ridiculous thing I've ever heard. Viv Albertine *is* the Slits. Without Viv, there is no Slits.' The panic starts to drain away, I feel the floor come up and press against my feet again. I'm grounded. I know that with Dennis Bovell on my side, I will be fine. Island respect him so much, he's probably the person they listen to above everyone else at the moment. I'm safe. And I'll never speak to that cunt Dennis Morris again.

None of his photos got used in the end.

Now we have to find a drummer. Who else can it be but Budgie? We've held auditions and a load of boring rock drummers have come through the door and banged away, smashing their cymbals all through the songs. None of them have a broad knowledge of music, none of them have heard any reggae. They don't like soul. Hopeless. Budgie is friends with Paul Rutherford (later in Frankie Goes to Hollywood), our friend from Liverpool. Paul and his friends follow us around when we're on tour. It takes a certain type of guy to feel that strongly about the Slits. A guy who is open-minded and intelligent and comfortable with his sexuality. Sometimes I feel like Paul is the only person in the world who thinks I'm lovely. He's gay, there's no agenda, he just likes me and I love him.

Budgie drums in a group called Big in Japan with Paul's friends Holly Johnson (also in Frankie Goes to Hollywood) and Jayne Casey. We know he'll have the right attitude, just because of the company he keeps. He comes down to London and plays with us. He's inventive, has a light touch, is rock-steady and, most important of all, has no problem whatsoever with Ari giving him extremely detailed instructions about the rhythms, the hi-hat patterns and no cymbal bashing. He's respectful and confident. Ari's getting stronger and stronger musically and needs a drummer who can play her vision as well as add his own ideas and technique. She's right and she's good, but still, to be able to take that from a sixteen-year-old girl who doesn't play drums, that takes a very special person. Budgie's in. Not completely in, just in for the album and a tour, he makes it very clear – he's a straightforward guy – he wants to keep moving on, not be in the Slits for life.

It's great to suddenly have this male energy in the room. His presence transforms the dynamic between us. He doesn't get involved in the squabbling so there are fewerarguments, the air between us feels different, the change is palpable. It's like the lid's been lifted off a pressure cooker.

Dennis relents and has his picture taken with us. Ridge Farm, 1979

54 CUT

1979

We work on the tracks that are going on our precious first album for a month in the rehearsal studio, then pack our bags and head off to the countryside to record.

Ridge Farm is a big old country house. The whole set-up is run by a talkative, charismatic guy called Frank Andrews. I'm more interested in his wife though, she fascinates me; she's pretty, petite, pale blonde and has a strong personality, the opposite of her looks – but the thing that really intrigues me is that she's on some sort of fast where she doesn't eat anything and only drinks her own piss. She looks perfectly OK on this diet. Maybe a little pale, and her skin is so translucent you can practically see her skull, but apart from that, nothing out of the ordinary. She says she's going to do it right up until after Christmas. I try and imagine her serving Christmas lunch to Frank and their little girl and then sitting down to join them with her cup of piss.

We all eat on site. The meals are cooked by a girl called Denise Roudette, huge heaps of food, vegetarian shepherd's pie, lasagne, fresh vegetables: I've never eaten so much or so healthily before. Denise is one of the sweetest, calmest, smartest girls I've ever met, she does a lot towards making the atmosphere at Ridge Farm harmonious. She's also a bass player and Ian Dury's girlfriend. Lucky him.

The recording studio is in a barn near the house. It's not what I imagined a barn would look like, it looks more like a country church inside. There are very high ceilings with wooden beams and wooden posts. The control room is up in the roof, the engineers look down on the studio through a plate-glass window. We all crowd around the mixing desk in the control room, pushing and shoving each other behind Dennis and Mike Dunne, the engineer, giving our opinions enthusiastically about the atmosphere of the songs, the sound of the guitar, the bass and the backing vocals.

The excruciating bit comes when we have to actually play. Up until now we've only recorded the Peel Session and 'I Heard It Through the Grapevine'; both those times we played live as a whole band. Now we're laying down the instruments separately and it's a completely different experience. First Budgie and Tessa do the backing track. Dennis keeps stopping them and making Tessa play her bass part over and over again to get the timing right. Every single second has to be in time. Every beat spot on. He's right of course, but she hasn't been playing that long, it takes years to get that sort of precision – still Dennis will accept nothing less than perfection. I go quiet as I stand behind him, looking down at Tessa in the studio. I know it's my turn next and I'm beginning to dread it. When the first backing track is finished, I descend the curved wooden staircase into the studio – feels like I'm entering a Roman arena, going to face the lions – with a knot of anxiety in my chest. Some of the songs I get right quite quickly but others, like 'Newtown', make me want to kill myself.

I stand alone in the darkened studio. Everyone else is up on high in the control room. Dennis's disembodied voice comes booming through my headphones, with Ari excitedly shouting instructions in the background. I try with all my might to concentrate and get the part right. I get a few bars into the song but the tape stops abruptly. 'You went out of time on the beginning of the intro, I'll drop you in,' says Dennis. I count the bars until I have to come in and start playing just before, so I'm up to speed when I'm dropped into the track. I'm completely focused on the task, absolutely determined to get it right this time. Phew, did it. The tape stops. 'You were a fraction early. Try again.' I can't believe it, seemed all right to me. I try again. On and on it goes. We spend half an hour on the first few bars of the song. I want to cry but hold it in. I honestly don't know what to do differently. I've lost all my self-confidence, all sense of judgement. I keep playing and replaying the part, not knowing what on earth to do to make it better. They play the tape for about the twentieth time, I flip. I thrash at my guitar furiously, not caring about timing, chords or tuning, I just smash my hand over the open strings, the tape keeps playing, I run out of steam and stop. I wait for them to tell me off for losing my cool. 'That was brilliant! Don't stop! Do it again!' And that's how the guitar part for 'Newtown' comes about.

Ari and Dennis bounce off each other well. I think Dennis recognises Ari as someone who loves and lives for music, like him. All of us are very willing to learn and there's no ego, no arguments regarding the songs, normally we argue a lot, but at Ridge Farm we are as one. We just want the record to be great, the song comes first.

'Instant Hit' is a new song; I can't believe it's turned out so well and is now the opening song on the record. I had a few lyrics about Keith Levene – the title refers to his smack habit – and we put them to music in the studio as a round or canon, which we remembered doing at school. Dennis thought it was a great idea. I love that he never dismisses an idea as childish. Keith's actual voice is on the end of the track, we taped a phone call where me and him have a bit of an argument: he says 'Thanks a lot' in a sarcastic voice. Dennis added the South American flute, it brought the whole song together, made it really light and ethereal. (*In 2013 this track was sampled and used on the single 'Consumerism' by Ms Lauryn Hill.*)

'So Tough' is the first song Ari and I worked on together in the Daventry Street squat. The words came out of that late-night telephone conversation I had with John Rotten about Sid. I used to phone John sometimes when he was staying at his mum's flat in Finsbury Park. He never answered the phone himself, a friend or brother screened his calls. John had just come back from Amsterdam, so when the bloke who answered the phone asked, 'Who's calling?' I made up the name 'Tulip'. He said, 'Hang on,' and went off to tell John that Tulip was on the phone. A minute later John answered, so I don't know what the point of the screening was. Anyway we chatted for about half an hour about Sid, wondering why he was spiralling down, out of control, what he wanted from life; when I put the phone down I wrote 'So Tough', using a lot of the words and expressions from the call. I already had the guitar riff so I tried to make it fit the words. When I played the riff to Sid, he said, 'Why don't you repeat the first part of the riff, do it twice?' It was a great idea and I liked that he contributed to the song about himself.

I wrote 'Spend Spend Spend', inspired by the pools winner Viv Nicholson. It's what she said when she won. It was the headline in all the papers the next day. She was the first winner to say she was just going to blow the lot, not 'I'm going to buy a house for myself and one for my mum and dad,' and all that safe stuff. I thought she was great and of course it resonated that she had the same name as me and I thought she was pretty. As the song evolved it turned into more of a comment on needing to own things to make yourself feel happy or complete, which I have a tendency towards, and the line about 'walking down the street looking in the windows' is something I've done since I was a child.

Palmolive wrote the words to 'Shoplifting', I just added the 'Do a runner' chorus. It's fun to record; we speed it up and Ari gets so excited when she does her part that she pisses herself when she screams. She laughs her head off and you can hear her on the track saying, 'I pissed in my knickers!'

'FM' is another Palmolive lyric. She's fantastic with words, and it's even more extraordinary when you think she hadn't been speaking English that long when she wrote it. Palmolive wrote the lyrics to 'Newtown' too. The song was originally called 'Drugtown', but I changed it to 'Newtown', thinking about all the new towns that are springing up around the edges of London, like Milton Keynes and Crawley. The young people growing up there are so bored, they take loads of drugs and drive around really fast or beat each other up at football matches, then they get up and commute to their dull jobs on Monday morning. Palmolive made up these great words like 'televisina' and 'footballina' as drug names, I think only a foreigner could do that. I'm too self-conscious about the language. I added the rap in the middle. We completely change the arrangement in the studio. After Tessa's deep, solid bass, my painful guitar part and Ari's extraordinary vocal performance the song is transformed – haunting, menacing, druggy and violent. We don't want to crowd the track with a load more instruments but something is missing. We sit at the mixing desk throwing ideas around but nothing excites us. In the end Dennis says, 'Let me try something.' 'What? What?' we want to know. But he won't say. Not sure he knows himself.

He goes down into the pit, turns the lights down low – it's quite theatrical – we all peer through the glass watching him search the studio for props. He lays a couple of things he's found on a table – a glass, a spoon, a box of matches – then says, 'Roll the tape.'

Dennis moves his body with the rhythm of the song, focusing on the table, completely in the zone: first he picks up the box of matches and, using it as a percussion instrument, gives it a shake, just one shake – he could have used maracas or any other proper percussion instrument, there are plenty lying around the studio but he chooses the box of matches – then he taps the glass with the spoon, drops the spoon into the glass, shakes the matchbox, taps the glass, drops the spoon, lights the match . . . bit by bit he builds a percussion track. He's so inventive he doesn't need any instruments at all to make music. We stand in a row in the control booth watching Dennis make magic. Nobody moves, nobody speaks, we don't want to break the spell. One take and that is it: 'Newtown' is finished.

Ari and I go through the lyrics of 'Ping Pong Affair' together, and I explain the emotions behind the words. We discuss that when she sings 'life's better without you', she doesn't mean it; she has to convey the underlying meaning of regret, not the actual meaning of defiance. The song is about me and Mick Jones. I rushed out of his flat in Ladbroke Grove one night in a fury, forgetting I didn't have enough money to get a taxi, and got a bit scared trying to get home. A couple of days later, looking at the pile of comics and records he'd left at my place, I started to miss him. Later when I was in the newsagent's in Shepherd's Bush looking at the magazines, I heard that beautiful soft voice behind me and knew I was still in love with him.

'Love und Romance' is a pastiche of a love song and all the expectations and traps of being in a relationship. Mick hates this one. During the recording of this track, our new manager Dick O'Dell visits Ridge Farm, bringing with him Bruce Smith, the drummer of the Pop Group (who he also manages). We all click with Bruce immediately. He has a friendly open demeanour and when we hear him play, we're knocked out. We know Budgie isn't into being in the Slits full-time, and Bruce says he'd love to play with us. We get Bruce to mumble on this track as if he were the boyfriend. I snog him before he goes home. Don't know what's the matter with me, I can't resist a kiss.

When I was writing 'Typical Girls' I sat cross-legged on the single bed – the same pale blue wooden one I'd had since childhood – in my tiny little bedroom, bored out of my brains in my mum's council flat in Highgate. After I moved out, my younger sister got the big bedroom, so when I moved back I was stuck in the box room. The flat was freezing, the only warm room was the tiny steamed-up kitchen. The living room was never heated, so none of us ever went in it. It was too cold to sit and watch TV so I never watched it. All the windowsills were rotting from damp and condensation. I wheeled the Calor gas heater into my bedroom; it took up most of the floor, I had to make a bit of space for it by kicking all my clothes into a pile. There was a big F scratched into the cream enamel paint on top of the heater where my boyfriend, Nic Boatman, started to write the word 'Fuck' before my mum caught him and went mad. I stared out of the window. Nothing was happening. Nothing for it, I'd have to write a song. I flicked through my lyric book and picked out snatches of words that suited my mood. I got distracted and started looking through a pile of books on the windowsill – they were sitting on top of a folded tea towel so they didn't get too damp. One was a sociology book called *Typical Girls*. It sparked off a train of thought and I went back to sit on the bed and write a list of all the traits a typical girl was supposed to have: *gets upset too quickly, emotional, can't control herself, worries about spots and fat and natural smells . . .*

I took the song – in my head as I can't write music – to rehearsal. I made sure I played the riff lots of times before I went to sleep so I wouldn't forget it. I learnt to do this the hard way; so often I've been sure the music is lodged in my brain, but can't remember it when I wake up the next morning.

Ari got 'Typical Girls' immediately; that I was taking the piss out of all the expectations and clichés, and she didn't change the timing of the guitar riff even though it's a bit odd, not 4/4. (When Mick heard the song he tried to persuade me to put it into 4/4 time. I didn't know what he was on about. I didn't know about time signatures, that this was in a strange time signature; it was just how the guitar riff came out. He said we'd have a hit with it if we changed it but we ignored his advice. We didn't have a hit.) Mick wrote 'Train in Vain' about me after we broke up the last time. When we were going out, he used to get the tube train from his gran's flat in Royal Oak to my squat in Shepherd's Bush. If we'd had an argument I wouldn't let him in, I'd leave him pining on the doorstep. There's a response to 'Typical Girls' in 'Train in Vain'. I say, 'Typical girls stand by their man' (quoting the Tammy Wynette song), and Mick replies, 'You didn't stand by me.'

'Adventures Close to Home', what a great title. Palmolive wrote this song just before she left the band. She said we could only use it on the record if Tessa sang it, she didn't want Ari to sing it. Tessa said she'd do it, which was very brave of her, she'd never sung before. Ari didn't mind not singing it at all, she didn't take it personally and leapt at the idea of playing the bass instead; she wrote a great bass line that weaves through the song like it's having an adventure of its own.

We want to use some holiday snaps for the front cover, taken on our trip across Europe with Nora last summer. We think we might even use the ones of us naked on the beach; I telephone Mum and ask her to look through them and post the ones we've selected to Ridge Farm. Mum calls me the next day and says something terrible has happened: whilst she was sorting through the pictures on the kitchen table, she knocked a cup of coffee over them and they're ruined. Ari and Tessa go mad. They're furious and I'm really embarrassed. It's not like Mum to mess up something so important. I call her back and ask if any of the pictures can be salvaged at all and she says absolutely not, they're ruined. So we decide to get a photographer to come to Ridge Farm to take a picture for the cover. We choose Pennie Smith to take the photographs, we've worked with her before and feel relaxed with her.

The night before the photo shoot, we discuss the kind of thing we might do; wild animals, warriors, woodland creatures – and

222

then go off to bed. Except I stay up and bleach the hairs on my legs with Jolen Crème, I don't want to look like a real animal.

In the morning we mess about on the lawn doing crouchy, crawly positions, playing off each other, putting makeup on like war paint. One of those shots ended up being the cover for the single, 'Typical Girls'. Then we go to the woods that border the farm and run about, chasing each other and peeping through the trees (the back cover of *Cut*).

A friend of Dick's turns up, he's just been in Africa. An older hippy guy, we don't mind him hanging about, he's very relaxed. He's watching the shoot and we're smearing mud from the rose garden on each other's arms and legs, mucking about and using our eye makeup and crayons to look a bit tribal. He gets what we're trying to do, and says we remind him of a tribe he saw in Africa; we ask him what marks we should do, he suggests he shows us how to tie a loin cloth . . . *Yeah! Let's cover ourselves in mud and wear loin cloths!* This is pretty late in the shoot, and we've been at Ridge Farm a couple of weeks so we're all a bit stir-crazy. We strip off in the garden. We wouldn't have done it if it had been a male photographer, but we feel safe with Pennie.

Someone gets an old sheet and tears it up. We dip the strips of fabric into the mud. I don't want too much mud on my face, I still want to look nice. Tessa and Ari are much better about that, they're not always worrying about looking pretty. They're more in the moment.

We know we have to have a warrior stance, not try and be all seductive. We're aware what we're doing could be misconstrued, we want the photo to have the right attitude, not be prurient.

After the shoot we jump in the swimming pool to rinse off. Dennis is already in there, he's horrified, can't get out quick enough. Says he can't be photographed with three naked white girls.

When we see the contact sheet we can't find a shot where we all look right so I'm cut out of another shot and superimposed. The designer Neville Brody, who later becomes famous (for *The Face*), does the artwork.

Twenty years later, Mum confessed that she deliberately ruined the holiday pictures because she was appalled that we wanted to use naked shots of ourselves on the record cover.

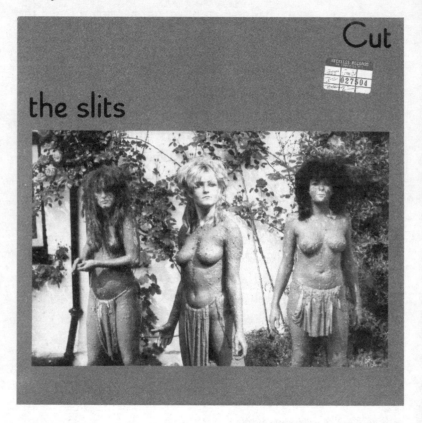

55 SIMPLY WHAT'S HAPPENING

1979

I meet Gareth Sager, the guitarist from the Pop Group, at Glastonbury. He's speckled with freckles, has healthy, ruddy cheeks and hair the colour and texture of pale English straw. His eyes are cornflower blue. I think of poppy fields and blue skies when I look at him. He's the opposite to the pale-skinned, dark-haired, intro-spective guys I've met up until now. We run around in the mud, he laughs a lot and says surreal things. His mind darts all over the place, he's bursting with enthusiasm and curiosity about music. I think he's extraordinary. I want him. I think he might fancy Ari, they get along really well. I'm a bit older and more balanced than they are. Maybe he's too clever or too wild for me.

Gareth lives in Bristol, so when I get back to London I start going into Dick O'Dell's office every day – he's managing us and the Pop Group – hoping Gareth will phone whilst I'm there, then we can have a quick chat. Gareth is the one in the Pop Group who does what I do in the Slits, all the organising. It's funny, but every time I'm in the office, he does call. Is it too much to hope that he wants to talk to me too? After he's spoken to Dick, he always says, 'Is anyone else there?' And Dick says, 'Viv's here, do you want to talk to her?' And he says, 'Yes.'

One day he tells me he's coming to London and we arrange to meet up: I say he can stay at mine and Tessa's place in Victoria if he wants. It doesn't take long before Gareth and I are together. The first time he has to leave me and go back to Bristol he doesn't seem too bothered. I'm upset at his lack of emotion, but after he's gone,

I go into the bathroom and he's scrawled on the mirror with my lipstick, 'Never can say goodbye.' I think it's beautiful.

Gareth is into free jazz and introduces me to music by Ornette Coleman, Dollar Brand, Charles Mingus, Miles Davis and Don Cherry. Even though he's a really exciting and proficient musician, Gareth thinks tuning and timing are arbitrary restrictions – passion and ideas are much more important. His approach makes me excited about music again.

Recently there's been no room for speeding up, slowing down, dropping a beat, turning the beat around, singing a bit out of tune; everyone's desperately trying to be a good musician, quite the opposite of why we started a group in the first place. I find it difficult to keep time but what kind of human being can keep in metronomic time? It doesn't seem natural to me.

I don't understand why time-keeping is considered such an attribute in western music. African drummers don't play one speed all the way through a piece of music, they speed up and slow down according to the mood, same with Indian music. It's like being told to keep the same speed and rhythm all through sex.

The Slits are off to Europe – Brussels, Germany and Amsterdam – to play some gigs and a couple of TV shows. At a Bavarian rock-and-roll show in Munich, I meet an improviser called Steve Beresford who's playing with the experimental band the Flying Lizards (they had a hit in 1979 with a cover of the Beatles song 'Money'). What impresses me about Steve isn't just his ability to play any instrument – piano, bass, trumpet, euphonium – or that he has a suitcase full of brightly coloured toy instruments which he also plays and takes great care of – but that like Gareth, he isn't a music snob. Steve's a classically trained musician and very accomplished. We hang out together in Germany and talk about TV shows, pop music and cartoon characters. Steve is my discovery.

Steve Beresford

When we get back to London, I go to see him play with a rotating group of musicians called Company at the ICA in the West End and again at the Musicians' Collective in Camden. I also see other great improvisational players like Derek Bailey, Evan Parker, Misha Mengelberg, Lol Coxhill, Fred Frith, Han Bennink and John Zorn.

I'm so excited by their playing; they're obviously all technically amazing players but they don't rely on learned formats, patterns or scales and compositions. They push themselves to respond to the moment, to the other players in the room, to the room itself, they are completely in the moment. It is very demanding and rigorous music but can also be playful and light. I find their attitude liberating and wonder if I could do it. I try it with my new housemate, Trace Newton-Ingham, and my neighbour, Tom Bailey, from the Thompson Twins (who were a large experimental band before they had hits). We do some pretty wild stuff in Tom's studio. It's not really something I can bring to the Slits yet, but it's a new musical path and it helps my confidence.

Knowing Steve Beresford helps me construct a mental framework with which to view myself musically, a context that validates my lack of ability. He's very open and non-judgemental and also extremely intelligent, so I trust and respect his opinion. I lap up Steve's views on jazz and improvisation: 'Singing in tune is

COMPANY

SIX SUNDAY CONCERTS
sunday august 5th–
sunday september 9th
at the ICA, the Mall, SW1

DEREK BAILEY · TOSHI TSUCHITORI · EVAN PARKER
(GUITAR)   (PERCUSSION)   (REEDS)
TONY COE · MAARTEN VAN REGTEREN ALTENA ·TEO JOLING
(CLARINET)   (BASS)   (CLOWN)
FRANK PERRY · PAUL RUTHERFORD · KEITH TIPPETT
(PERCUSSION)   (TROMBONE)   (PIANO)
BARRY GUY · KONDO TOSHINORI·TRISTAN HONSINGER
(TRUMPET)   (CELLO)

Admission: £1.60... + .ICA day membership)   Doors open: 8.00pm

Flyer for some of the improvised Company shows I went to

overrated,' he says. He also tells me a little story about the great
free-jazz saxophonist Ornette Coleman. 'Ornette Coleman was
always a semitone sharp when he played,' says Steve. 'When a
producer told him to play a semitone lower, Coleman tried it but
said, "It doesn't sound like me any more."' Now I can see a way
forward despite my limitations. Even though this point of view
is supposedly one of the main doctrines of 'punk', in reality all
the bands except us and the Raincoats, and a few other people
dotted around, can play to a high standard and want to be rock
gods. Because Gareth and Steve are so talented and proficient,
Ari respects them and I gradually start introducing some of the
principles of free improvisation and experimentation into the
Slits. Funk, jazz and disco are very uncool in the 'punk' scene, so
it's quite radical of the Pop Group to be playing those rhythms;
Bristol has an enlightened music scene. The Pop Group are all
good dancers too, we go down to the Dug Out (Bristol night
club) and they dance wildly all night. I've never seen white boys

228

do that before – either they headbang to heavy rock or throw themselves at each other at Sex Pistols gigs, a few can dance to reggae – but these Bristol boys really let go.

Because of the Pop Group and Steve Beresford's influence on our taste in music, when we plan our first headlining tour, we decide to mix up the musical genres on the bill and introduce our fans to the music we're listening to. One of the records we love most is *Brown Rice* by the trumpeter Don Cherry, with its African and Arabic rhythms. The title track is long and meandering but full of energy, drive and menace. 'Brown Rice' is hypnotic and trancelike and the lyrics mix nursery rhymes with whispered voodoo-like chants. It's trippy without being hippy.

We invite Don Cherry on our *Simply What's Happening* tour and he says yes. We also fly the reggae singer and 'toaster' Prince Hammer and his band over from Jamaica (we've blown most of our advance on arranging this tour). We decide to rotate the line-up, with a different one of us headlining every night.

Ad for our tour, 1979

On the first day of the tour, to my delight I find myself sitting at a table on the tour bus with Don Cherry and a couple of his band: I feel so privileged and excited. We're chatting away all friendly and relaxed, I'm holding my own, trying not to get nervous that I'm talking to this cool, talented American musician. I don't remember how, but the subject gets on to junkies. 'I hate junkies,' I say. Everyone goes silent. I don't understand. I look from one stony face to another, no one speaks, no one smiles. Something's wrong. I start to feel very alone at the table, the other three guys seem to grow bigger and loom over me as I shrink smaller and smaller. Then in a slow, measured and very cold voice, Don Cherry, looking me straight in the eye, says, 'I hate hate.' It's a complete and total putdown. I know it's the title of a song by Razzy – the DJ used to play it at Dingwalls – and I love the song; but what a fool I look and feel for hating anything. How unworldly, narrow-minded and judgemental I appear.

I have a knot of anxiety in my stomach all through the rest of the tour because things are so awkward between me and Don. I feel like an outsider on my own tour. I can't wait for it to end. I can't look Don in the eye, he doesn't look at me either. Don's trumpet playing is amazing but his band are disappointing – he must have thought that because he was playing with young people he should bring rock musicians – he's brought Lou Reed's backing band with him, the music isn't pure and trancey like we expected, more like muso rock.

Ari makes great friends with Neneh Cherry, who is Don's stepdaughter. She has bright red dyed hair, and although she's only about fifteen, she has this grown-up, wise, maternal air about her – at the same time she seems very cool. I've never seen maternal look cool before.

The idea of pregnancy did not become a beautiful thing for me, or having a baby an acceptable life choice, until I saw Neneh Cherry performing pregnant on Top of the Pops *in 1988. Never on TV, in public, in magazines or in a club had any girl worn pregnancy the way Neneh did that night. She was beautiful, but not in a glowing earth-mothery way, she was sassy, full of attitude, sexy, powerful and a great dancer.*

Luckily for me, my friend Paul Rutherford and his mates come on some of the dates so I hang out with them. In Plymouth we all stay at a boarding house. I smuggle Paul and his two friends into my room for the night. I go off to the bathroom, which is across the hall; the house is very suburban and claustrophobic, patterned carpet, embossed cream walls, plastic flowers in a vase on a three-legged table. As I pass the top of the stairs, I jump because there's a boy standing very still in the shadows. He's about ten years old, short dark hair, navy school uniform. He's holding something, I look down, both his hands are wrapped around his huge, erect cock. The whole thing is bizarre, even more shocking because his giant cock looks so out of proportion to his pre-adolescent body. In a panic and trying to normalise the situation I say, 'Very nice,' then turn round and walk steadily back to my room. I tell Paul and the others what I just saw. They're terrified, especially the boys. We discuss what sort of mental state the boy must be in to do that, we think that his mother probably takes in a lot of sailors and maybe they've fiddled with him, corrupted him. A piece of paper slides under the door. Paul screams. On the lined schoolbook notepaper is written: *I think you are very nice too, please come outside*, in childish writing. Now we're too scared to leave the room, the boy might still be standing there, might stand there all night. We lock the door and piss in the little corner sink. The next morning he's nowhere to be seen. We haven't got the nerve to tell his mother, as she serves us scrambled eggs on toast, although we think she should know.

Two months after the tour, Tessa mentioned that Don Cherry is a heroin addict.

56 SPACE IS THE PLACE

1979

We listen to 'Space Is the Place' by Sun Ra whenever we travel through Europe on tour. It works especially well in Switzerland; we put it on at the beginning of the Gotthard Tunnel. Bruce Smith, our drummer, has his ghetto blaster on his lap and the rest of us hover around him, going, 'Not yet, don't press it yet.' As soon as we enter the cool shade of the tunnel, we shout in unison, 'Now!' He jabs 'Play' and we sink back into our seats, losing ourselves in the music, each one of us in a completely different mental space. The track lasts exactly the length of the journey through the tunnel, twenty minutes. It builds and sways, it's shamanic and uplifting. If we time it right, the track ends as we burst out into the light on the other side. Orgasmic.

We love Sun Ra, we're very inspired by him, his music feels accessible to us, the way he mixes childlike rhymes into his repetitious, overlapping rhythms. We go to see him play live every time we're in New York. We think that if someone as extraordinary as him can use songs from childhood, then so can we. We need to feel validated; we aren't taken very seriously in England, especially within the music industry. But here is someone we respect doing what we want to do, and no one calls him silly or unmusical. Lots of girls' history of music is playground songs; chants, folk songs and nursery rhymes, passed down through mothers, aunts, older sisters and friends. I want to incorporate these rhymes into our songs, they are all I have in terms of a musical background and I intend to use them, however small and insignificant they are to other people. This is one of the ways we can build an identity for ourselves

– we're starting from zero, no rules, no role models. Of course we're going to be derided by people who haven't heard music used in this way before, played by a bunch of wild, scruffy girls: new things are often threatening or considered frivolous and take a while to sink in. We have to take little snatches of ideas and inspiration wherever we find them: a conversation overheard on a bus, Rotten coming from a council estate, Vivienne Westwood's fearlessness, Sun Ra and Don Cherry validating the use of nursery rhymes . . . and stitch it all together like a patchwork quilt to create the Slits' sound.

At Ally Pally gig, 1980. A rare outing for my Rickenbacker. Body paint, harlequin dress from Angels (a theatrical store that sold off its old stock). Spalding hi-top trainers. Pink lurex knickers from a Berlin sex shop

We incorporate a whole a cappella rhyme and chant section into our live set, using Sun Ra's 'Quit that jive, Jack, put it in your pocket 'til I get back, I'm going out to space as fast as I can, ain't got time to shake your hand' (which is adapted from a Slim Gaillard song). We've added the rhyme that Don used to sing to Neneh Cherry when she was young, 'Ooh ah, ooh ah ah, who stole the cookies from the cookie jar?' And two from my school playground: 'Milk, milk, lemonade, round the corner chocolate's made,' and 'Chinese, Japanese, dirty knees, what are these?' (point at chest).

We play in America twice. First we do three nights supporting the Clash at Bond's Casino, in New York. They're playing a two-week residency. It's nice of Mick to invite us, he's going out with a pretty American singer called Ellen Foley, so it could be quite awkward, but he's very loyal to his friends. We fly on Freddie Laker's airline, it costs fifty quid each way. Even waiting in the taxi queue outside the airport is exciting: our yellow cab pulls up and we pile in and set off to the Iroquois Hotel in Manhattan. We drive under a bridge with graffiti saying *Wheels over Indian Trails*. As we're looking up at the words and agreeing solemnly with the sentiments, the bonnet of our cab springs open, obscuring the driver's view of the freeway. A few minutes in New York and we're already dead. The driver steers blindly to where he thinks the verge is, accompanied by a soundtrack of blaring horns. We're too terrified to scream, our senses are heightened, the world has gone into slow motion, I look ahead trying to summon superhuman powers and see through the bonnet. We make it to the edge of the road without a collision. The driver gets out, ties the bonnet down with a piece of string and sets off again without saying a word.

Steve Beresford, who plays in the Slits now, can't play the Bond's Casino shows with us because he has a gig in Amsterdam. Dick's found us a brilliant replacement though: Raymond Jones, who plays keyboards with Chic. Ari is overawed by Raymond, very unusual for her; she frets and worries that we'd better be great for him, she's not worried about the audience or the Clash. All day before our first night at Bond's, Ari refuses to speak and will only communicate via written notes, to preserve her voice. Every now and then she lets out a little trill to test her throat. As we get closer to show time, Ari starts saying she doesn't think she will be able to sing tonight, her voice isn't up to it. None of us take any notice of her, she does this before every show, she's always holding us to ransom over her voice. I don't know whether it's nerves or a power trip. Tonight we indulge her and tell her not to sing at the soundcheck, to see how she feels nearer the show. I'm not worried, there's no way she's not going to sing tonight now that Raymond's in the band.

It gets to a couple of minutes before we go on and Ari's still saying she's not sure if she's going to sing. This is one of the most important gigs we've ever done, our first in America and in front of thousands of people. Right up until the last minute she keeps us guessing. In the end she doesn't do it. We are defiant and go on without her. Raymond is game, 'Yeah let's do this!' So is Tessa. Ari can't believe it. She thought we'd give up. But we go on and play the whole set as an instrumental and just sing backing vocals. God knows what the audience think, they seem to be into it, dancing and smiling. Halfway through Ari comes on and does her skank dancing. I don't think she can bear us to be on stage without her. I feel we've let the Clash down as well as ourselves and the audience. The next two nights go without a hitch and Ari doesn't mention her voice again. We're supported at Bond's by two really great bands, the Golden Palominos with Shelley Hirsch and John Zorn one night, and a three-piece girl band called ESG (Emerald, Sapphire and Gold) the other two nights. Howie Montaug is on the door, he's a gay Jewish New Yorker who writes poetry. He is *the* guy you have to have on the door turning people away, that's how it works in New York.

On the second visit to America, Ari doesn't use her voice as a weapon again, but she does cause chaos wherever we go. In every town she runs around the back of the cafes we eat in and tries to talk to the immigrants working in the kitchens. They're very suspicious of her: possibly they don't have visas and Ari looks like nothing on earth to them, with her tower of dreadlocks and layers of skirts over dresses – she shows them how she dances and shouts into the kitchens that they're being exploited and shouldn't be treated like slaves.

Me and Ari bothering a fit boy from a restaurant kitchen in LA, 1981. Vintage straw hat. Sarong, Brixton Market

When we arrive in Philadelphia, we decide to pay Sun Ra a visit in homage to his great music. We don't know how to find him so we do what we'd do in England and look him up in the phone book. Phone directories are inside public phone booths in America, same as England. We look under Sun, but find nothing, we feel a bit foolish but we also check under Ra, and there it is: Ra, Sun – followed by his number and address. Someone suggests we call and check he's in (not to ask if he wants to see us), someone else shouts, 'No no! It's destiny, of course he'll be in!' We all agree we should just take a chance and turn up, so we pile back into the van (Ari, Tessa, Bruce, Steve Beresford, Christine Robertson – who co-manages us with Dick O'Dell – and Dave Lewis, who later plays guitar with us) and navigate through Philadelphia, past rickety clapboard houses with stoops, stopping and asking directions whenever we get lost. It's Hallowe'en, we're dressed in our usual stuff but the people we stop peer past Christine, who's driving, into the back of the van and ask if those are our Hallowe'en costumes. We arrive at Sun Ra's small terraced house; it's very ordinary and modest with a front gate, short path and plain front door. Not what I imagined at all, I thought there'd at least be a plaster planet on the gatepost or something. We knock, hopping from one foot to the other like children on the doorstep of a birthday party – Christine and Dave stay in the van so we don't overwhelm Sun Ra – no answer. We knock again. The next-door neighbour opens her front door: 'You lookin' for Mr Ra?' 'Yes!' we chorus. 'He's away on tour right now.' She gives us a quick look up and down and immediately shuts the door. Still, we got to see Sun Ra's house and Sun Ra's street and talk to Sun Ra's neighbour. Result.

DEAR SUN RA FAN,
    For information and a membership application for the RA-LEGION, please fill in this card, affix a stamp, and mail it back to us.

RA LEGION

P.O. Box 8167
Philadelphia, Pa. 19101

NAME_____

ADDRESS_____

                            ZIP_____

WARNING: MATERIAL IS SPIRITUALLY X-RATED! MAY BE HABIT-FORMING.

My old Sun Ra fan club application

By the time we reach Madison we're exhausted but have to go straight to WORT Radio for an interview. Ari's in a foul mood, she's young and all this touring is difficult for her. As we sit down in front of the microphones, I say to Ari, 'The only way we're going to get through this is if we make it fun.' Every time the interviewer asks a question, we mess around, drum on the desk and shout out the answers, luckily the DJ joins in the mayhem. Next there's a competition, the winner gets tickets to our show tonight. The DJ asks us what the question is, I say, 'Ask the listeners to list the colours of the stains on a girl's knickers throughout her monthly cycle.' Me and Ari have been talking about writing a song around this subject ('Girls and Their Willies'), we think it could be quite beautiful. The switchboard lights up, we get loads of insults, which we laugh hysterically at, then a girl comes on the line and says, 'White, pink, red, dark red, pink, white.' 'Yeah! She wins!!'

In LA we're picked up at the airport by a big burly guy, the manager of a reggae artist we're playing with. As he drives us to our hotel, he tells us he's a Vietnam veteran and he's seen some terrible things. He was in the vanguard of men who slashed and burned the villages and killed the inhabitants. He says he's now a changed man, has discovered reggae and wants to put things right by promoting artists from Jamaica. When he laughs, his face twists into a hideous tortured death mask, full of pain. Everything he wears, his trousers, his shirt, his underwear – which we can see poking over the waistband – even his wallet, is camouflage-print. This guy is in charge of us for our stay in LA. We say we want to go to the desert, Death Valley – he takes us, says he knows how to camp out in the desert. We believe him. Off we go. The photographer Anton Corbijn comes half the way with us and takes some shots of us looking like we're in a Diane Arbus picture – I've got socks tied in my hair and am holding a child's parasol – they're for the Christmas cover of the *NME*. We arrive in Death Valley, I can't believe Americans come here for a holiday, it's barren, bleak. The Vietnam vet says it takes time to see its beauty.

We set up camp and I go off to have a pee behind a cactus. I look up and see the vet a couple of feet away, staring at me pissing. He stares at me all the time; wherever I go he's watching me. I can't sleep, I lie on the hard ground in a sleeping bag, listening out for any movement, not of wild animals, but this madman. I thank god when the sun rises and the night's over; the desert is freezing at night and boiling during the day. We set off back to our hotel. Driving through the endless flatness is oppressive, just white plains, they look like salt, stretching ahead of us as far as the eye can see. I discover that I'm a bit agoraphobic: I can't bear to look out of the window, I get anxiety attacks from the nothingness, I have to look down at my lap the whole time. We wrap up in dark clothes and tie scarves around our heads, it seems the only way to protect ourselves from this relentless heat.

The photos from this trip were used as the basis for the cover of our second album, Return of the Giant Slits. *This artwork was also by Neville Brody.*

Our hotel in LA is called the Tropicana, on Santa Monica Boulevard, which is on Route 66. Jim Morrison, Rickie Lee Jones, the Byrds, Janis Joplin and Tom Waits have all stayed here, and you can feel the history oozing out of the walls. It's the most exotic and deliciously foreign place I've ever seen. It's like a building in a film noir or a Raymond Chandler novel. There's a sign reaching way up into the sky, saying 'Tropicana Motel' in fake Tahiti bamboo-style lettering. Wedged underneath the hotel is an ordinary-looking cafe called Duke's Coffee Shop. Ari says she'll meet us at Duke's in ten minutes, she's going there straight away because she's starving. She comes running to find us later, all excited because she sat next to the singer of Rose Royce for half an hour, chatting about music. We soon realise that Duke's is the place to hang out in LA, it's always packed and there's always someone interesting in there. The most amazing thing about Duke's, for me, is the breakfast. There are pancakes, bacon, maple syrup and cream squirted out of a can, cottage cheese, three types of melon, exotic fruits like mangos and kiwis, things I've only ever seen pictures of, all piled up on top of French toast. You never look at your plate with disappointment here, eating seems to be a penance back home but in America they make food fun.

Our first show in LA is at the Whisky a Go Go; we walk onto the stage acting like Stepford Wives because we've just watched the film back at the hotel and we think it perfectly describes LA – a tranquil surface with sinister undercurrents, I'm surprised how much I like it. Whilst we're here, we try to meet up with a friend of ours called Ivi, a sweet, gentle Jamaican guy Don Letts introduced to us in London, but when we call his apartment we're told he's been shot dead in a drug feud. We dedicate *Return of the Giant Slits* to him.

With Ivi at Regent's Park

57 RETURN OF THE GIANT SLITS

1981

The greater the success, the more closely it verges upon failure.
                                             Robert Bresson,
                                Notes on the Cinematographer

There are two kinds of people in the 'punk' scene. There are the psychopathic, nihilistic extremists and careerists, who are very confident because they have no fear, lack empathy and don't care what others think of them. The second kind are drawn to the scene by the ideas – I hope the latter will endure much longer than the first type, who are like the collaborators during the Second World War, just want to be on the side that's winning. It's new to me, this mercenary streak in people. I didn't notice it in my teens, but now I'm in my twenties I see it more. Or maybe this attitude only started to rear its head after Margaret Thatcher became prime minister in 1979.

I'm doing an interview on my own with a journalist from *Melody Maker*. Halfway through, he asks me what I think of Island Records. I say, 'I think they're great, they really get us.' 'They've just dumped you,' he replies. He tells me he rang Island for a quote and spoke to Jumbo, an A & R man at the label, who said we're rubbish and they've dropped us. So that's how I found out, with a journalist watching my expression keenly to see what he could write down. It's devastating news, but I keep my composure, I've learnt a few tricks by now. That's the music industry for you; no manners, no kindness, no morals, not even from a so-called 'indie' label.

We don't find out why they've dropped us; we delivered a great album, we loved the label, got on well with Chris Blackwell: it doesn't make sense. I tell Ari and Tessa, they're shocked and upset too, but after a couple of days we rally and start to make plans to find another label and make another record.

We have fresh energy in the group as Neneh Cherry has joined us as backing singer and dancer – 'vibe master' I think the term is – and she stays with us for two years. Neneh really is lovely to be around, warm, friendly, calm and enthusiastic. Her attitude is a great help in getting us back on our feet emotionally after the Island blow.

We hear that CBS are interested in us and make an appointment with a guy called Howard Thompson. When he turns up at the cafe in Covent Garden for the meeting, I look him over. He has white-blond hair, pink cheeks and blue eyes, it can only be him: Howard Thompson from my junior school. It's so extraordinary that we both went to this tiny little tin-pot school in Muswell Hill, it creates an immediate bond between us – he's a lovely man, so we sign to CBS. It's not much of a deal, but 'punk' has had its day already as far as the majors are concerned. We've already made our next album, *Return of the Giant Slits*, in different studios, bits and pieces here and there. It's more experimental than *Cut* and brings in even wider musical influences. In some ways I think it's a better record.

There is a mistake with the artwork, the cover comes back with the title written as *Giant Return of the Slits*. I have to argue for it to be put right, trying to explain that it really matters that it's the Slits that are giant (either us the band, or giant vaginas), not our return. The title is based on science-fiction films and comics, like *Attack of the Fifty-foot Woman*.

Even though we love our new record, it was exhausting to make without any support and things are disintegrating within

242

the group; the musical climate has changed in England, it's more careerist, bands go to record-company meetings dressed in suits with briefcases and do business deals. It's not an environment the Slits fit into at all. Honesty and outspokenness are yesterday's papers. In the back of the van on the way to one of our last gigs

The Slits memorial photo, 1982. L–R: Tessa, me, Ari, Bruce Smith, Neneh Cherry

Ari tells us she's pregnant; as she talks, she tugs absent-mindedly at her eyebrows, pulling them out one by one. By the time we arrive in Bristol, she has no eyebrows left.

We played our last show at the Hammersmith Odeon in December 1981. It was a great show, with Neneh Cherry and Steve Beresford in the band; we were really 'tight', for what it's worth. Touring America had really sharpened us up. One of our support acts was the London Contemporary Dance Theatre. I loved modern dance and wanted to give them the support slot instead of a band.

58 OVERDOSE

1981

Physician, heal thyself.
Luke 4:23

'Wake up, Tessa!' For fuck's sake. I can't believe anyone can sleep so much. It's midday and she's still crashed out on the sofa fully dressed. I'm so pissed off, I'm going to put a record on full blast and dance around the living room to spoil her sleep. I feel exhilarated by my naughtiness and anticipate a bit of a showdown when she wakes up. I pirouette round the room for five minutes to 'Dancing in Your Head' by Ornette Coleman, a deliciously annoying piece of music. I keep glancing over at Tessa to see if she's woken up, but she doesn't stir. I turn the music up even louder. Still nothing. I'm bored with this now, I go over and peer at her. She's very pale, extremely white, even for her.

'Tessa!'

I put my hand on her shoulder and shake her. She flops up and down like a rag doll. I look at the coffee table in front of the sofa, there's an empty bottle of pills and a tiny scrap of paper, and written on it in Tessa's elegant script is:

I'm sorry, some people just don't have the courage . . .

A feeling shoots through me but I don't know what it is so I ignore it. What does she mean? Is it a lyric? It dawns on me: she's taken an overdose. I have to be grown up. I have to be very calm. This is important. I think back to a party I went to when I was thirteen, a boy had taken acid and was threatening to jump out

245

of a window. My friend's parents were terrified, they didn't have a clue what to do. I told them that I'd heard of an organisation called Release (founded by Caroline Coon) which gives advice on drugs, it's non-judgemental and run by volunteers, they have a helpline that's staffed twenty-four hours a day. The parents phoned Release and the volunteer told them what to do. This is all I can think of to do now, *no need to call an ambulance, this can't really be anything serious. Don't want the police coming round.* I get the telephone book and look up Release. That was so long ago, does it still exist? Yes, thank god. I tell them my friend's on the sofa, she won't wake up, she's limp, there's an empty bottle of pills. No, I don't know what kind of pills, there's no label. They tell me to get her on her feet and walk her round the room. I try to lift her but she's a dead weight, I drag and pull but it's hopeless. I call Release back and say it didn't work.

'Is she unconscious?'

'Yes, I think so.'

What does unconscious look like? This must be it.

'Dial 999. Call an ambulance.'

For a second I think they're being dramatic and overreacting. There's nothing seriously wrong, is there? Tessa's just a bit out of it, don't want to call an ambulance unnecessarily, I've got too much respect for what they do to waste their . . . A voice in my head cuts in, *Do it, Viv.*

I feel a fool, but I make the call. The paramedics arrive and carry Tessa out of our basement on a stretcher and slide her into the back of the ambulance. I put my coat on and walk alone to the hospital. It's only a few streets away. I feel stupid and guilty. Tessa might die. From the hospital payphone, I call Don Letts, who Tessa's seeing off and on. He's out so I leave a message on his answering machine telling him she's in hospital. I call our manager, Dick, he says he's on his way. I'm so relieved. I'm out of my depth and Dick's grown-up and capable. I call Ari and tell her what's happened. She says she's going out to meet some friends and has no respect for people who do things like that.

I go and visit Tessa every day. I sit by her bed and talk to her even though she's unconscious. So does Dick. Her family come and go, they get a priest to say something. She remains unconscious, so still, her body 'a rock of blue-veined stone', like Lizzie in 'Goblin Market'. Tessa's pale face is framed by tumbling black hair spread out across the white pillow, her expression serene – she reminds me of Snow White lying in her casket after she's taken a bite of the poisonous apple – beautiful, fragile, in eternal sleep.

At the end of each day I walk back to our flat through the streets of Victoria. Such a soulless, transitional place. I stop and stare into the window of Cornucopia, my favourite second-hand shop. A man approaches me:

'Are you on the game, love?'

'No. Are you?'

He slithers away. I'm bereft, but not just because of Tessa. If I'm honest with myself, if I look myself in the eye and the heart, I have to admit – hateful and weak as it is – that visiting Tessa every day gives me something to do. Something important. Something to live for. The Slits have split up, Ari's already making music with new people, I have nothing. Twenty-seven years old and all I've got ahead of me is living in a box room at my mum's. No band, no money, no job, no husband, no children. I'm finished. I tried to do something different and I failed. I'm using Tessa's situation to make myself feel good, needed, worthy, useful. I'm no better than Ari who isn't interested in coming to see Tessa; in fact she's more honest than me, I'm just pretending to be good.

Tessa wakes up and smiles the most radiant smile I've ever seen. She's transformed. I ask her if she minds that I brought her to the hospital, that she's come back to life, and she says, 'No, no, I'm happy.' She keeps apologising for what she did. I feel so differently about Tessa now. I love her. I've watched her sleep day after day – looking so innocent and vulnerable – thinking she might not come back. I feel differently and she acts differently. She's open, communicative, happy, reborn.

59 THE END

1982

I smell the stench of peace.
Gabriele d'Annunzio

Tessa and I can't afford to keep the flat in Victoria any more, so I move back to my little bedroom at Mum's. I dye my hair back to brown and wear dull, drab, shapeless clothes. I want to disappear. Other people disappear too. They vanish from my life in an instant, no invites, no calls, no interest. Boys in bands find it so easy to have girlfriends, there's always a pretty – even smart – girl to be found who's willing to be a sidekick, but it's very difficult for girls to be in the music industry and keep a relationship together. Boys don't like it, not many of them feel comfortable in the supportive role that's required.

I call Mick. Even though we're not together, he's always been there for me. I burst into tears of relief when I hear his voice. 'Mick, it's all gone wrong. Life's gone wrong, not how I thought it would go.' He says, 'Come over, I'll pay for a taxi, I've got a bottle of champagne.' Mick is a success. A survivor. I thought I would be too, but instead of being the equal I expected to be, here I am asking him to rescue me again. We sleep in the same bed but I don't want to have sex – I do want to, but I want him to love me, I couldn't bear to have sex with Mick and not be in a relationship with him. I hope he'll tell me he loves me tonight, but after I've said no to sex (I thought rather coyly) he snuggles down under the quilt and falls asleep.

The next morning he has to go out and suggests I come back later if I'm still feeling upset; I say I'll come back in the afternoon. At four o'clock I ring on his bell but there's no answer. I stand on the doorstep and ring the bell every few minutes for an hour – *maybe he's fallen asleep.* I go for a walk and try again: *he'll be back soon.* After two and a half hours, I have to face it: he's forgotten. Mick's forgotten me. I understand, he's moved on.

The pain I feel from the Slits ending is worse than splitting up with a boyfriend, my parents divorcing or being chucked out of the Flowers of Romance: this feels like the death of a huge part of myself, two whole thirds gone. Now the Slits are over and Tessa has recovered, I've got nowhere to go, nothing to do; I'm cast back into the world like a sycamore seed spinning into the wind. I'm burnt out and my heart is broken. I can't bear to listen to music. Every time I hear a song I feel physical pain, just to hear instruments is unbearable, it reminds me of what I've lost.

The Slits naked on Malibu Beach

Side Two

CONTENTS

Side Two

1 LOST

1982

That awful yawn which sleep cannot abate.
Lord Byron

The only music I can stand listening to now is by This Heat. At least three times a week I go to their rehearsal studio, Cold Storage, a concrete room with a thick metal door in Coldharbour Lane, Brixton. I sit on a speaker for hours as Charles, Charles and Gareth play the loudest, purest, heaviest, ugliest, most beautiful machine-music noise in the world. A sound so honest and passionate that even a broken person can tolerate it.

I need some love. I know a nice drummer who likes me; I invite him over to the flat I'm house-sitting. We go to bed, we have sex. The second it's over, I want him to leave. I feel terrible. My skin is crawling with a thousand insects, Curse-of-the-Mummy type thing. I lie next to him, counting the seconds until it's 7 a.m., then I can get up without looking rude. I don't want to be rude, I like him. It just feels wrong.

Lying here, staring across the room at the white veneer wardrobe, trying to see shapes in the lines of fake grain, I make a decision. I'm not going to have sex with anyone again unless I can bear to have their baby. Not that I want a baby, the thought still horrifies me, but that's surely the purpose of sex. If I can't bear the thought of having a man's baby, then I shouldn't be having sex with him. I think this caveat will bring meaning back to the deed. At the moment, sex is like scoffing a box of chocolates and then feeling a bit sick afterwards.

After three years with no sex, I gave up on that rule.

As soon as the drummer leaves, I pack up my carrier bag and get the 31 bus back to Mum's – she's moved into a housing co-op flat on the top floor of a large Victorian house in a tree-lined street off Finchley Road – where I have a small bedroom with a skylight over the bed.

I lie under the skylight whilst a rain storm drums on the glass just a couple of feet above me. I think, *I'll have a go at masturbating, everyone's always going on about it.* I take all my clothes off and stretch out, imagining the rain hitting my body. I put my hand between my legs. *Boring.* Wanking doesn't work for me. I've got to have a man in my life that I have feelings for to be sexually excited, but I don't think I'll ever fancy a guy again. It's difficult to like someone else when you don't like yourself.

I trot after Mum to the launderette, pulling a brown plastic old-lady's shopping trolley after me up the road, the dirty washing stuffed into a black bin bag inside. I'm so broken that this seems like a good thing to do on a Saturday night. I sit on a plastic chair, glazed eyes fixed on the rotating washing, and listen to Mum talk about her work as an estate manager at Camden Council. I have nothing to say, but she's a good storyteller and makes me laugh. Most nights we eat too much – healthy stuff, lentil roast, potatoes, salad – but huge portions, so we link arms and go for a late-night walk around the streets of nearby St John's Wood to try and get rid of the bloated feeling. I can't find meaning in anything, so I may as well do meaningless things like go to the launderette and stare in rich people's windows.

2 WISHING AND WAITING

1983

Hofstadter's Law: It always takes longer than you expect,
even when you take into account Hofstadter's law.
                                                    Douglas R. Hofstadter

It may seem like I'm just drifting, but I have a strategy: wait. Yep,
that's it. Wait and something will turn up. I've always hustled life
but this time I'm going to do what I've seen other people do and
let something come to me.

A year goes by and still nothing happens. I'll still be sitting here
in another year's time at this rate. I'm obviously not the sort of person things just happen to. I ask myself the same question I always
ask when I'm lost. What do I find most interesting right now? The
LA fitness boom. I've been going to Pineapple Dance Centre and
the Fitness Centre in Covent Garden every day, keeping fit. I love
being physical, I haven't used my body so fully before. I've always
hated sports but envied the way boys get to use their bodies, not
only by doing sport but mucking about and play-fighting. I've got
so good at the classes that a couple of the teachers ask me to take
over for them whilst they're away. When one of them leaves, I'm
given her class to teach. I build up more and more sessions until
I have the busiest classes at Pineapple, much to the annoyance of
the regular dance teachers. I teach aerobics. I'm only the second
person in the UK to teach it. It was made popular by Jane Fonda
in LA. I work on the front desk sometimes too. I like answering
the telephone, 'Good morning, Pineapple Dance Centre, Viviane

Teaching aerobics at the Fridge night club in Brixton, 1983

speaking, how may I help you?' I find it soothing. I like the people I work with too, they're funny and down to earth, we have a laugh. Something weird happens when I laugh though, my face crumples up into a cry. Nothing I can do about it. I turn away so the others can't see me. It reminds me of the Vietnam vet we met in California; maybe you can tell how much pain a person is in by watching them laugh.

I'm aware I'm undereducated in all areas, especially music. I hated that I couldn't ever jam with anyone when I was in the Slits. I want to put this right, otherwise I'll never be able to make music with other people, so I go to evening classes at Goldsmiths College in New Cross, to learn how to read music, practise playing guitar and develop my ear.

But although I'm earning good money teaching aerobics and enjoying going to the music classes, I feel time is slipping by and my brain is atrophying. I've got to do something that stimulates my mind. So again I ask, what, for me, is the most interesting thing happening in the world at the moment? It's got to be filmmaking. With directors like Scorsese, Tarkovsky, Godard and Cassavetes making great films, and experimental filmmakers Maya Deren, Chantal Akerman and Stan Brakhage being reassessed, independent film is challenging how people think and feel much more than music. Even more interesting is film theory, especially feminist film theory; it's changed the way I watch a film, questioning what part the audience plays in the experience and the responsibility the filmmaker has not to reinforce stereotypes. The influential film theorist Laura Mulvey (author of 'Visual Pleasure and Narrative Cinema', published in 1975) is teaching at the London College of Printing, so that's the college I want to go to. I want to do a degree in filmmaking at LCP and be taught by Laura Mulvey. I'm never going to enter into a discipline again without knowing the background of the subject. I learned that lesson in music. So now I have a goal: get a portfolio together and get into LCP.

3 GET A LIFE

1983–1988

I join a filmmaking evening class and a life drawing class, and I visit Don Letts to ask if I can have some of the Slits footage to edit so I have something to show at the interview when I try and get into film school. He says, 'Why don't you make your own film?' At first I don't think I can do it. But I ask my friend Jeb, who can do anything, where to start if I want to make a film and he says, 'You need a camera.' Oh yeah. Jeb says if I tell him what to do, he'll shoot the film. I decide to give it a go.

I'm not going to cook up a story, that's too daunting a task; I'll just film three interesting girls I know and then cut the footage together to the Slits song 'Typical Girls'. I don't know how to edit a film either, but I'll face that problem when I come to it. My three girls are the dancer and choreographer Gaby Agis, my friend Helen, who's in a girls' netball team, and the chanteuse Anne Pigalle. I choose a location for each of them and hire a Super 8 camera, splicer and Steenbeck editing machine. I know about long shots, medium shots and close-ups from my evening classes. I film Anne Pigalle getting up in the morning, I shoot Gaby in one very long sweeping take, running along the wall of a formal garden in Chiswick Park, and Helen and her netball team meeting up and playing a match in Hackney.

I take the finished film, my life drawings and other bits and pieces, including the Slits' records, to the interview. I'm so passionate about my work and want to get onto the course so badly that my hands tremble and my voice wobbles with emotion; they must think I'm a nutter. I've done my best, nothing left to do now but wait. I feel my life depends on whether I get into film school or not, and I know that Mum does too, even though she's trying not to show it. Every morning as I go off to teach aerobics, she watches me out of the window to see if I've received a letter from the college. I shake my head up at her every day and mouth, *No.*

One day there's a letter from LCP on the mat in the communal hallway. I don't panic, I don't feel anything, it's too important. I scan the contents: I'm in. As I close the front gate behind me, I look up and there's Mum at the window of our top-floor flat looking down at me. I smile and wave the letter at her and start to head up the road. She flings open the window, 'Wait, wait!' She runs down the stairs and makes me tell her face to face that *I've got onto the film and photography degree course at the London College of Printing.*

Over the next three years I learn a lot of new words and expressions, like *mise-en-scène*, the male gaze, sexual objectification, counter cinema, second-wave feminism, semiotics, signifiers, scopophilia and orientalism, and read texts by many film theorists, including Laura Mulvey, Molly Haskell, E. Ann Kaplan, Richard Dyer and Christian Metz. I study Freud and Lacan, Derrida, Foucault and Nietzsche (*all forgotten now, so don't stop me and expect that calibre of conversation*). I learn to deconstruct films by Alain Resnais, Chris Marker, Douglas Sirk, Michael Powell and John Ford. I also make short films and begin to get to grips with expressing myself in a new medium. I understand sound, and I have a strong visual sense, but being responsible for the message I convey through the medium of film is something I'm having to learn. I'm out of my depth, but so is everyone else on the course. I'm daunted by the essay writing but get a great piece of advice from Laura Mulvey: 'Think what you want to say and then say it as clearly as possible.' I work hard, I never miss a lecture. I try and overachieve, like all mature students. People given a second chance know the value of their reprieve.

Whenever I get a free period, I set off to the college library and work systematically through the Dewey system, taking each book off the shelf one by one and adding, in black biro, '/she' and '/woman' to every 'he' and 'man'. I do this for the whole three years but I never finish (and luckily I never get caught). I do it with righteous indignation; there is hardly one book in the whole library that doesn't use only the generic male pronoun. As if only men think and feel and discover and read. We've been taught on this course that every single mark and sound on film or the page is important and laden with meaning, and yet every book in this library talks only to men. Language is important: it shapes minds, it can include, exclude, incite, hurt and destroy. If language isn't powerful, why not call your teacher a cunt?

4 CAMERA OBSCURA

1984

They always say time changes things, but
actually you have to change them yourself.
Andy Warhol

I keep thinking about my father; I don't think I'll have a healthy relationship with a man whilst my relationship with him is non-existent. Over the years he's blown up in my head to Michelin Man proportions. His stocky French frame is always there, at the back of my mind, but due to lack of contact and bad memories, his image has distorted into the shadowy figure of a bogeyman.

Both my parents have tendencies towards reclusiveness, especially my father. After my parents' divorce, he moved back to Toulon to be near his family. Most of them have died now, leaving him isolated for the last ten years. He can't be bothered with the effort it takes to make and keep a friend.

I write and ask him if he'd like to meet me in Perpignan, where I'm teaching an aerobics holiday course for a week. He replies by return that he'll be there. I can feel his excitement coming off the page.

On the day I've arranged to meet my father I pop out onto the balcony of our holiday apartment to hang my bikini up to dry. I hear a scuffling noise in the courtyard below and look down to see a hunched little man with a greying Beatle haircut, scurrying about with an anxious look on his face. He's dressed in old-fashioned flared jeans from the 1970s and a short-sleeved blue shirt, unbuttoned to reveal a large gold medallion nestling on his greying hairy chest. He's muttering to himself. Rumpelstiltskin springs to mind. My heart explodes. I just know this peculiar little hobgoblin of a man is my father. You know when your mates at school used to point at a homeless man shuffling across the road and say, 'Hey, Viv, there's your dad!' for a laugh? Well, that *is* my dad. I rush back into the apartment before he sees me. I don't understand; when I look back at photos of him, he's really good-looking. Maybe it's like Oscar Wilde said, a man's face is his autobiography. I suppose if I had seen him age, day by day, it wouldn't be such a shock, but he's stuck in a fashion time-warp and he's all bent over and . . . *Oh god, please don't let him find me. And please don't let the girls see what a strange, ugly, mad-looking dad I have.*

A knock on the door tells me god isn't listening and the crazy man has found me. How do I address this man I haven't seen for fifteen years? I can't call him 'Dad'. I hustle him out of the apartment and we go and sit on the beach, throwing pebbles into the sea as we make small talk. Not easy: I have years of anger, confusion and resentment bottled up inside me, and I let it all out. He gives his side of the story, and slowly we arrive at a truce. As we talk, the comic-book baddie in my mind peels away, layer by layer, to reveal a vulnerable, simple man. A relationship with my father has begun.

I decide to get to know him and visit him in France once a year, staying at his apartment. He talks in his sleep, I can hear him from my room. He keeps a baseball bat beside his bed (it's a southern French thing, they keep them in their cars too). I'm worried that if I go to the bathroom in the middle of the night he'll come flying at me and smash me over the head with it, forgetting I'm staying with him. He seems very disturbed by my visit, or maybe he thrashes and frets like this every night. He swears to himself as he washes up. Really bad swearing, I think it might be about my mum: 'Fucking cunt, she's a fucking cunt.' When I talk to him about it, he's totally unaware of what he's doing. I'm scared, revolted. No one has a dad as bad as mine. Obviously there are worse fathers in the world, it's just that I don't know them, so in my world, I've got the worst one.

I try to communicate with him and tell him about my life, what I've been doing. 'I was in a group, Dad. Made records and toured.'

'Don't talk about it. I don't want to know. Never mention it again,' he says.

I have a choice: I can get all upset and self-pitying about his attitude, *boo hoo, my dad doesn't love me, isn't proud of me*, or accept that he is damaged. I decide to be calm and level-headed about it: *This man is incapable of love. He is to be pitied.* And I never mention my life in music again. From that moment on I only talk to him about neutral things – health, weather, history – because I understand that for some reason, that's all he can cope with. It's not me, it's him who has a problem, and I really can't use up any more time and energy on being a victim of my father's inadequacies. I have got to get on with my life.

5 THE PACT

1987

To fear love is to fear life, and those who
fear life are already three parts dead.
Bertrand Russell

I graduate from film school in July 1987 with a 2.1. My boyfriend, Olly, who's on the course with me, and nine years younger than me, gets a first. I'm furious. We split up.

I'm ejected out of the protective environment of film school and into the world of work, at speed, like zooming down a water chute, legs in the air, and landing hard on my arse on the mat of real life. I begin working immediately with an independent video production company called Dogray Productions, directing videos for alternative bands like the Mekons. I churn out music videos, a couple a week, and all of them get selected by the new music station MTV. I'm too busy to be scared or smug. I go through all the usual stuff that happens in the world of work: I'm stabbed in the back a couple of times, lose jobs, win jobs, get tougher, shag a runner (hello, Dom), work too hard, fuck up sometimes, blag and hustle and get better at directing. I film early live performances by Big Black and Butthole Surfers. I make two short films. I work for Channel 4 and the BBC non-stop. I earn good money, buy a little flat in Balham, save up for my tax. I buy nice clothes: Azzedine Alaïa, Romeo Gigli, Katharine Hamnett. I'm living in the 1980s. I'm not in love though – it would all be so perfect if I were in love. Loneliness gnaws away at me, the ache in the middle of my body keeps me awake at night. I call Mum every evening. 'I'm so lonely, Mum. I just want someone to hold me.'

My friend Mo and I are so fed up with being single, we decide to do something about it. We make a pact, which has three parts:

One: We're going to go out with any guy who asks us. Any guy. Old, young, fat, thin, rich, poor, ugly or beautiful. And we are going to give that guy three dates, even if we want to kill ourselves after the first one. No man is to be dismissed until he's had three chances. That's because it can take time for a person to reveal themselves and for us to override our own prejudices and nerves.

Two: Mo and I have to ask out two guys a month. It doesn't matter who they are, if we like them or not, it's the act of asking that's important. We've just got to fulfil the quota, two a month. By asking guys out, we begin to understand what a man goes through when he asks a girl out – the nerves, the fear of rejection, the courage, the humiliation. Until now, I haven't really been rejected because the way a girl usually lets a guy know she likes him, with looks, hints, smiles, telling a friend of his, means we don't directly experience rejection. And the first couple of times it happens to me, it hurts. But after a while, I think, *Oh well, I've filled my quota. On to the next one. Who can I ask out next? Mustn't let Mo down.* By reporting back to each other, the humiliation is easier to handle. And the more I do it, the quicker I move on.

Three: Whenever we go out, men must be included in the party. It's so much easier to take refuge in the company of your girlfriends after a hard day's work but it's not going to help us meet anyone. So we always make sure a couple of guys are invited along, even if they are just friends. At least that way we can practise talking to men, it's a whole different thing from talking to girls.

This pact does something amazing to both of us: after three

months of dating any guy who comes along, our expectations are considerably lowered and we become realistic.

During this time, I come across a lot of dodgy guys. There's the one I meet in Groucho's, who I'm brave enough to ask, 'Do you have a girlfriend?' 'No,' he replies, so I say, 'Do you want one?' We go out a couple of times but he's rude to waiters, so that's the end of that. A guy I date for a few months slaps me round the face. We're outside a pub in Soho, he points across the road as a friend of his walks by. 'You see that guy over there?' he says. 'He's a millionaire.' The millionaire is scruffy and young. 'Really?' I answer. That's when he slaps me. I just walk away. Mum instilled that into me from an early age, 'Never let a man hit you twice. If a man ever strikes you, never go back. If you go back, he'll do it again.'

I see Malcolm McLaren at a club one night. My girlfriend Debbion comes over to me and says, 'I just overheard that guy Nils [Stevenson] asking Malcolm, "Who do you like?" And Malcolm said, "Viv's nice." Then Nils said, "I'll get her for you."'

I bump into Malcolm quite often over the next few months and we become friendly – we are at a lot of the same parties, we're both trying to break into film. We often go out to dinner together, to the Ivy or somewhere in Notting Hill Gate. Once, at the end of the evening, he asks me to come up to his room at the Westbury Hotel where he's staying, but I laugh and say, 'No way, you must be joking.' He looks hurt. I don't trust him. It's not that I don't trust him because I think he wants my body, that's OK if I want it too; I just don't trust him as a person, his morals.

We talk about very bourgeois things like house prices and good neighbourhoods. I tell him about my flat in Balham, which I paid for with the money I've earned teaching aerobics. Malcolm's looking for somewhere to buy but can't decide on the area. 'Not Notting Hill. Maybe northwest? Regent's Park? What do you think, Viv?' And, 'Why does everyone like Queen Anne furniture?'

Then we get on to love. Talking to Malcolm McLaren about love, how lovely. He's good on the subject too, interesting and insightful. He tells me that when he first went to LA, Lauren Hutton made a play for him and he completely fell for her. Head over heels. He didn't know you could feel like that. It shocked him. He says he felt very sexual with her, she made a man of him. They were together for a while, then she dumped him – in that way that famous Americans make you feel the centre of the universe for five minutes, then get bored and turn their beam on someone else. It's shocking the first time you encounter it, but once you've seen it happen, you never fall for it again. She broke his heart. He speaks very honestly about the pain; he doesn't hate her, he loves her: they're still friends. He says Debra Winger made a play for him too but he wasn't interested. She wouldn't give up though; so bold, these American women.

The last time I see him is when he calls me up and asks me to meet him at Hazlitt's, a little hotel he likes to stay at in Soho. I wait in the lobby for an hour, he's always really late, but this time I've had enough – there's something so unmasculine about a man who's always very late – so I give up and go home. Later that night Malcolm gets his mate to call me and take the blame. 'It's all my fault, Viv,' he rambles, 'please come back, we're here now, Malcolm's very upset, it's really not his fault.' *Nah, can't be bothered, thanks for calling though.* I've never regretted letting someone go who was taking the piss, although sometimes I miss them for a couple of months. I think you can get a bit addicted to people and often these piss-takers are good fun to hang around with. In the end, the 'relationship' isn't worth the damage that's done to your self-respect, though.

I keep on with the pact, but after most dates I can't wait to get back home and shut the door. *Thank god that's over.* I think fondly of my lovely empty bed, my faithful friend, as I race up the stairs.

One night I arrange to meet a bunch of people in the bar at the ICA on the Mall. I tell them, 'Ask a guy, any guy.' My old boyfriend Olly, from college, is there (I've forgiven him for getting a first). One of the group, Emma, says, 'My friend's coming later, oh, here he is!'

I look up and ambling down the long white corridor towards us, almost in slow motion – a real movie-star type of entrance – is a young guy in black leather motorcycling jeans and jacket, swinging a crash helmet; he has tousled blond hair and a clear, happy face. *He's too good-looking for me. Out of my league,* is my first thought. He has a wide smile and rosy country-boy cheeks. He doesn't try and act cool, he's friendly and interested in everyone. As he's listening to someone talk, he turns to the side and I sneak a look at his profile. He has a nice big nose and full sensual mouth but he looks sad, his green eyes cloud over, he drops the happy mask for a second; now I *really* like him. We all go on to Groucho's, he rides his motorbike (turquoise Harley) and I drive everyone else in my car (black Ford Capri). I ask Emma what he's like. 'A bit mercenary. He's an illustrator, he'll do any job for money, no scruples.' *That's interesting,* I think, *he looks so scruffy and unkempt but he's into earning money. I like those contradictions. He's a survivor, a realist, good for him.*

The Biker and I sit next to each other on a banquette in Groucho's bar and he tells me about a flat he's just bought in Ladbroke Grove, which he's moving into in a couple of months' time. His voice has a slight west-country burr which is mellow and comforting. He draws the layout of his new flat on a napkin. I envy his girlfriend, such a nice uncomplicated guy. Emma tells him I was in the Slits, his eyes light up, he becomes more interested in me, says he used to have a poster of us on his bedroom wall. I'm a bit suspicious that he perks up when he hears I was in the Slits; I make a point of not mentioning it nowadays, I like to see if people are interested in me without knowing about that. I like him though, so I decide to sow a seed; I tell Emma that I fancy the Biker, and to let him know. I'm not going to make a move because he's got a girlfriend, but you never know, I'll just keep casting my net and then get on with life. Take each day as it comes and give it my best shot.

6 NAB THE BIKER

1990

The next time I meet the Biker it's six months later, and he gate-crashes my birthday party, which I hold at my friend Jane Ashley's house in Fulham. I've forgotten all about him. Jane and I dress the garden with candles wrapped in coloured tissue paper. Flickering orange, pink and red cornets dangle from the trees and bushes, lighting the guests' way down the stone path to the open front door. It looks like fairyland.

After doing the pact for six months, I'm starting to put men into perspective – no more fantasising about some perfect unattainable guy, I'm cured of that nonsense – and when Mr Ordinary rocks up, he looks like a god. Ordinary *is* godlike actually. An ordinary guy is a blessing and a very rare thing.

The Biker has two cheap gold necklaces with him that he bought from a guy with a suitcase on Oxford Street. He lifts his arms up to fasten them round my neck. 'Happy birthday,' he says. He's soaking wet from dancing, all sweaty under his arms. As I lift the hair off the nape of my neck for him to fasten the necklaces, he closes in. *Well, this is it, make or break, if I don't like his smell, this is going nowhere.* He smells of good honest sweat, no poncy deodorant for him. He's a vegetarian so it's not a meaty, kebabby smell, not overpowering, but strong enough to let me know, *here is a man.* I like it.

The stereo breaks down. The Biker squats down and rewires it. I see the waistband of his black Calvin Klein pants poking out from the top of his jeans, his strong back, smooth, tanned skin. He mends things. He's handsome and funny and works hard . . . and he mends things. Doesn't get much better than that.

Later in the evening, the Biker walks towards me purposefully with a lustful look in his eyes; I think, *Better not take it any further, Viv, he's just split up with his girlfriend, should give it some time, he won't be ready* . . . then another, quite strident voice cuts in: *If you don't take him, someone else will.*

We start to dance, our bodies clamp together, the sexual chemistry is intoxicating. Jane whispers to a bystander, 'Who's that embarrassing couple practically *doing it* in the corner?'

I know everyone says never sleep with a guy the first time you meet him, but I did. And I married him. So bollocks to that.

My eighties look: silk top from Whistles, skirt from Vivienne Westwood's shop, Nostalgia of Mud, 1983

7 THE WONDERFUL WORLD OF WORK

1987–1995

Work's going well. Life's going well. Me and the Biker are going out together, we've said the L word, but more significantly, he's bought me an expensive black Arai crash helmet, so I think he might be serious. We've been on holiday together – camping in Ireland, riding round on his Harley; a minor upset when I mentioned I might need to have a baby soon, seeing as I was thirty-six. He said he wasn't ready, he's twenty-seven. Oh well, plenty of time to bring it up again later. At least it's been said.

I've had some good jobs. First I work as a freelance second assistant on commercials. Most of the set-ups are the same, what's termed in the industry 'Two Cs in a K' (two cunts in a kitchen), but I earn good money. Next I'm given my own office at *01 for London*, a listings magazine on TV – I nearly ran out into the main office and said to the producer, 'No! No! There must be some mistake!' – and worked with a great team of people there, intelligent, fun. The office was in Denmark Street, right in the middle of Soho. I had to think on my feet and improvise, guerrilla filmmaking, four or five locations a day, in and out of a van with a small crew, meeting interesting people, Anthony Burgess, Roald Dahl, Spike Milligan, up and coming bands like the Cranberries, the Black Crowes and the Black-Eyed Peas.

Next I write and direct the short film *Coping with Cupid* for the BFI, and another for Channel 4 – *Rachel's Dream* (1992), starring Kate Beckinsale and Christopher Eccleston in their first film roles – and do a stint directing at the BBC, using actors to reconstruct crimes that have happened recently. It's difficult, coming into contact with victims of crime, especially when they are the parents of murdered children. I keep going over the crimes in my head, *Why has it happened to them? What is the common thread?* All I can come up with in the cases of the murdered or abducted children is that the majority of them were either too young to say no to an adult or brought up to respect adults too much. I promise myself that if I ever have children, I will make sure they are not in awe of people in authority. I'll bring them up to understand that sometimes you have to speak up and tell an adult to fuck off, and know that even if you're wrong, your mum will back you up every time. One of my colleagues had to make a film about paedophiles. She interviewed one of them in prison – she said she felt like Clarice Starling faced with Hannibal Lecter. She asked him, 'What can parents do to keep their children safe?' He said, 'Never take your eyes off them.'

This was a very difficult job. I couldn't sleep properly for a year afterwards. I felt vulnerable and suspicious all the time because now I knew that crime doesn't happen to other people, it happens to normal people, randomly.

At least I'm functioning in the world, working and earning money. My face doesn't crumple any more when I laugh. I can listen to music too; I love choosing obscure soundtracks for the films I make.

Then I get a couple of duds. I'm hired to co-direct a film with a writer, he's new to directing, and the producers want someone to oversee him. It's not ideal but I haven't been offered much work lately. The recession has hit film and television badly, so I accept the job.

At the interview, the producers say to me, 'He's quite difficult to work with, do you think you can handle it?'

'More difficult than Sid Vicious?' I laugh. *Yeah, of course I can handle it.*

On the first day of filming Writer says, 'Hey, you weren't wearing a wedding ring at the interview. Was that a ploy to get the job?'

'No, my boyfriend proposed to me over the weekend and he bought a wedding band instead of an engagement ring, he's quite naïve about those sorts of things.'

Writer doesn't believe me. *Fucking women*, I can see written all over his face, *always trying to trick you.* He takes me back to his house 'to collect something' and keeps putting his hands on me in front of his wife. I find out later she's having an affair and has moved her lover into the house. I realise Writer was trying to make her jealous. *Christ, the situations you walk into innocently, without knowing what's going on.*

We set off in a car to do some location hunting out of London and get stuck in a snow storm on the motorway; the car is steaming up, it's freezing outside and Writer's hot air is clouding up the windows. He starts talking about rape, says there's no such thing, and I should give him a sympathy fuck: 'What's the big deal anyway? Why are women so fucking mean about their bodies? It's just a fuck.' He snorts. 'We're going to have to get a hotel and share a room tonight, there's not enough in the budget for two.' I tell him I'll pay for my own room, thanks. I act calm; it's important not to appear scared. I look out of the car window and clock the road; because of the heavy snowfall, we're not going very fast – I'll throw myself out of the moving car into the road if it comes to it. I can do that. I'll rely on the kindness of strangers to get me to a hospital. Hopefully they won't be as bad as him. I'll take my chances. There probably aren't many people on the planet worse than this one. I think the only thing that stops him attacking me is the fear that he'll get caught and go to prison.

My next job is really interesting. I'm directing three episodes of a twelve-part kids' sci-fi series. There's something odd about the producer though (I'll call him 'Anal'). He seems to be trying to mess with my mind; he lies, changes meeting times at the last minute so I'm late, takes me to meetings with the American producer but doesn't brief me about what we're going to be discussing so I have to scramble mentally to catch up. He's definitely trying to undermine me and keep me off balance. Another one with an agenda. It transpires the US producers want me to direct the series, but Anal doesn't, he wants to direct it himself, not have this ex-Slit girl do it. He's resentful. The whole crew can't stand him, but they need the work and go about their business with a lacklustre, uncommitted ennui. I want this series to be great, I'm constantly trying to motivate them, get them excited about the locations, the costumes, the casting, to infuse the series with style and creativity, but they can't be bothered.

I start bleeding heavily on the coach when we're going to recce a location. *That's weird, it's not my period, I never bleed in between periods.* Something's not right. I discreetly ask a girl if she has any tampons.

Anal's ears prick up: 'What's going on? What are you talking about?'

'I've started my period,' I say, to shut him up.

The nastier he is to me, the clumsier I become. I keep forgetting things, I'm absent-minded. It's not like me, I'm usually very efficient. Maybe it's because he's watching me all the time, hoping I'll fail. At the end of the first week's shooting I feel I've done OK. Negotiated Anal's weirdness, and – apart from a few shots that need to be picked up – I've got through the insanely packed schedule. Ringing round the next morning to find out where we're all meeting to look at a new location, I can't reach anyone. That's funny, surely they're not all sleeping in? The cameraman, the location guy, the costume designer and Anal himself are unavailable. It takes a while for me to get suspicious.

'Do you think they're avoiding me?' I eventually say to the Biker.

'No, of course not,' he replies.

Then I get a call from Anal, can I come in to the office for a chat? I dress quite sternly, a fitted jacket, white shirt, jeans and biker boots, I have the feeling I need to look strong. The Biker takes me in on his Harley and drops me outside the office.

'I think you know what I'm going to say,' says Anal, rubbing his bald head, like the weight of the world is crushing his skull (I wish).

'No.' I'm not going to make it easy for him.

'I'm going to have to let you go.'

I've never heard this expression before, it takes a few seconds for it to sink in that I've been sacked. He says he'll pay me the full amount for the job, but I have to sign a confidentiality clause and never speak about what's happened. *It's all right, no one's died,* I tell myself as I go reeling out into a wall of horns, cars and crowds, all mushed together into the big grey blur that is Tottenham Court Road.

Anal got his wish and directed my part of the series. I watched the first one and a half episodes later that year and was happy to see he made a right pig's ear of it.

With Anal's pay-off I buy my first computer, an Apple Mac, and the scriptwriting programme Final Draft and start to write a feature-film script about a girl gang in Scotland in the 1970s, based on my friend Traci's upbringing. I call it *Oil Rig Girls.*

I move in with the Biker. I sell my flat in Balham and go halves with him on his place in Ladbroke Grove. I'm living with a handsome, surfing, motorbike-riding illustrator. We're getting married at Chelsea Register Office in June and when I go to the doctor about the bleeding, she tells me not to worry and to take it easy, I'm pregnant.

8 BABY BLUES

1991–1995

I lose the baby. It starts to go wrong when I'm at my accountant's. I have stomach cramps and feel wet between my legs, I say I need to go to the loo. Thick juicy slices of blood slither down my legs and onto the floor. I spend ages in there cleaning it up. I go to Selfridges to look at hats to take my mind off it but it happens again. Blood everywhere. I run out onto Oxford Street and get a taxi home. The Biker calls the doctor and they send an ambulance. How embarrassing. I've never been in an ambulance before. As the paramedics wheel me into the red-brick Victorian hospital on Euston Road, a couple stop to let us pass. I look up from the stretcher and say, 'Sorry.'

The Biker stands by my hospital bed, he looks shocked. Tubes going into my arm, a tank of oxygen attached to my face with a clear plastic mask. 'You're so white,' he says. I'm losing so much blood. It's all draining out of me.

Baby's gone. Another baby gone. Not my fault this time. I'm determined to be positive. I *will* have a baby. Nature was just telling me this one wasn't healthy. I get on with my *Oil Rig Girls* script. I'm also co-writing a girl-gang script with a writer called Lisa Brinkworth. We've actually been commissioned, paid money, to write it. I'm finding it hard to concentrate though because I still feel pregnant, like baby's been left behind after the miscarriage. I don't tell anyone; they'll think I'm mad. I pop up the road to Boots and buy a pregnancy test. It's positive. *Must be a residue from the pregnancy*, I think, *probably happens after a miscarriage, still some of the pregnancy hormone left in your body*. I don't know what I'm talking about. Should I tell the doctor? I might just be mad or a bereft lunatic. Lisa is downstairs waiting for me to start work on our girl-gang script. I call the doctor quickly and tell her I've just done a test and it says I'm still pregnant. 'Probably doesn't mean anything, sorry to bother you,' I say. Her voice goes very stern and steady and monotonous, like a Dalek: 'Call a taxi and go to the hospital right now.' 'OK,' I say. 'No, I mean immediately, do not even pack a bag. Do you understand? Immediately.' Now I'm scared.

I call the Biker and he races home and tells Lisa to leave. I don't want to go downstairs. I'm scared to say anything out loud to her, it will make the situation real. I'm scared to get off the bed. I'm scared. After a scan, the doctor at the hospital tells me I have an ectopic pregnancy, the baby's growing in my fallopian tube, trapped in my stringy, mangled, fucked-up tube, never made it to the womb. It could rupture any second. If that had happened and I wasn't in hospital, I'd have bled to death.

I'm knocked out and cut open and my baby and my fallopian tube are removed. I've lost this baby twice. The operation is more complicated and takes much longer than the surgeon anticipated so I'm heavily sedated; I come round to a man shouting angrily at me, 'Viviane! Viviane!!' I don't want to come up from the bottom of the soft silt seabed I'm lying on, it's nice and dark and quiet down here. The nurses shout angrily when you've been under a long time because it brings you back quicker than a soft soothing voice. You don't respond to a seductive siren calling your name, you just float off towards the calm deep waters of oblivion. Anger rouses you, makes you passionate, fires you up. I'm wheeled back to my bed. I feel sorry for the Biker. He was young, handsome and carefree when we met and now he's creased and haggard and in and out of hospitals all the time, living through these dramas because he's lumbered with me. I think my body collapsed as soon as it knew it was loved.

I wake up and look down at my stomach, it's been cut open and stapled back together with huge steel staples. It looks disgusting, like a crumpled fleshy fish's mouth puckering right across my body. I'm getting married in two weeks' time but my face is yellow, my eyes are red, my stomach is stapled and my baby has gone. Not quite the fairytale ending I'd imagined.

I cancel my hen night, and my oldest school friend, Paula, comes to visit me in hospital with a tub of soya ice cream instead. The Biker tries to have his stag party, playing baseball in Hyde Park, but his heart's not in it; he leaves early, goes home and shares a spliff with his brother. I comfort myself by writing pages and pages of baby names. Arlo, Roseanna, Ariana, Frick, Freda, Ava, John . . . my friends are using up all the good baby names as year after year goes by and I don't conceive . . . got to keep ahead of the game . . . 'It's all right, I'm OK,' I say to Mum rather too brightly, pen and list in hand. But I can see she thinks I've lost the plot.

I'm very thin now, so my wedding dress has to be altered. I buy long satin gloves from a fancy shop in Bond Street, to cover my knobbly elbows.

And then it's my wedding day.

I stay in a beautiful boutique hotel the night before. My sister has flown over from America and sits on the end of my bed and chats to me all evening. In the morning, my friend Charlie Duffy, a fantastic makeup artist, performs a miracle on me. I will never forget what she does for me today. She mixes exactly the right shade of foundation (Hospital Yellow) and paints my features back onto the death mask that is my face. She is an artist, she makes me look human, pretty even. This is not an easy thing to do when your subject has lost every spark of life and colour that makes a person attractive. My hair is swept up and dressed with fresh blue ranunculus buds. My dress is ivory, floor-length, empire-line, with silk chiffon wisps trailing from the shoulders; Grecian with a touch of Audrey Hepburn in *My Fair Lady*.

My tall, handsome cousin Richard gives me away (I've gone all traditional now I've had a brush with death). We walk slowly into Chelsea Register Office – I'm physically frail, I have to cling onto his arm for support but I'm not nervous – to the calm, wistful strains of Eno's 'Another Green World'. After the reception, Hubby and I go back to the boutique hotel, no making love on our wedding night for us, I'm still stapled up. Can't even stand up straight without difficulty. So we lie on the double bed, propped up by a pile of down-filled pillows stacked against the rattan headboard, surrounded by a fresco of cherubs and doves, and watch TV. It's the happiest day of my life.

Throwing the bouquet after my wedding, 1995

9 HELL

1995–1999

Abandon all hope of fruition.
Zen saying

I turn down directing work that's offered to me if it means being out of London for long periods of time because I want my marriage to work. Hubby works very long hours, so one of us has to compromise our career and I'm happy for it to be me. He earns more than me anyway.

Now I've recovered from losing the baby, we're all geared up and committed to trying again. We've been told that I won't be able to conceive naturally because my remaining fallopian tube is also mangled, so we sign up for IVF at the Lister Hospital in Chelsea.

I inject a solution into my stomach for a month to suppress my natural hormones, making me menopausal. Next I inject pregnant cow's urine into my stomach for a month to stimulate my ovaries so they produce lots of eggs, then I'm ready for the eggs to be harvested. I make about twenty. I've swollen up, I look six months gone, it's called ovarian hyperstimulation syndrome, looks like elephantiasis (a teacher at my school had it). My legs, feet and waist are huge as barrels. It's a complication, quite dangerous; I overreacted to the drugs, now I can barely walk and am constantly nauseous. My eggs are mixed with Hubby'ssperm in vitro, and the most viable three are placed back inside my womb. We wait four weeks then do a pregnancy test. I'm pregnant again.

I waddle back and forth over Chelsea Bridge to the Lister, the doctors and nurses are thrilled that it worked first time for me, but at the next appointment I start bleeding, gushing blood – *hello darkness my old friend* – and baby's gone again.

I am wildly insanely bug-eyed crazy with grief. I don't want to live. I think of ways to kill myself. Throw myself under this passing car? Jump off Chelsea Bridge and drown in the Thames? Or just lie face down in this puddle and stop breathing? Poor, poor Hubby, he is hitched to a raving lunatic. But he is my rock, solid, grounded, steady. I love him so much that life is just about still worth living. If it's just going to be me and him, so be it.

We keep on going to the Lister, I keep on trying to get pregnant, months turn into years, fail after fail after fail. I am not a person, I'm a shadow, creeping along walls, quivering along pavements, my body itching, my mind wild, my patience stretched tight, ready to snap at the slightest provocation. I can't stand to look at pregnant women. I hate them. I can't even bear pregnant friends – I stop seeing them. If anyone walks too close to me in the street or at a bus stop, I want to kill them. I *will* kill them, *just let that fucker take one step closer, it's nothing to me, I'm dead anyway.* My body feels like one of those diagrams you see on posters in doctors' surgeries: skin stripped away, palms turned out, vessels, organs, arteries on show, blood raw.

Lying on the doctor's table, week after week, my feet hoisted up in stirrups, I transport my mind outside of my body; I'm not here, it's the woman who is longing for a baby who's lying down there, legs wide apart with a man she's never met before sticking his arm right up inside her. *Do it for the baby. It's not you, Viv, you're up on the ceiling looking down. My, she's pale. Sweating desperation. Saddest thing I ever saw. Been crying a couple of years I'd guess. Glad it's not me. I'm lucky. Mum always said I was a lucky baby. The nurse told her that when I was born. It's part of my history.* At another hospital, where I'm sent for more tests, the doctor doesn't use gloves, sticks two fingers inside me and circles them round and round inside my vagina whilst he looks into my eyes. I think it's called abuse. When I get dressed and sit opposite him at his desk, I burst into tears. He looks petrified but I don't report him, I haven't got time. I'm on a mission. Next time I go to this hospital I say I don't want him; the nurse says, 'Don't worry, he doesn't work here any more.'

I have to stop working, I'm mentally unfit to work. I become reclusive, hiding away at home, occasionally venturing out to get food. Every ounce of my energy goes into my husband. I love him, I want to keep him, I make his dinner, we sit on the sofa together holding hands and watching TV. We are very close. It's us against the world.

I am accepted at St Mary's Hospital miscarriage clinic – run by the world-famous Professor Lesley Regan – and put on a blood-thinning regime, injecting aspirin into my stomach every day; then I go back to the Lister to start trying again. Still nothing. No baby. Just purple, black and yellow bruises all over my stomach. I couldn't look less like a mother. I have a sharps bin under the sink. Every day, every day I inject. I go to see *Trainspotting* at the Screen on the Hill, but have to leave halfway through. I think it's glorifying needles; needles aren't rock 'n' roll to me, nothing glamorous about them – to me they signify heartbreak and failure. Back home that night, the tiny pale grey mosaic tiles in our bathroom pulse like millions of mini TV sets as I sit on the bog, head in hands, staring at the floor and worry, worry, worry if I'm doing the right thing. Is this is a safe or ethical way to conceive? IVF is in its infancy, not many people have done it. A little girl's voice cuts into my thoughts, loud and clear, *I don't care how I get here, Mummy. Just get on with it.* The voice is reassuring and confident. Or am I just barking mad? I shouldn't watch surreal films whilst I'm in this state.

I hear of an IVF clinic in Belgium that has a better success rate than English clinics and because they have different fertility laws over there, they can put more than three embryos back into the womb. So Hubby and I start trekking over to Belgium. Altogether, I've had eleven attempts at IVF and thirteen operations under general anaesthetic, including two lost babies and the removal of my gall bladder as it was overstimulated by the IVF drugs. No wonder I'm bonkers. I lie on the bed and stare out at a Belgian industrial estate; hundreds of magpies gather on the grass outside. *Dear god, just send me a sign if this is the wrong thing to be doing* . . . Hundreds of magpies, thousands of pounds, heartbreaks, train trips, international phone calls, blood tests . . . and still I fail.

Failure has become my middle name. Do I sound sorry for myself? Fucking right. Why don't I give up? Because I want a baby more than anything in the world. I didn't want a baby for thirty-six years but now I've met a man I love and I want a baby. Simple as that. I'm gripped and driven by a desire way out of my control. Mum is being destroyed along with me. She tries to tell me that having a baby isn't the be-all and end-all: 'Why do you want one so badly?' 'I JUST WANT TO HOLD MY BABY.' No logic, no sense, a compulsive biological urge. I see a baby in a pram outside the gym. How lovely it would be just to pick her up and hold her. I look down at the sweet little bundle, *I just want to hold* . . . *Oh god, I am that close to stealing a baby.* That vile, unbelievable crime, I understand it now, I get it, that's what the crazy bad lady always says, 'I just wanted to hold her.' You pick her up for a quick cuddle, and baby feels so warm and soft, and that lovely newborn smell makes you close your eyes in ecstasy, and you can't put her back down again. Ever.

As a project, to take my mind off everything, Hubby and I start looking for a house to buy. We want something modern, can't stand those cornices and uneven floors and dust coming out of the walls made of lime and horsehair. We find a great house in a mews full of one-off architect-built houses in Camden Town. Lots of people are after it but we get it. It's the first thing that's gone right for years; I hope it means my luck has turned. I wasn't expecting it. I will never just presume I'll succeed again. I am not that person any more. I am a person that bad things happen to. We move in, it's huge. 'Please don't leave me alone in this big house,' I say to my husband. I love the house though, it's the first time in my life I have walked up to a front door and been proud to put my key into it. This means a lot to me; it sounds shallow but my home is important to me, I'm ashamed to say it defines me in a way. I've lived in horrible homes all my life, now at last I am in a great one.

My career has gone down the toilet with my failed pregnancy tests. The BBC have offered me a short contract. I don't want to do it but I've accepted it. I need to start contributing to our finances again; I've sold all my guitars, amps, Sex clothes and Sid's bits and pieces at auction to pay for a couple of the IVF attempts (if one of those attempts had worked, I was going to call the baby Sid if a boy, Sidonie if a girl). We've decided to have one more try and then stop. When I've healed emotionally I'll think about adoption.

Hubby and I plod off to the hospital in Chelsea for one more go and I start working at the BBC in White City again. On my last day of the BBC job, I meet a very kind woman who is a reiki healer. She does a 'hands on' healing session on me, as I'm stretched out on a desk in an empty office. She won't take any money for it, she's a true healer. I go home feeling good for the first time in years. I keep telling myself, *Whatever happens, I can take it.*

It's Saturday, time to do our last-ever pregnancy test. Negative. Of course it's negative. I'm resigned to it now. We've arranged to meet some friends at Kenwood House for a picnic and to listen to the open-air concert tonight. I'm not going to let my quest for a baby dominate our life any more, so we go anyway. Hubby and I lie on the grass and Handel's *Water Music* floats over the lake. I can't smile. I can't talk. Hubby says, 'Why don't you get drunk? At least you can do that now.' But I daren't, in case baby is still there. I have a feeling baby might still be there.

I secretly do a pregnancy test every day. It's always negative. I just want to be sure, seeing as this is the last try. I'm going to do a pregnancy test every single day until my period comes. If I'm still doing tests, I've still got something to live for. Still got hope. But it's the hope that kills you. Every day I torture myself looking at the little window on the white tester stick, waiting and waiting. No blue line.

Except one day there *is* a blue line. Very faint but I think I saw it. Or imagined it. Hubby squints at the stick and says he thinks he can see a blue line too. Is it possible that you can get negative after negative reading and then a positive? The next day I do it again. The blue line is stronger. Not imagining it. We go to St Mary's, where my consultant does another test and confirms I'm definitely pregnant. I've become quite friendly with this woman, but today we can't look at each other. Her best friend, the TV presenter Jill Dando, has just been murdered. I'm so unstable that it all feels like part of my curse.

A baby is growing inside me. I know it. And I know Baby is healthy. I don't trust myself, don't trust my own health but I have no doubt that Baby is strong, mentally and physically. It's just up to me now not to let her down, to be a safe and stable home until she's ready to be born. (I found out the sex, I can't bear any surprises, it's gone on too long. I have to be ready.) Surely I can manage that? Of course I can't. Dear old Blood starts showing up again, pouring out of me. I'm carted off to hospital and stay overnight. The woman in the bed next to me is handcuffed to the bedstead. She's a prisoner, a warden sits on a chair next to her bed. The prisoner is so excited to be out and about that she gabbles away excitedly all night. The bleeding stops, Baby seems to be OK, I'm sent home. But I keep bleeding on and off throughout the pregnancy; every time it happens I go back into hospital but Baby hangs on in there. Doesn't let go. Thank you, darling girl.

10 HEAVEN AND HELL

1999

It's days before I'm due to give birth, and I am suddenly convinced that I shouldn't have the 'natural' birth I've planned and was so looking forward to; I should have a Caesarean in controlled circumstances. I follow my instincts and book the operation for 12 April 1999. Baby is lifted out of my womb: *Bloody hell, I don't know much about babies but she looks the size of a toddler!* For the first time in my life, I know what it is to cry with joy. If I die now, I will be happy. She is swaddled and handed to me, hollering her head off. As the nurse advances towards me with this wailing hole wrapped in a white cotton blanket, I panic. *I won't be able to stop her crying. She'll know I'm a fake. Everyone is going to see I am a useless mother.* I hold her and whisper, 'It's all right, Baby, Mummy is here, Mummy will look after you.' And she stops crying. I don't put her down again, unless I really have to, for three years.

The three days in hospital with my baby are three days in heaven. She's a beautiful, soft, dimpled little dumpling. I gaze at her all the time. She clings to me like a baby koala bear. I'm standing on the steps of the hospital with her in a car seat, she's dressed in her Baby Gap pink hat and jacket, we stop a passer-by and ask him to take a photo of me, Hubby and Baby. Now we're in the car, Hubby is driving. I'm horrified. What the hell is he doing driving like this? He is going to kill my child. Everything is heightened and distorted. Being a new mother is more psychedelic than taking acid. The whole world is different. Dangers are exaggerated, smells are intensified, speed and distance are stretched. Back home with another fish-mouth scar across my stomach, I sit in the rocking chair feeding Baby, listening to Hubby moving about downstairs, and think to myself, *Please go. Just leave now and put a cheque through the letter-box every month.* What a filthy thought. I am filled with hate and fury and mistrust towards my husband, who has stood by me through years of IVF and never once threatened to give up on me, not even in a temper. I loved him with all my heart until the second we set foot on the pavement outside the hospital. I confess my feelings to the visiting midwife. She tells me to give it a year and then reassess the situation, she explains that it's biological and not uncommon. She's right: after a while, the familiar warm feelings I had for Hubby creep back into my cold heart.

I'm nervous. After so many years of trying for a baby, deep down I don't think I deserve a child. Someone is going to take her away from me; my mum will lose her in Camden Town, a paedophile will snatch her, Hubby is going to trip up whilst he's carrying her: every night I imagine going to her funeral.

Hubby is going out tonight for the first time since Baby was born, she's six weeks old. I feed her and put her to bed. I think, *Shall I just lie here and go to sleep?* I'm exhausted but decide to get up and make beans on toast. Got to look after myself. I'm sitting on the sofa eating when I hear a thump. I ignore it. Another couple of thumps. I put my beans on toast down, wander into the hall and drift towards the sound, not in the least bit worried. The noise is coming from the garage. I open the garage door, look up at the skylight and see a figure spread-eagled across the glass.

Oh, just some kids messing about, I think to myself, *probably climbing across the roofs of the houses for a laugh . . . NO, VIV. THIS IS IT.*

A man is climbing into the house through the open first-floor window at ten o'clock at night he wants my baby he's come for her I'm alone she's upstairs I'm downstairs I'm a new mother I don't know what

I'm supposed to do I don't know how to save someone else I've only ever looked after myself before does he have a lookout outside should I run upstairs and grab my baby or will that make us both vulnerable . . .

I think all this in a split second and decide to confront him, hopefully luring him away from Baby. I decide to leave her up there alone. I might be wrong. I open the front door – if he has an accomplice, I'm in trouble – and look out into the silent black street. Fucking modern houses, not one of them has a window onto the mews, just brick and render as far as the eye can see. I remember being told that criminals hate noise, it draws attention to them and makes them nervous, so I let out the loudest, most blood-curdling scream I can muster. Two lives depend upon it – I give that scream everything I've got. The man drops off the roof and lands a foot away from me as I stand trembling at the open door. I try and slam the door shut but time has gone elastic, my hands have turned to rubber and the door is made of lead. It takes a lonely lifetime to push it shut. An army of men could have come through that door, it seems to take so long.

Once the door is shut I stand in the hallway and scream again. I don't know if there's another man already in the house, I want to give him the chance to get out. Then I run upstairs to Baby, who is crying. She's never heard her mother make such a frightening noise before. I've rehearsed an emergency like this so many times in my head. I've always thought I'd lock myself and Baby outside on the balcony, so this is what I do but the moment has passed. All that worrying and plotting my escape I've done in the past was useless; when it happened, I had to improvise.

The police come, they think it was an attempted robbery. 'Did I do the right thing?' I ask.

'You and the baby are safe,' says the officer. 'That means you did the right thing.'

11 BLOOD ON THE TRACKS

1999

I'm walking with Baby and Hubby on Primrose Hill when I get a terrible, cramping stomach ache, so I go into the nearest pub. I'm losing lots of blood, it's a wonder I've got any left. Something's wrong. Baby's only three months old and I'm breastfeeding so I shouldn't be bleeding at all. I have a feeling that something bad is happening. I'm in the bog for ages; Hubby snaps impatiently through the door at me as if he thinks I'm staying in there to be annoying.

I go straight to the doctor's surgery and a trainee nurse does a smear test. I bleed like a stuck pig and the nurse runs out of the room to find a doctor. Fat fleshy steaks slide out of me, they pile up on the white paper sheet covering the examination couch, looks like a butcher's shop window. I can't stop it. Where is everyone? Anyone?

A doctor appears as I'm standing in a pool of red liquid, stuffing slices of liver into the flip-top bin.

'Get in a cab. Go to A & E. Now.' Not again.

I'm sitting with Hubby, Baby on my lap, in Dr Jeffer's office. She says, '. . . burble, burble, burble . . . cancer . . . burble, burble . . .' I must be looking a bit dazed because she fixes me with her glinting birdy eyes and says: 'You will never have any more children. Do you understand?' Well yes, put like that, I do understand.

I must appear in control, still in charge of my own destiny. 'How do you get this sort of cancer? How does it happen?' I ask.

'Cervical cancer can only be contracted by people who are sexually active.'

Shut up. Stop talking. You're making me sound like a right slag. What must Hubby be thinking? That he married a loser who not only has cancer but slept around and is now going to die and leave him to bring up Baby alone? I stutter through the rest of the consultation. When I try and say my address, no words come out, just gasps. I leave with an appointment for an MRI scan.

I lie on the conveyor belt, put on the headphones that protect your ears from the loud noise and grip the little buzzer tightly, which I'm told to press if I want to come out. The machine is so loud they won't be able to hear me scream. I tell the radiologist I'm claustrophobic. She says, 'You'll be fine, you won't go in very far. Just up to your head.' There's a sense of urgency. MRI machines cost thousands of pounds a minute to run. There's no time for a chat. The radiologist retreats into a side room and peers at me through a glass window. 'We're taking you in now,' says a disembodied voice. The conveyor belt slides slowly into the machine. There's a soft wind blowing. My feet are deep inside the tunnel, my head is at the entrance now, but I don't stop moving, the conveyor belt keeps sliding deeper into the tunnel. She lied. The roof is almost touching my face, I'm enclosed, entombed, on and on it goes, further and further in, until I'm a long way down the shaft. I can't stand it. I press the buzzer, 'Stop! Stop!' I want to scramble out but the space is too tight, like a pothole, I can't turn round. Any second now, I'm going to start clawing at the walls. The stretcher reverses slowly, and I'm back in the cold white room. So ashamed. I've wasted the hospital's time and money. I've let the doctors down. I've let my daughter down. I'm hustled out of the door and told briskly to make another appointment. There's a queue of people in the waiting room ready to be scanned.

You'd think you could overcome anything if your life depended on it.

I go home, empty out three large cardboard boxes and stick

them together so they make a long thin coffin shape. I lie in the coffin – in the middle of the living room – every day. And every day, I draw a blanket closer and closer to my face, until by the third day I can stand it covering my face for five minutes. When I can lie in the box for half an hour, I go back and have the MRI.

This time I'm fine. Some things you just can't do without practice.

I'm fucked. I've got a huge tumour at the top of my cervix. If I had gone ahead with a natural birth, I would have bled to death. Having a Caesarean saved my life. The tumour went undetected somehow, even though I paid to have a smear test annually instead of every three years. Cervical cancer is one of the few cancers that are viral. You catch it from shagging. You could shag only once in your life without protection and get it. The doctors say they'll do what they can, but I should make arrangements 'just in case'.

Now the guilt descends. Is this the consequence of too much careless sex? Of wanting and needing love? Am I shallow? Immoral? I confide in a friend who has HIV, and he asks me, 'Do these thoughts help you get better?' 'No.' 'Then don't think them.' My sister flies over from America and takes care of Baby, so she doesn't have to go into a nursery. My mother comes round every day and forces me to eat, spaghetti with salt and butter is all I can face. My friend Tricia accompanies me to hospital appointments – otherwise I can't remember anything that's said – and another friend, Erin, delivers a home-cooked meal for Hubby every night. These women, and a grant from the charity Macmillan Nurses, keep me from going under.

Hospital, doctor. Doors opening. Doors closing. Fourth floor. *Lift going up.* MRI. Endocrinology. Oncology. Train. Home. Baby, cuddle, sleep.

Hospital. Blood test, endoscopy, scan, anaesthetic. Vomit. Bleed. Results. *Worse than we thought, I'm afraid.* Bus. Home. Baby, cuddle, sleep.

Lift going down. This may sting a little. Did you take a number?
You need a ticket. Blood levels. Drip, chemotherapy. Vomit. *A little*
tattoo. Lie very still. Think of the machine as helping you get well.
Radiotherapy. Vomit. Bleed. Taxi. Home. Baby, cuddle, sleep.

Close your eyes. Open your legs. I'm important, me, I'm ill. Poke,
test, weigh. Vomit. Diarrhoea. *Please use the hand gel. Follow the*
green line. You are here.

Thank god that's not *my* life. I can't feel anything, so it must
be happening to someone else. It's all happening to that woman
who was so desperate for a baby – it's her who is being prodded
and irradiated and her veins flushed with platinum (cisplatin, the
chemotherapy drug, is made from platinum), not me. Anyway, *I*
would never shit in my pants. I'm quite elegant actually, so it can't
possibly be me – standing at the junction of York Way and Camden
Road, face screwed up like a bunched fist, legs trembling from the
effort of holding back the poo. Look at her with her knees clamped
together, clutching the black iron railings that surround the council estate (*great rock 'n' roll moments*). She's probably a drug addict,
or a wino. Tut tut. So many of them in Camden Town. Even posh
ones. 'Please can I use the loo? Thank you so much.' *Use best voice*
so don't sound like a junkie desperate for her next fix. Act calm, just
a few more steps. Too late, can't stop it. Disgusting filthy stinking
soiled low-life . . .

I see life differently now. I can't ever go back to the well side, I've
crossed over. And I'm glad. Now I have patience and compassion
and I'm not scared of ill or dying people. People who haven't been
to the other side, or aren't close to someone who has – they seem a
bit half-baked to me, lifeless.

At the end of the radio- and chemotherapy, I have one last
treatment to go through. Brachytherapy. This involves the doctors
shoving a stick of radioactive material inside my vagina (it looks
like that glowing green bar that Homer Simpson gets caught in

his shirt in the title sequence of *The Simpsons*), then they all scoot out of the room and lock the nuclear-attack-proof door behind them, peering through a triple-glazed window at me as I lie on a trolley, legs in the air, green thing up my whatsit. I spend most of the week after this treatment on the polished wooden floor of our bathroom, writhing in agony and vomiting bright green liquid as blood pours out of my arse, which feels like it has been slashed with a razor.

I write a long letter to Baby in case I don't make it. I've read that's a good thing to do. I'm so angry with myself; *what kind of a mother are you, to bring a child into the world and then immediately go and die on her?* I vacillate between damning myself for dying and thinking I'm a burden to Hubby and Baby and should top myself. Do them both a favour.

Night-time is the worst though. Death waiting patiently just outside the half-open bedroom door. I know he's out there, and he knows I'm in here. Even if I beat him and get through another night, he's not bothered, he knows his time will come. 'I'm scared,' I whisper to Hubby. 'I know,' he says. What else can he say?

When you're facing death, you have to walk that walk alone.

12 THE WHITE HOUSE

1999–2007

Out of your vulnerabilities will come your strength.
Sigmund Freud

I'm still drained from the radiotherapy and chemotherapy. I'm as dead as an alive person can be without actually pegging it. I really should eat a vegetable occasionally. During the treatment I drank wheatgrass, shiitake mushroom juice, miso soup, ate vegetables, no carbs, no sugar, no wheat, no dairy, oh and before the chemo started I drank my own piss – only to be done if you're not taking any supplements, medication, etc. – but now there's something about the smell and taste of chlorophyll that makes me gag. I'm so thin that I can't lie on a mattress, I have to have two pillows under my body.

I wish I could get up off the sofa. Wish I could smile and laugh. I can't remember the last time I laughed. I wish I could think of one thing in the world that interested me apart from my daughter. I'll spend today trying to think of something that makes me a tiny bit excited. I look at the lampshade for a couple of hours. I like looking at the lampshade, it's neutral, has no feelings, no agenda. There's nothing about the lampshade that upsets or frightens me. That's also why I think about that female gardener on TV, Charlie Dimmock. I don't wonder about her, I just picture her. She's neutral too. The other person I picture is Heather Mills. Heather Mills lost her leg but still thinks of herself as an attractive woman. If I get very scared that I might die, I chant to myself,

'Heather Mills, Heather Mills, Heather Mills, Charlie Dimmock, Charlie Dimmock, Charlie Dimmock.' I can't think about anything that will make me feel. That's the trouble with serious illness, and depression, you can't imagine being well – like on a cold day you can't imagine warmth – you live in the everlasting dread-filled moment.

The only thing keeping me going is my daughter. Because of her, love courses through my body like a drug. I can feel it there all the time. This must be confusing the cancer, this intensely happy feeling pulsing through my veins all day. I'm determined to get well enough to enjoy Baby's first Christmas; she's eight months old. The only time I spend with her nowadays is holding her when she and I are both asleep. Hubby does all her feeds and changes her nappies. She's started looking to him eagerly for cuddles, she feels safer with him because he's the provider of comfort.

I watch as the intense bond I had with my daughter slips away. I'm losing the child I fought so hard to have in my life. It's unbelievable, inconceivable, we were telepathic. Tied together in love.

I lie awake all night watching Baby sleep in her cot next to us, remembering how happy we were. After a few hours of sniffling, the self-pity starts to evaporate and my brain kicks in, *Hang on, maybe I can do something about this. I can at least try to turn this around. Not many things in life are irreversible.* I'm so down, I've forgotten that I can control things in my life. Cancer can make you feel so worthless.

The next morning I say to Hubby, 'From now on I do all Baby's feeds and changes. No matter how tired I am.'

I don't have the energy to do it but it's that or lose my daughter, so I find the strength from somewhere. Doing all the day-to-day chores for her pulls me back to life. Through these actions I learn what matters to a baby – the one who takes care of her physical needs, the one who plays with her, feeds and changes her, that's the person she wants to hold her when she cries. Clever baby. After two weeks, she's back. And over the next few months we grow closer than ever. She needed time and effort from her mother; I'm rewarded with her love.

Holding Baby (tight) on Primrose Hill, 2001

If I'm not looking after Baby, I barely get up off the sofa. I don't watch TV, I just sit there. I don't even stare into space, I just exist in the tiniest amoeba-like way. I never go out. I don't want to see or talk to anyone. It never occurs to me that I might be depressed. I know there's nothing apart from my daughter and my husband that holds any interest for me and I've become very lethargic and antisocial, but I just think I'm a bit burnt out and jaded from all the hard work I've put into life, followed by the traumas of IVF, childbirth and cancer. I mention to my doctor that I can't laugh, but I don't want to say too much in case she takes my baby away.

During all this I get a call from Ari. I haven't heard from her for ten years, she's living in New York now and wants me to re-form the Slits with her. I am terrified of Ari being back in my life. I can't take the madness and chaos that I know will ensue. I tell her *no way*. She tries very hard to persuade me. I don't mention the cancer, it all feels too raw. She's very upset that I won't countenance being in the band again, but I can't possibly do anything that would be disruptive to my daughter or my physical and mental health.

One morning I find myself sweeping the kitchen floor. Pushing the broom around in front of me, I don't remember deciding to sweep the floor, getting up and going into the kitchen, I just notice that I'm doing it. I used to enjoy sweeping up, it was the only household chore I liked. I remember thinking to myself, back when I was well, *Poor old Madonna, never gets to sweep her own floor, someone does it for her, she doesn't know what she's missing.* I think there's something very healthy about keeping your own cave clean. It is a good barometer of how your life is going, the state of your home. If it's a complete tip, you're taking on too much or depressed; if someone else has to keep it clean for you, it's too big or you're too busy.

As I sweep, I realise that this is the first time for a year I've felt motivated to do anything that's not absolutely necessary, and I know that a little shift has occurred. It gives me hope that maybe, if more little shifts start to happen, I might get better.

From that day, when I realised I'd got up off the sofa and was sweeping the kitchen, it took ten years until I could honestly say: 'I am well.'

I think I'll go back to the gym. I sit on the exercise bike and picture a phoenix rising out of the ashes to give myself a boost. I set the resistance level to 1 – the easiest setting – I used to be on 10 but I need to give myself time. The bike doesn't bloody work. The pedals won't go round. I flap my hand at an instructor as he wanders past. 'Excuse me, excuse me.' He comes over, has a fiddle with the controls, says it seems to be all right. I slide off and he hops onto the bike to test it. The pedals go round. I climb back on, the pedals don't go round. I've got nothing. Nothing in my legs.

London is full of bad memories; Hubby and I think it might help me get better if we move to the coast – the fresh air, slower pace of life – and it will be good for our daughter too. I sell my guitars – it surprises me how pleased Hubby is that I'm selling them – but I don't throw away my picks. I keep them in my lady-like purse. I like seeing them every time I get money out; a gold one with a serrated grip and a heavy-gauge pale grey one.

Hubby and I view a house by the sea. To get to it we have to walk up a narrow dirt track, across a wooden bridge – where we pause and look down into the stream as two swans sail underneath us – past lilac bushes and an apple orchard, a row of flint fishermen's cottages, until we come to a white clapboard A-frame beach house, like an American holiday home from the fifties, perched on top of a slab of rock that drops away to the English Channel. The white shingle path to the front door winds around enormous sword plants and yuccas – just walking up the path is an adventure – but as we round the last bend, we come across a rabbit splayed out on the doorstep, its throat and stomach ripped open. The estate agent scoops the limp carcass into a plastic bag in one deft movement. I step over the entrails and joke that maybe this is a sign we shouldn't buy the house. We enter the large white open-plan living room and straight ahead, as if there's no wall, is sea sea sea. We decide to buy the house, sign or no sign.

13 HASTINGS HOUSEWIFE REBELS

2007

I promise myself I will do two things when we move to the coast:

1. I will do a class at art college.
2. I will get fit.

I sign up for a ceramics course one afternoon a week at Hastings Art School. My husband is annoyed, I don't understand why. Perhaps he's jealous. I register him for a life drawing class, so I'm not the only one having fun. I choose ceramics because it fits in with my daughter's school timetable and, since the cancer treatment, my hands are so shaky I probably can't draw or paint any more. This is the first time I haven't agonised over a decision. The other people on the course are a mixture of old and young, unemployed, part-timers and loners, like me. I love them. They're clever and interesting. I love their conversations. They discuss hearing aids and the war. 'Women used to put a box of Omo washing powder in the window to signal to the American GIs, "Old Man Out".' They make me laugh. Coming to this class once a week is healing. I feel relaxed and comfortable for the first time in a decade. Best of all is the teacher, Tony Bennett – *When the student is ready, the teacher appears*. A good teacher is a gift, they bring a subject alive and that's what Tony does for me. He watches me for a couple of months, like I'm a nervous animal. He doesn't get too close. Occasionally he appears behind me – the way art teachers do – and makes a comment about my interpretation of a subject; he never criticises, never picks at my technique, always talks about the emotion in the work, until one day, when we've become relaxed with each other, he says gently, 'Viv, why don't you try expressing *your-self* in your work?'

I'm horrified. I'm surprised at the vehemence of my response. 'I don't want to express myself! I'm sick of expressing myself! I've expressed myself to death! I just want to make nice brown pots to put in the living room.'

He lets me blow off steam and leaves it at that. Next week he comes up to me and says, 'I know why you said that, I heard you on Radio 4 last night, it was a different surname but I recognised your voice, you're Viv from the Slits.' (It was a rerun of an old interview.) We talk about the Slits and how hard it was being a girl who forged the way, who took the knocks every day on the street and in the industry and that now I just want to be invisible.

But he's sown a seed, something in me changes and I let go. I create my first piece of real work. It's like the work I used to make at art school when I was seventeen; erotic and a bit funny, combining ancient and modern, fertility symbol and fetish. I take it home. Husband doesn't like it. He sneers at it, says he won't have it in the house, 'Put it in the garden.' He also says our daughter mustn't see it because it's sexual. It's not sexual, it's a representation of a naked female. I think children can make the distinction between entertainment, art, humour and real life from a pretty young age. Do all artists who draw life models have to hide them from their children? Of course they don't. What about artists like Yoko Ono and Louise Bourgeois? They make extreme work and both have children. Not that I would ever call myself an artist. I wouldn't dare. But I'm not going to hide my real self from my daughter any more. This is what her mother is doing. If she's got any questions or worries about it, she can come and talk to me. I put the ceramic on the sideboard.

Husband works all day in the open-plan kitchen/living room, the one room we have apart from the shared bedroom. He still has

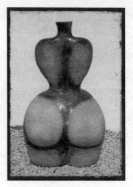

My first ceramic, 2007

a studio in London, but won't ever go to it. He's becoming very insular and curmudgeonly out here in the country. I'm beginning to wonder if moving was such a good idea.

I'm craving my own space, so I rent a studio (which I offer to Husband, but he'd rather work at home) in Hastings with a fellow student called Robin, and I go there every day for a couple of hours – after dropping my daughter off at school – to work on my ceramics. I don't like touching the clay at first. It's too squelchy, gets under my fingernails and messes up my clothes. It takes a couple of weeks before I can plunge my arms deep into the big clay bins, right up to my elbows, and grab fistfuls of the stuff and slam it onto a bench. I find kneading and pummelling therapeutic – I never would have chosen this medium if it hadn't been for my circumstances, but now I've found it, it's just what I need. The shaping and moulding, scraping and smoothing are very natural, organic actions, you only have to half concentrate, so a little bit of your brain is unaware of what you're doing, letting the instinctive, intuitive part come forward. This is good for me, it gives the hamster on the wheel inside my head a rest.

My daughter comes home from her new school in tears. She came last in the cross-country race. She says she doesn't mind not coming first, but she can't bear coming last. I say it's because you haven't practised. No one can do anything well if they haven't practised. Let's practise together. We run round the field next to our house every evening after school. It's muddy and lumpy with mole hills; there are boggy patches with reed beds that we have to leap across; startled sheep trundle out of our way; little piles of sheep poo are dotted around like mounds of Maltesers. She trots off, but I can barely walk. My asthma is so severe I have no breath, no lung capacity. My legs are tired after a few steps, she goes round twice to my once. I hate running. After a couple of months my daughter comes third in the cross-country race (subsequently she opts to stay at the back with the cool girls) and I decide to start trying to run along the top of the sea wall, see if it's a bit easier running on a flat surface. I'm like Rocky at the beginning of the movie, out of breath, falling onto each foot, no control, I remind myself of the pensioners I've seen on TV at the end of a marathon. I manage a quarter of a mile but I'm dizzy with lack of oxygen. I lean on a flagpole panting for a few minutes before turning round and half running, half walking back home. Gradually, I improve, the asthma clears up, I can feel my muscles firm up and I start to love running. It's like a meditation to me, I *have* to do it; I don't even notice the effort any more.

I run in all weathers at all times of day; rain, cold, dark, hot. On one side of the sea wall is a road and flat fields of tall grass. I watch the swans gliding along a little canal, which was built to ferry ammunition up and down the coast on barges during the First and Second World Wars. I wave at the shepherdess driving her tractor, long blonde hair whipping around her brown face, her collie eager and alert on the passenger seat. On the other side of the wall is the sea; the grey waves roll onto the pebbles, gulls squawk and dive, and in the far distance Dungeness power station is lit up like a floating gin palace, perched on the horizon. These days I cruise past the quarter-mile flagpole and after two miles of straight running I reach the beach cafe at the end of the wall – its front door propped open with a tub of margarine – no need to rest now, I turn my face into the wind and head back.

The paranoia I was left with after the cancer – that I would get ill again – is beginning to lift. For a while I kept going back to the hospital, thought I had this, that and the other. They were very patient and tested me for everything; I swallowed tubes for them to look into my stomach, had loads of blood tests for food allergies, then they stuck a camera up my arse . . . that one finished me off. I think I almost had a touch of Munchausen's Syndrome (hospital addiction syndrome); I couldn't leave the safety of the hospital and all the attention and ritual behind. But a camera up your arse will sort that one out.

After so long worrying and being fearful, living by the sea and running is giving me the mental space to think creatively again for the first time in years. With the salty wind on my face, feet pounding on the shingle, Kate Bush, *The Hounds of Love*, on my iPod, new thoughts enter my head. *What do I think about that architecture?* as I run past a white modernist house: 'I like the shape of the house but the windows are too small.' *What do I think of the asymmetrical stairs, the sculptures in the garden?* 'Those stairs don't look right with the house; the sculptures are interesting.' *Who am I now? Am I the same person I was when I was seventeen? The person I was when I married? Or has my personality been completely eroded and I must start again, creating myself from scratch, like an amnesia victim?* It doesn't matter what the answers to the questions I'm asking myself are, how uncool, how ordinary; they just have to be the truth.

Each morning I start again with the questions, easy stuff, like colour – I've always been drawn to colour. Mum made colour interesting for me, when I was little; she would say, 'See the colour of that woman's skirt? That's called elephant's breath.' Or, 'See that ribbon? It's mint green, this one's duck-egg blue, that flower is dusty rose, and that one's salmon pink.' I interview myself as a way to discover the new me. *What colours do you like?* 'Eau de nil, pale, calm and mysterious; mauve and lilac, delicate, gentle, sensual.' *Why do you like those colours?* 'All I could think about after chemo was the colour purple, I decorated the whole Christmas tree in purple and wrapped every present in purple, it felt healing.' *Good, there's a story there, a meaningful answer. Make a story out of your experiences.*

I've started to laugh again too; mixing with the non-judgemental people at art college, I realise I'm quite playful. I reignite my love of detail in clothes: a puffed sleeve, a side or a front zip on a leather jacket, the shape of a heel or toe of a boot. I'm enjoying looking: I used to look at everything and everyone. I notice marks on a stone, the haggard sea-worn groynes; *it doesn't matter what you like, just be truthful and observant*, I tell myself. I don't let myself off the hook; if I make a statement, I have to justify it.

Running also helps me accept my body. After all the years of medical intervention, I feel violated. All those unknown men's hands up me for years. To cope, I reacted like a rape victim, disowning my body, floating above it, not *in* it whilst it was happening. I would chant to myself, 'I'm doing this for a baby, I'm doing this for a baby. I'm doing this to get well.' At last my body is beginning to feel like it belongs to me again and it's strong and healthy, serving me well instead of constantly letting me down.

I'm also trying to learn to play tennis. It's not me, I'm hopeless at it, but I want to fit in with the other mothers. I swing my arm listlessly as the tennis coach lobs me a ball. 'I wish a man would come into my life to inspire me,' I say to her. Where did that unfaithful, insurgent little thought come from? I'm shocked at myself. I haven't strayed, even mentally, in all my fifteen years of marriage. And now it's occurred to me I need a muse to get me going, someone in my head to make me step up, give me some inspiration. *Be careful what you wish for.*

14 BEAUTIFUL FORTRESS

2007

In every dream home a heartache.
Roxy Music

I go to my doctor, Dr Shah, for a check-up. He says he saw my husband in the surgery last week about a minor complaint. 'He doesn't love you, you know,' he says matter-of-factly. 'He doesn't care about you. I've seen it many times, when the weaker of the two becomes dominant and tries to undermine the stronger one.' What an extraordinary thing for a doctor to say. I should be shocked and worried, but I'm not. I know my husband loves me. We're going through a rough patch, that's all.

How does anyone make it through marriage and children and remain a whole person? Perhaps it is unavoidable that the individual has to be sacrificed for the unit. Rachel Cusk describes marriage and family as 'institutionalised dishonesty', 'a cult of sentimentality and surfaces'. Robin Wright Penn called it 'a beautiful fortress'. And Virginia Woolf, never one to hold back: 'I loathe marriage. I hate its smugness, its safety, its compromise and the thought of you interfering with my work, hindering me.' All I know is I wasn't brought up for this. I was brought up a feminist, a rebel, a creative person. Not a cleaner, cook, pacifier and compromiser. I think I could cope with a bit of each, but not just the domestic side on its own.

Looking back, I don't think I could have been a full-time wife and mother without the illness but I had no choice, I wasn't well enough to work, I did the best I could in the circumstances and I was happy to do it. But even though I've willingly put my whole heart into my home life, it's been difficult. I've earned my own money since I was seventeen years old, motherhood is a huge shift in freedom and status. No one ever says, *You're good at this, well done.* No one pays you. If you fuck up and drop the baby, then you'll get some attention, but if you keep your head down and do a 'good enough' job, you're ignored.

One day during an argument Husband says to me, 'I own you.' And it dawns on me: *It's just like the fifties. If you are a full-time mother without a private income, you're a chattel, a dependant. It's 2007 and nothing's changed.* Husband wants me to stop dyeing my roots and having my legs waxed, to save money for the school fees – to turn me into a greying, frazzle-haired yeti. But I still have to function in the world, I still have to present myself to people every day, to hold my head up. This is a sacrifice too far for me: 'If we can't afford to pay for a couple of leg waxes a year, then we can't afford to send our daughter to private school,' I say and I mean it. I'm not going to martyr myself, it's not healthy. I've already started down that road, it's time to stop or there'll be no turning back.

I never look out of the window and appreciate the sea any more. I don't even glance at it on my way to the kitchen with an empty cup. There it is, spread out across the whole back of the house, undulating like a jewelled cloth forever being shaken out for my delight – and I ignore it. And that's how my husband and I are becoming: we don't notice each other enough, we don't touch each other enough. If you can take something as majestic as the sea for granted, because it's there every day, what chance does a mere mortal have? The balance between us, the ecological system that was our relationship, has shifted: he used to be my rock, but after having Baby and surviving cancer I've become a rock myself. We either have to shuffle about and rebalance together on the raft that is our marriage, or we're going to topple over the edge and drown. We need to renegotiate our roles – I think you need to keep doing that throughout a marriage. There's a fine line between a rock and a dead weight. *A thin line between love and hate.*

At this point we decide to rebuild our house. Want to know if you're really suited to someone? Move to the middle of nowhere together, where you don't know anyone, and then proceed to build a house. That'll sort it out. There are five Polish builders here all day, starting at eight o'clock in the morning, and Husband is still working from home. He's doing this to save money, so we can afford to pay the builders, but it's taking a toll on our marriage. We have one large open-plan living area and one loft-style bedroom. 'You must have a very strong marriage,' say the other mothers doubtfully when they hear how Husband works in the middle of our home every day. He constantly comments on the state of the house: what's (not) in the fridge, crumbs left on the bread board, washing up not done, the sheets, the bathroom, where I've been, who I'm emailing, what I've bought, why am I making another appointment for a leg wax, 'Again? Didn't you have your legs waxed last month?' 'Any chance of a coffee? What's for lunch?' Now he doesn't go to London to work at his studio any more, home is his only domain, and he's becoming obsessed with it. I recognise that feeling only too well from my Year on the Sofa, and of course it will never come up to scratch, it can never be perfect. He has the disgruntled air of someone who's saddled with an incompetent employee and thinks they've made a big mistake hiring them. I get the feeling he wishes he could sack me, *would* sack me if he didn't have to pay me off.

I often sit in the car outside our house and cry. I don't want to go in because I have no space, nowhere to go once I'm in there, there's no kitchen, no living room – that's become the office – Husband, Baby and me all sleep in the upstairs bedroom, which, because of the works, we reach by a ladder. The contractor is inept, so time and again the building work is delayed. I sit in the car after doing the shopping or dropping our daughter at school to put off going inside for as long as possible. It doesn't feel like a home any more. I watch as the slow and painful rebuilding of the house slowly and painfully demolishes our marriage.

15 THE LETTER

2007

Every human encounter is an adventure.
Tony Bennett (not *that* Tony Bennett;
my ceramics tutor at Hastings Art School)

I lie on our white king-sized bed, in our minimal white bedroom, inside our gleaming modernist glass box beach house, and look up through the skylight at the clouds drifting by. I can hear seagulls shriek and scuffle on the roof as they take off to dive over the Channel, and sheep bleating outside in the fields. Dozing here on the cool cotton bedcover like Lady Muck, whilst a young, fit local fireman called Dan is down in the garden building a fence made from reclaimed railway sleepers, I think, *Things aren't so bad. We've made it through the hard times.* Dan's stripped to the waist, tanned and sweating, with a little brown cheroot dangling from the corner of his mouth. He's hot, but he doesn't interest me. I hum quietly to myself, challenging the gods:

> Nothing you can say can tear me away from my guy.
> Nothing you can do could make me untrue to my guy . . .
> He may not be a movie star . . .

Husband and I have been married for sixteen years, we've had some extremely testing times, and things aren't too good at the moment, but even so, no fit fireman, no handsome young guy from the village, no millionaire, nope, not even a film star, could turn my head or my heart away from the life we've created together.

312

Two days later, I'm struggling up the winding shingle path, weighed down with orange plastic Sainsbury's bags. My back's killing me. I'm hot, stressed and late. I need to get in, unpack the shopping and get back out as quickly as possible to pick up our daughter, whose school is fifteen miles away. On my way up the path an exotic pointy plant stabs me in the eye. Husband watches me from the wooden decking. Why the hell doesn't he get his arse down here and help? And why is he flapping a piece of paper in the air?

'You've got a letter from Vincent Gallo!' he shouts across the tops of the agaves and the yuccas.

'Who?'

'Vincent Gallo. That guy in films.'

What on earth is he on about? I give him a withering look as I push past him and dump the bags on the kitchen counter. My fingers are swollen and sausagey from the handles cutting off the blood flow. He dangles the envelope in front of my face. I snatch the bloody thing. I work on instinct. I work on details. I'm suspicious, like a detective. A slightly defective detective. I scan the envelope. My name and address are handwritten in black ink in a mixture of lower case and capital letters. The writing isn't joined up, it's spiky and seems out of control, shooting off in different directions. There are grooves dug into the paper from the pressure of the pen. I make a guess that this person is not formally educated and probably quite volatile. My first name is written in full – 'Viviane'. This is unusual: any handwritten mail I get is usually addressed to 'Viv'. It makes me suspicious. It's too considered. *What's he after?* The return address in the top left-hand corner is Sunset Boulevard, LA. *Oh yeah, right. Like that's his real address. It's probably there for effect.* This deconstruction of the envelope takes a couple of seconds. Husband is peering over my shoulder.

'You know the guy,' he says. 'Not very nice. He was in that film, *Buffalo '66.*'

'Where he plays an independent movie director?'

'No. That was Steve Buscemi. You know, he got his cock out in a film, the one with the blow job.'

Doesn't sound like my kind of thing.

I open the envelope whilst Husband trots off to his computer to pull up a picture to jog my memory. He calls me over. I hover behind him but I can't concentrate, I keep looking across the room to the clock flashing on our Bosch oven. I haven't got time for this.

Then an image pops up on the computer screen of – well, what is it? I lean in for a closer look – is it a prosthetic? Nope, definitely never seen him before. I would have remembered that. I pull the letter out of the envelope. Just a couple of typed lines saying as little as possible. Can he email or call me about something? Kind regards. Formal. I like formal. Most people contacting me think they have to sound cool. It's also mysterious. I don't like mystery, I like clarity. Then that spiky black scrawl again. 'Vincent Gallo'.

Either he wants money, thinks I'm still in the film business and wants to hassle me about work or, at best, wants to use the Slits' music in a film. Like I said, defective detective. I pick up the car keys and head to the door. I look back at my husband, who's still sitting at the computer scrolling through images. 'Whatever this guy wants, I haven't got it,' I say, stuffing the letter into the cutlery drawer on my way out. Then I run down to the Audi to get the rest of the shopping.

I've received letters like Vincent Gallo's before, although not for about ten years. Some really interesting guys too. I never answer them. It's the whole 'punk' ethos of 'nobody's better than anyone else' – we didn't encourage fandom and that's still with me – also I'm a very private person. But mostly, it's that I don't think I've got anything to give. It's not like I'm going to meet them and shag them, and I haven't got anything interesting to say: I will only disappoint. So best if, in the unlikely event that Vincent Gallo is a fan, he thinks of me as the wild and rebellious blonde guitarist I used to be, not the dull Hastings housewife I've become. Anyway, it's nice to have a letter from a handsome American bad boy in my cutlery drawer. If I don't answer it, maybe that nice feeling will last forever.

'I really think you should find out what Vincent Gallo wants,' Husband badgers later. He's more excited about the bloke than I am. He goes on about it a couple more times that day.

Walking along Rye Harbour Nature Reserve the next morning with my friend Gina, I ask, 'Anything interesting happened to you this week?'

She tells me about her knitting business and an argument with her colleague about which pieces should go in the shop window. 'What about you?' she says.

'Nothing much. I got a letter from a guy called Vincent Gallo.'

She stops in her tracks. Her mouth drops open, her eyes grow bigger and rounder. 'You let me prattle on about knitting, when you've had a letter from *Vincent Gallo*?'

'You know who he is then?'

After a few more enquiries, it seems a lot of women know who Vincent Gallo is. And they think he's delicious. I'm surprised, and enjoy the status his attention has conferred upon me. I email him and ask what he wants. He responds immediately that he wants to talk to me about something. After waiting two weeks, during which he sends the same email to me a couple more times, I reply and get another immediate response: can he call me or I call him? He sends me two phone numbers.

I can't call him! I don't know how to talk to a man of the world. What will I say? I put off answering the email, but my husband is intrigued. He wants me to write back. He must think there's absolutely no risk at all in opening up a dialogue between me and a handsome, talented girl-magnet. Even if he does live across the

315

Atlantic, would you really want your wife emailing such a person? I wouldn't.

I write back and say again that I'd rather he writes than calls to tell me what he wants. I'm stalling. I'm so green, so out of practice, feel so boring and bland that I don't think I can handle a conversation, I won't be able to think fast enough. This goes on for a while, us emailing backwards and forwards, him coaxing, me resisting.

I remember from my BBC days that you must do research on a person before you speak to them. I decide not to Google him – I like to get to know people in real time – but I rent his films *Buffalo '66* and *The Brown Bunny*, and watch them with a girlfriend, tucked up on the sofa, giggling away together. They are funny and sad. I have a twisted knot of discomfort in the pit of my stomach all the way through them, especially *The Brown Bunny* – just how I like to feel when watching a film. I love movies about broken men, and this is one of the most honest I've seen.

The scene with the young girl at the hotel reception – that was me when I was her age. Waiting and hoping and believing such a romantic thing would happen – that a handsome man would come into my life and whisk me off. My heart broke for her when he drove away without her. I played out the rest of the scene – which wasn't in the movie – in my head: her coming out of the house with her bags, him gone, thinking he'll be back in a minute and waiting and waiting, but he never returns. How it hangs over her for the rest of her life.

How nice to have someone who's doing interesting things with their life show some interest in me. Vincent's attention is like an exotic present from a mysterious distant relative who lives abroad, totally unexpected and just what I want, even though I didn't know it. I decide to call him.

Sunday morning. I'm dialling Vincent Gallo's number. I have no idea what to say, I've only spoken to children and other mothers for the past ten years. Vincent's the opposite of everything that's in my life: tennis lessons, pony club, fresh-faced, blond-haired, well-spoken children, shopping, cleaning, walks, sheep, fields. I think I will be very easily manipulated by a man I imagine is a player and a womaniser. I'm out of my depth and off the scene. What can he possibly want? He mentioned in an email seeing me play in New York when he was eighteen, and being quite smitten. Maybe he has a terminal disease and is rounding up all the girls he's ever wanted to kiss before he dies.

I decide I'll just have to be myself. I'm sick of pretending any-way – of policing my words and editing my thoughts. Husband never wants me to talk about the Slits or my ceramics or make rude jokes, I'm losing every ounce of the person I used to be. I know she wasn't all good, but she wasn't all bad either. I'm not going to pretend to be something I'm not for this bloke who lives miles away across the sea. I'm not going to try and be nice and seductive for him. There are so many people in my life that I'm putting on a front for, I don't need one more. If he doesn't like me for who I am, forget it.

It's a sunny morning so I sit outside on the garden wall looking at the turquoise sea sparkling and listen to a phone ring some-where in America. *I feel strangely calm*, to quote Charlie Brown on the morning of an exam he hasn't prepared for.

A highish man's voice with a New York accent answers after a couple of rings.

'Hello?'

'Hello, Vincent, it's Viv Albertine. Is this a bad time?'

'No, it is a very good time. Let me call you back. I'm sure I can afford it more than you can.'

Cheeky fucker.

My daughter runs in and out of the open glass door, showing me her drawings. The cat throws up on the grass in front of me, butterflies flit around the hawthorn hedge and my husband works at his computer inside the house. Meanwhile me and Vincent Gallo chat away about this and that like it's the most normal thing in the world. Like we've known each other for . . . ever. I love that word. Forever. I love that forever doesn't exist, but we have a word for it anyway, and use it all the time. It's beautiful and doomed.

We talk about architecture, food, exercise, love, the Slits, what he's doing, *The Brown Bunny*, loads of stuff. After about an hour I have to go. I tell him I'm surprised that he's so easy to talk to and not pushy or after anything.

'Did I disappoint you?' he asks.

'No.'

Did I disappoint you? Insistent, masculine, sexual.

My voice disappears into a whisper.

'No.'

Bloody hell. No guy has talked to me like that for a very long time. I'm high as a kite. For the first time in years I've been spoken to like I'm a woman, like I'm a girl, and most exciting of all, like I'm an artist. Not just a mother, not just a wife. OK, maybe this is the oldest trick in the book to get a girl's attention, but it doesn't matter, because the life force that was in Viv Albertine – that has been bottled up for so long – has been released.

Husband's not too pleased. Sitting in our glossy Italian kitchen a couple of hours later, looking across the solid oak Habitat table at his wife twinkling away, waving her arms around excitedly as she talks and laughs too much, having ideas above her station, he realises that through someone else's eyes – someone he quite admires – I appear interesting. And that worries him.

Everything looks and feels different as I go about my usual daily routines. I watch myself, I listen to how I talk. I'm seeing myself through fresh eyes. Vincent's eyes. You know how it is when you meet someone new, someone you admire or fancy: you imagine them watching you and you glide about, a superhero in your own little universe. And my universe is very little; I can only glide up and down the aisles in Sainsbury's, reaching balletically up on tiptoe for the rice and Marmite. I start dressing a bit differently: younger, more stylish. I feel more confident with the posh mums. I've found someone who gets me. It's OK that I don't fit in here, I fit in somewhere else, so I can relax. I'm not mad, I'm not wrong, I'm just not in the right environment.

Since she was born, I've wanted my daughter to have everything I didn't have – a happy, stable family, access to books and art, a good education, a beautiful home – but this quest has become my whole world. I get upset if she's had a bad day at school. Last week I broke down and cried at the thought of her leaving home when she's eighteen. That's eleven years away. I've suppressed myself so she can have the perfect upbringing. I monitor everything I say and do. I want her to fit in with her posh mates, so I go to coffee mornings and garden centres and listen to conversations about rearing Labradors or pot-bellied pigs, growing organic tomatoes and making Aga towels (don't ask). I like the women very much, but I don't fit in. I chose private school for her so she would have confidence and an excellent education. So she would learn how to work hard and be self-disciplined. So she would be Nothing Like Me.

Now Vincent and I chat regularly on the phone, I begin to rediscover myself. My old self and my new self. And he helps me do this. He laughs at my jokes, listens to my tales about past boyfriends (you don't talk about them in a marriage, but those relationships help define you). He asks me about my musical past – also a taboo subject at home – and finally, one day, he says to me exasperatedly:

'Viv, *do* something.'

Although I'm a bit miffed at his insinuation that bringing up a daughter and running a home is not doing anything, I choose to take his call to action as a challenge. Permission to go ahead and do anything I want. Something artistic, not something domestic, which is all I'm facing for the rest of my life and which would be fine if I was happy, but as I get fitter and healthier, I realise I'm not. I'm so lacking in confidence, though, that I can't believe that I still might have something to give, or that anyone out there would be in the least bit interested.

Vincent Gallo believing in me is like a secret door being opened again to a world I left a long time ago. This world is not fame or fortune, I never had that: it's self-expression. And in this man's opinion, it's not impossible for me to take the journey from Hastings housewife to . . . well, whatever I want. It's possible to believe him because he is so sure, he's a force of nature, a tornado. Like the tornado that ripped through our hamlet a couple of months ago . . .

. . . it was a hot summer's evening. The doors and windows were open. We were pottering about doing normal family things. Making toast, playing on the computer. There was a sudden stillness. Funny how you can notice stillness. 'There's a difference between stillness and doing nothing,' as Jackie Chan said. It has a power of its own. I looked up from the computer and saw a piece of paper on the dining table lift up into the air, hold there for a second, and then float back down. It was eerie. I glanced out of the window: the sky had turned black, as if a swarm of insects was gathering over the sea. The blackness was moving towards us. Really fast. A woman screamed. A door slammed. I rushed around shutting all the windows. Husband and I hustled our daughter upstairs; she jumped onto the bed and curled up into a ball. I shouted at her to get off, because she was under the glass skylight. She burst into tears. The room went dark.

We huddled together and watched as our beautiful exotic garden, our new roof and our fancy Audi were torn to shreds and stoned with huge balls of ice. It lasted about ten seconds, then it was gone. The sky was blue again. The sun came out and beamed on the devastation. Windows were smashed, trees felled, gates torn from their hinges. Nothing left standing. The giant agaves, decades old, were in ribbons.

We went out onto the lane and met groups of neighbours, wandering around, picking their way through the debris. I saw Anne Crosby, an intelligent feisty older woman I loved.

'Just like the war!' she shouted.

I was in tears.

'You wait,' she said. 'It'll grow back even stronger.'

And she was right. It did. Within a year, that garden was lusher and greener than it had ever been . . .

. . . well, Hurricane Vincent is what it took to raise me from my torpor. No doubt there will be devastation. Let's just hope that I grow back stronger too.

I start to look forward to Vincent calling. Our long telephone conversations inspire me and spur me on to meet new people and try new things. The calls become more frequent, two or three times a week, at the end of his day and the beginning of mine. He sounds sleepy and intimate after a long day's filming. 'You don't know how to love,' I tease. 'You don't know love until you have been loved by me,' he replies.

This is getting out of hand – for me, anyway. Instead of talking to my husband, I'm sharing my new thoughts with a virtual stranger. I'm being emotionally unfaithful. It's easy for Vincent to be all supportive and funny and sexy from thousands of miles away: he has nothing to lose. My husband, on the other hand, doesn't look so cool, he's suspicious and angry, but that's because he can see the balance of our life tilting precariously, a balance we've spent sixteen years creating. He is – quite rightly – pissed off and threatened by what he perceives as my passion for Vincent

Gallo, but it's what Vincent makes me feel about *myself* that is intoxicating, not what I feel about *him*. If Husband had encouraged me, even a little bit, in my creative exploits, I wouldn't have been blindsided by Vincent Gallo.

I'm driving through a perfect little English village after dropping my daughter off at school one winter morning. As I tootle past the old stone church and village store, braking for three fat white ducks to waddle across the road, I decide it has to stop. I can't keep talking to Vincent. It's just not an appropriate thing to be doing, being married and all. This decision is not easy for me; I've nothing much in my life. My daughter is growing up, I have no work – I'm virtually unemployable – and I'm living in the middle of nowhere amongst the country set, mixing with people I've nothing in common with. I swerve up onto the grass verge, scratching the side of the car with the hawthorn bushes, turn off the engine and burst into tears.

The thought of giving up Vincent is unbearable. But this isn't the shocking bit. The shocking bit, I realise, is that it isn't Vincent I'll be giving up, but *myself*. He's helping to feed and water the old me so she can blossom and flourish again. But I'm not even a bud yet. Just a tiny green shoot poking out of the ground into the light. I'm not ready to let go of the only person who is part of this rebirth. I don't think I can make it happen on my own. My eyes have been opened, I can't go back, but I feel too unsure of myself to go forward alone.

Later that night, I'm in the bathroom cleaning my teeth, Husband is in the bedroom getting ready for bed. I call out to him, through a mouth full of toothpaste, 'I'm not going to be in touch with Vincent Gallo any more, it doesn't feel right.'

He comes up behind me. I turn round and look at him, toothpaste on my chin. I feel ashamed, I got carried away. He's been a good husband. Stuck with me through difficult times. We've shared everything, every thought. He doesn't deserve this. I'll tell him the truth, even though it's a bit embarrassing to say in case I'm imagining things, no one's given me a second glance for years as far as I'm aware.

'And I get the feeling he may be coming on to me.'

He comes back immediately: 'Not unless he wants to fuck his mother,' and with that, climbs into bed.

I turn on the tap and catch some water in my cupped hands, pressing them hard together so I have a little pink pool quivering in my palms. I lift them up carefully and splash my face. I feel so still. So cold inside. Not shivery cold. *Cold like steel.*

I have a wry little laugh to myself as I pull the bedcovers over me, switch off the light and turn my back on my husband. He's five years younger than Vincent Gallo.

16 THE YEAR OF SAYING YES

2008

I've decided not to let go of Vincent just yet. I'm in a full spin now, like a kamikaze pilot. I'm going to see where it takes me.

I have two voices in my head. A rational daytime voice: *You've sacrificed yourself for this dream of domestic perfection. It was your choice to do it this way. Your decision. Don't go and mess it up now, you're too far down the road.* But at night another voice slinks in. It snaps and snarls like a wild dog. *Go on,* it growls. *Take it all the way. Dive. I dare you.* I can't believe that the loving mother and committed wife I was just a matter of weeks ago is turning into a selfish monster, putting herself ahead of all others. I lie next to my sleeping husband, my eyes wide open, staring into the darkness, terrified, ashamed and exhilarated.

On Christmas Day Vincent writes that he loves me. I'm furious.

Each morning I get up exhausted, my cheeks hollower, my body thinner. The weight is dropping off me. I imagine lumps of flesh left behind in the bed. I'm becoming deranged from sleep deprivation. You can fool some of yourself some of the time, but you can't fool all of yourself all of the time.

I'm tidying up when my mobile rings and for once it isn't my mother or my daughter's school, it's Tessa Pollitt, the Slits' bass player, asking me to meet a female journalist who's thinking of writing a book about the Slits. My heart sinks. Who would want to write about a band that was happening twenty-five years ago? I can just imagine what she's like: one of those people who lives in the past, probably dresses all punk and retro with a couple of face piercings. *No, got to stop thinking these negative thoughts.* Since Vince, I've decided that this is going to be the Year of Saying Yes. My natural inclination is to say no to everything; I over-filter. Well, I'm going to give it one year of saying yes to everything (except sex with anyone but my husband). If it all goes horribly wrong, and I make a complete fool of myself, I'll stop saying yes and go back to saying no. I don't have to think about any decisions any more. I just have to say yes.

I drive to Hastings Station with a heavy heart to meet 'Zoë the Journalist', expecting an ageing goth with holey fishnet tights, pink hair and a ring through her nose. This is how I imagine Slits fans must look. I've become narrow-minded and judgemental living out here in the sticks. I lean against the barrier outside the station, scanning the emerging passengers, looking for a 'punk'. There aren't any. What appears is a beautiful, fresh-faced, bright-eyed girl in a red coat, heading towards me smiling. This is Zoë Street Howe. Zoë is writing the book. Zoë is not any old girl, she emanates light and health and intelligence. I can't believe such a gorgeous creature is interested in the Slits. I keep asking her *Why? Why? Why?* It's quite simple, she says, she loves the music, thinks it's still relevant. Loves the look. Loves the attitude. 'But that was twenty-five years ago,' I say. She tells me lots of young people like the band. And the message is still as potent today as it was back then. I'm astounded. Then she comes out with another bombshell. Tessa wants to know if I'll reconsider joining the New Slits.

I'm just about to say *no way,* like I did when Ari asked me a couple of years ago, then I remember my New Year's resolution: *Just say yes.* I don't have to think about it, I don't have to wonder about whether it's right or cool or practical. I just have to say yes. At least give it a go. When will I ever again in my life be asked to join a band?

Tessa is thrilled to hear I'm considering being part of the band again, and asks me to come to New York to see them play an actress's party. She says it's the only show they're playing this year, if I come it'll help me decide if I want to join.

'Who's the actress?' I ask.

'Don't know, Chloë something.'

'Not Chloë Sevigny?'

'Yes, that sounds familiar.'

'Tess! She's fantastic! OK, I'll come.'

Just keep saying yes. See where it leads.

And of course I'm thinking, *I might see Vincent. Chloe was in his film* The Brown Bunny. *Maybe he'll come to her show.* I've only got a few days to arrange the trip, which is good because if I overthink it, I won't go. My friend Lindsay says, 'If you wax your legs, I'll know you're thinking of sleeping with Vincent.' Of course I'm waxing my legs. And having a pedicure. You don't go to New York without a little grooming. But I won't be sleeping with Vincent. I email him to say I'll be in New York for a couple of days. He replies that he'll try and get there to meet me, he's filming in LA. I don't expect him to turn up. I sort out the tickets and hotel, then tell my husband I'm going to see the New Slits in New York, and I may meet Vincent whilst I'm there. I'm not going to lie. He must know I won't sleep with the guy, I've been faithful for sixteen years. Affairs are for people who haven't the courage to terminate the relationship they're in, or the imagination to go out and entertain themselves in a more creative way. And I shudder at the thought of anyone except my husband putting their hands on me or seeing me naked. I ask my friend Kate to come with me, she's always wanted to go to New York and she's great company. I can't face it alone.

I haven't slept for four months. Not one night. I'm in a highly nervous state. Thin as a stick. Not terribly attractive actually. Shame, I would like to look my best, but I can't do anything about it. No matter what I eat I just keep losing weight. My face is so gaunt, I can't bear to look in the mirror any more. My arms are like twigs. My breasts are empty and sexless. My bum is flat and square (on the plus side, I look great in jeans). And my labia . . . well, is this what all very thin girls look like? I ask a couple of beauty therapists. Yep, it's not just me. Extremely underweight girls have floppy fanny flaps (FFFs). No wonder so many more girls are getting 'ripped and snipped' as they say in the cosmetic-surgery business, what with the fashion for thinness and no pubic hair, there's nowhere left to hide.

This is the most spontaneous thing I've done for a long time – it's my first trip away from my daughter in all her seven years. Until recently I've accepted that my own life is over. As my husband said, 'You've had your life, now it's her turn.' (I'm forty-eight.) And a part of me sees motherhood like that. My own mother martyred herself for her children. A lot of the mothers around me seem to be just living for their families, and maybe a bit for the dog: their lives revolve around family, food, dogs, tennis, dinner parties and charities. These are very rich women, career wives; if their marriages broke down, I don't know what they'd do. They've put everything into these arrangements – although one confesses to me over a cup of herbal tea, 'Marriage is a crock.'

At last there is an unknown element back in my life. This is how it used to be. This is how I used to do things before the eighties and jobs and money and careers and Thatcher and marriage and mortgages. I was spontaneous, free, even reckless. Things often didn't work out, but I felt alive. Painfully alive. For the last few years I've been feeling painfully dead. That drive, that lust for life that everyone expects you to have after surviving cancer, well it took ten years to arrive, but here it is. I don't care what anyone thinks of me any more, I'm going to live life to the full, starting with New York.

17 FAIRYTALE IN NEW YORK

February 2008

> I feel as if I have been through something
> very exciting and rather terrible, and it was just
> over; and yet nothing particular has happened.
> Mole, *The Wind in the Willows*,
> Kenneth Grahame

On the plane I feel as if a magnet in my chest has grown so strong that I can't resist the tug any more. Like I'm being pulled on a rope towards Vincent, and the discomfort won't go away until I've seen him. I stare out of the window at the clouds, daydreaming about the conversations we might have and the things we might do – I have such innocent daydreams about him. He doesn't seem to get it. 'If you aren't imagining me fucking you, what are you imagining?' he asks me.

What am I imagining? That we will sit together on a sofa and talk for hours. That we'll arm-wrestle or he'll cook me a meal, and afterwards we'll throw stones at tin cans like we're in *Badlands* or *Bonnie and Clyde*. If he knew what I was imagining he'd think I was a simpleton. I think I might be sexually retarded. Or I've been hanging out with children for too long. I really must get round to watching some porn.

As the plane begins its descent, it occurs to me: *I'll be asked by New Yorkers what I do.*

'Kate, what on earth can I say to Americans when they ask me what I do?'

'Say you were the guitarist in the Slits.'

'But that was years ago. What can I say I'm doing now?'

'Say you're a sculptor or a ceramicist.'

'They'll want to know about galleries and shows.'

'Then say you're a full-time mother.'

'Oh god.'

Kate and I dump our stuff at the Washington Square Hotel, and I get the subway to Ari's flat in Flatbush Avenue, Brooklyn College. Not trendy Brooklyn, Brooklyn College is at the end of the 2 and 5 lines. The very last stop. As instructed, I wait on a corner for someone to come and meet me. It's night but no one bothers me. I know how to stand, how to look relaxed. I've done this kind of thing before, albeit twenty-five years ago. It comes back to me in a flash; you never forget how to be streetwise once you've learnt it.

I'm met by a sweet girl called Maria, who I think is some kind of assistant to Ari. Maria chatters away as she walks me to Ari's place. I haven't seen Ari for twenty-one years. She opens the door to her small apartment. It's got a council-flat vibe. She's wearing a yellow scarf round her head as a turban, keeping her waist-length locks in place, a yellow mini skirt, yellow and green T-shirt, fancy trainers. She looks good. Tanned, strong. A couple of people are scattered around the living room – Adele, the guitarist in the New Slits smiles shyly; sitting next to her are a pretty young Jamaican cousin of Ari's and a guy. I'm not nervous, but Ari is. She's awkward and self-conscious with me, so twitchy she can barely look at me. I don't understand why. I'm confused. She's also very stressed. She's constantly on the phone, trying to arrange flights and rehearsals for the New Slits' show in two days' time. She's doing what I used to do and she's copying the tetchy way I used to do it. I can see my mannerisms and expressions in her.

I remember a New Yorker in the music business telling me that when he met Ari a couple of years ago, she told him that I was the scariest person she'd ever known. Ari scared of anyone is incredible

329

enough, but scared of me? Still, it explains a lot. How she acted towards me in the past. It might explain her wariness tonight.

A cool-looking guy who works with Lee Perry arrives, Ari introduces us. He's very pleased to meet me, he knows of me, compliments my guitar playing. I can't believe it, I'm nothing in my own eyes. Ari starts to twirl and dance in the middle of the room, just like old times. I thought we'd have a nice chat together and bond, but she's performing. I'm tired, so I order a taxi and leave, say I'll see her tomorrow at the show. I hang about outside the building and when my cab eventually arrives, the driver doesn't know the way to Manhattan. It takes us hours to find our way to the West Village, but we chat and have a laugh along the way. Just a couple of hours in New York, and I feel more alive than I've felt for years in England.

Vincent makes it to New York. Not just because of me, I suspect, but because it's Fashion Week, which he attends every year. I ask Kate to be with me when I meet him: I'm weak from lack of sleep and need to protect myself from doing something stupid. I have to be very careful. My whole life, everything I've built – my marriage, my lovely safe home, a haven after years of uncertainty and illness, my daughter's security – will be blown apart in an instant if I don't control myself. Vincent's a free agent, he can do what he likes, have fun, but I've made my choices and I've worked hard for this life I've built. I'm not going to throw it all away on an impulse, a quick fling. If that's even what he wants. I don't know what he wants; he's evasive. My friend Traci says he's like a burglar who breaks into your house but doesn't steal anything, just shits on the bed.

A knock at the hotel-room door. My knees are so weak I'm not sure I can stand up and open it. And there he is.

Standing in the doorway, framed by the dark brown architrave, bathed in golden light like a Caravaggio, he smiles. I swear light

Vincent Gallo. Well, you would, wouldn't you

bounces off him and zings all around the room. *On the day that you were born the angels got together* . . . His greased hair is just past his ears and pushed back from his face. He has stubble. He has cheekbones. A pink felt Homburg-style hat. Soft brown velvety top with a little white mark on the right shoulder (did he dribble in his sleep on the plane?), a beautifully cut black wool three-quarter-length coat (Gucci: I check the label later when he's not looking. I smell it too, but rather disappointingly it doesn't smell of anything) . . . *and decided to create a dream come true*. He's everything I like all rolled up in one beautiful bundle. All my girlhood fantasies come true. *So they sprinkled moondust in your hair and golden starlight in your eyes of blue* . . . (Except the blue eyes, I prefer brown, but hey, who's going to complain about one little detail? That would be churlish.) Just for a few delicious moments, I will let myself be attracted to another man. I haven't thought of, or looked at another man this way for years – just let me enjoy it for a couple of seconds, god. I promise I won't do anything. Except maybe vomit with excitement.

Get a bloody grip, Viv. Say something.

'Oh my god, you're so handsome.'

May as well tell the truth, I'm probably gaping open-mouthed at him anyway. He thinks I'm teasing him and flips me the finger. I ask Kate to go, I want him all to myself. I've waited a long time for this moment and I'm going to make the most of it. I've got myself under control, I'm not going to collapse into his arms.

I make a point of sitting as far away from Vincent as possible, to signal there will be no physical contact. He looks confused. The sexual tension just sort of hangs there in the air between us. He flops backwards onto the bed and stretches his arms above his head. I can see the top of his grey Calvin Klein underwear peeping out from under his trousers. I can see a line of hair leading from his navel to . . . I know what's down there. I've seen it on film. Kind of weird to know what a man's thing looks like before you've ever met him.

Vincent paces around as we talk. He's not all nice and friendly like he was on the phone. He seems a bit cross. He slides his back down the wall and sits on the floor, drawing his knees up to his chest. He says he's cold and pulls a blanket off the bed, wrapping it around himself. Then he starts to shake. His whole body trembles. I look at him coldly. What's he up to? I like him, but I don't trust him. I talk to him in my head. *Stop it, Vincent.* Then his eyes start rolling back like he's having a fit. He says he's got a type of narcolepsy. I don't believe a word of it. I think he's trying to make me go over to him. I don't know if I'm right, but that's what I think. I ain't going. If this is something real, it will wait.

We get out of the hotel and walk along the streets of New York to a restaurant. *Why do birds suddenly appear, every time you are near . . .* Girls keep coming up to him. 'I just want to say I really love your work.' Yeah, right. Back off, girlie. Today he's mine. A band plays on a doorstep. He makes a cynical comment. A flurry of spring snow is followed by sun. I feel like I'm on the cover of *The Freewheelin' Bob Dylan.*

My senses are heightened from lack of sleep and the newness of the situation; I try to read every little bit of body language he emits. Data scrolls behind my eyes, like the Terminator. I'm on red alert.

He looks over at me, unsmiling.

'We're never going to have sex, because you're *married*.' He says the word 'married' like he's just stepped in dog shit and is trying to shake it off his expensive shoe.

We walk a few more steps.

'Do you know the Dusty Springfield song "Some of Your Lovin'"?' he asks.

'I prefer her singing "You Don't Own Me".'

'Not the best version.'

His hands are thrust deep into his pockets, his shoulders hunched, he walks very fast without any thought as to whether I can keep up (I can). And then it hits me, in a moment of divine clarity, like someone has struck a big old brass bell in my head, a true, clear note sings out: *This is a man who walks alone.* That's it. He walks through life alone. That's how he wants it. That's how he likes it. That's how he's always done it and is always going to do it. It's plain as day, the truth, revealed through the simple act of walking. I try with all my might to fight my insight, but there's no going back, it's lodged in my brain, and from this moment on it informs everything I say and do with Vincent. Underpinning all my words and actions is my belief that he's not someone who can deliver on an emotional level. He's lots of other interesting things, but he's not that. And my subconscious steers me steadily away from him, even though my heart and my ego are begging to stay.

We sit opposite each other in an empty, low-key Japanese restaurant. He reaches out across the table and gently pushes my hair back from my face.

'Don't be against me, Viv.'

I'm not against him, it's just that at last I've realised: *This man can't give me back my self.* No man can. They can only reflect my anxiety, my confusion and my insecurity, straight back at me. I've got to rebuild myself on my own. *Bollocks.*

Enter Patti Smith.

No one else in the entire place, and in walks Patti Smith with a friend. She and Vincent nod at each other a tad frostily. Could there be a clearer sign to get on with my life, to resurrect the person that I was back in 1977, to pull my finger out and finish the job, than the woman who unlocked me appearing at this crucial moment?

It's time to go to the New Slits' gig at Webster Hall. It's fun getting all dressed up in the hotel room with Kate and my friend Angela. I first met Angela Jaeger in New York in 1980. She came backstage after the Slits played their first show at Hurrah on New Year's Eve – an extremely pretty, creamy-skinned, straightforward young girl – she told us that her sister, Hilary, had a little club called Tier 3, she couldn't pay us, but it was a very cool place, would we consider doing a gig there? So we went with her and played a show (and that's where Vincent saw us play when he was eighteen). Angela and I have kept in touch ever since. She's a great singer and was in Pigbag.

For the New Slits show I wear a floaty cream Jim Morrison-type silk shirt by Kate Moss for Topshop and very wide black Balenciaga trousers – I've dwindled to a size six, that's a US size two – trousers look great when you're thin. I think thin girls look good dressed, but fuller girls look better undressed. We arrive at the hall. Ari has sent Maria outside to look for us and we're waved in, skipping the queue. We all chat in the dressing room but the girls are busy being interviewed and putting on makeup; I don't want to get in the way so we go out onto the balcony and dance to the music. I'm introduced to Chloë Sevigny, although I've met her before, I was going to cast her in my feature film, *Oil Rig Girls* (not been made yet). I'm tempted to ask her about Vincent, but what's the point? I'm pretty sure I know what she'll say and anyway, tonight's all about the girls: the New Slits playing at a celebration of Chloë's first collection for the label Opening Ceremony.

I don't feel jealous of the band, or wish I were part of them. I'm relieved to be in the audience. The place is packed, there's a real buzz. They come on stage and start to play. Ari is still one of the best front people in the world. Up there with James Brown in my opinion. She's as cheeky, sexy and irreverent as she was the first time I saw her perform, at the Coliseum in Harlesden back in 1976, when she was fourteen. It's so strange to hear my old songs played back at me. I'm proud of them, they sound good, but I feel a bit territorial, like my children have been taken away and brought up by someone else.

This evening has been so uplifting, I decide that if I can learn to play the guitar in time, I'm going to do a couple of shows with the New Slits and see how it works out. I'll have some explaining to do when I get home, but seeing Ari and Tessa up there having fun, connecting with the audience, makes me think it's not so ridiculous a concept.

Vincent and I meet one more time before I leave for England. As we walk to a cafe, he tells me he's so happy because he's just found a rare record by the Poppy Family. He says it with exactly the same inflection that he used when he told me a couple of months ago that he was so happy he found me, like I was a rare vintage record or guitar for his collection. As we talk, I realise that since seeing

Ari and Tessa play, I've already got stronger. I've got plans. I've changed, I'm not so vulnerable to his charms. Before we part, we hug – the first and last time we touch. Of course being held by Vincent Gallo is no ordinary affair, nothing about him is ordinary. He avoids my friendly kiss and pushes his cheekbone across my face, grazing me with his stubble, his mouth is in my hair as he crushes me into his chest – like Heathcliff – holding me so tight I can hardly breathe. I can only imagine what the rest would be like. No, better not. We separate and head off in different directions. I turn and watch him beetle around the corner and think, *That is the last time I will ever see him.*

I go back to the hotel and bawl my eyes out in front of Kate. Not because Vincent and I aren't John and Yoko, but because I have a feeling of dread in the pit of my stomach signalling to me that without the crutch of an affair to distract me, without any money of my own to protect me, despite being unemployable and a very certain age, my marriage is over. *Going to see Vincent in New York was like trying on a couture dress you know you can't afford (a little trick of mine). Nine times out of ten it doesn't suit you anyway, and it's good you know, because then you don't hanker after it any more. The truth is, Vincent is not my princent. And nor should or could he be. That's a ridiculous thing to ask of anyone – god I'm such a slow learner, I bore myself.*

I walk back into my home, into my life, a different person. Husband is standing at the hob frying mushrooms. He looks over at me.

'Did you have a good time?'

'Yes.'

'Did you see Vincent Gallo?'

'Yes.'

He winces. 'Did you fuck him?'

'No.'

I take my suitcase upstairs and press my forehead on the cool glass of the bedroom window. Rain splashes onto the shiny tropical leaves, slowly transforming the garden below from a fresh minty green blanket into a muddy brown pool. Our relationship is broken, and I have played a part in the breaking of it. My judgement became clouded – it was rusty – I haven't needed it, safely swaddled in marriage and motherhood. I can judge a cake all right, and I can judge whether a necklace goes with a blouse. But I can't judge if a man is sincere or not.

I still can't.

18 TO PLAY GUITAR

2008

If you bash into the web of a spider, she doesn't get mad.
She weaves and repairs it.

Louise Bourgeois

I don't know what size I've dwindled to now, but I look disgusting.
The mothers at school are concerned and ask if they can do anything to help. I take all my clothes in to the dry cleaner's to have
them altered because they're hanging off me. The man behind the
counter is worried about my weight, even though he's never seen
me before. I laugh it off, I'm not *that* thin. I think I'm looking
quite svelte. A friend's husband tells me I look awful, he says, 'You
looked better before.' My friend shushes him. Well, somebody had
to say it.

I've developed a terrible chesty cough. It's agony. I go back to
Dr Shah, he looks up from his desk, 'You're much too thin. What's
happened?' I tell him my marriage is in trouble. He listens to my
chest and tells me I have pneumonia. He prescribes me antibiotics
and says, 'I'm giving you one week to start putting some weight
back on. If you haven't by Friday, I'm sectioning you, admitting
you to Hastings Hospital and putting you on a drip.'

No way I'm going to that hospital. I buy a load of protein drinks
and force myself to drink them, as well as eating as much pasta
and bread as I can bear. I lie in bed. I can't function. I can hardly
breathe. I think I might be dying. What I'm actually doing is facing the truth: Husband and I don't love each other any more, no,

it's worse than that, we don't like each other any more.

After two weeks I've put on enough weight to satisfy the doctor I'm getting better and the pneumonia is showing signs of clearing.

I have a goal: learn to play guitar in five months and be ready for the New Slits gig. I feel like a contestant on the reality-TV show *Faking It. Take a bored Hastings housewife and turn her into a punk-rock guitarist in five months.* I go to the local music shop – in the sleepy old town of Rye – which just happens to be a great guitar shop run by Richard Kingsman, the guitarist with the band Straight Eight. It was his pedals Ari pissed over at the Music Machine, back in the seventies. I buy a second-hand Fender Squier for eighty quid, a little practice amp, a guitar lead and a couple of picks. I think Richard will laugh at this middle-aged woman coming in to buy an electric guitar but he's encouraging and acts like it's the most normal thing in the world; he even shows me a couple of 'vamps' (chord sequences) to practise.

I set up the little amp next to the kitchen table, cut the nails on my left hand right back to little stumps, and after my daughter's gone to bed I try to get my fingers back around those chord shapes that I used to be able to play twenty-five years ago. I've completely lost it. I have to start from scratch. I remember the shapes, but my fingers can't make them on the neck of the guitar, so I sit there night after night, my tongue sticking out as I concentrate on spreading my fingers apart and keeping them pressed on the strings long enough to strum a chord. I ignore the pain of the wire cutting into the pads of my fingers. I don't watch TV, read newspapers, meet anyone for coffee or lunch or do anything that will take a second away from my playing. I just do the minimum I have to do domestically and that's it. Everything else stops. I take the guitar with me wherever I go, it's always in the back of the car; if my daughter's at a tennis lesson, I sit in the car, push the front seat back and practise whilst I wait for her. I take it to my studio in Hastings and play for a couple of hours before I have to drive back to school and pick her up. I play it in the car park at school for ten minutes until the bell goes and she comes out; I even play it on the train if I'm in an empty carriage. I'm seething and burning with determination and drive. I will do this. I have no idea why, or where it's going, but nothing in the world is going to stop me. I play to survive. I've got to express myself to stop imploding into depression, so I write songs. I buy a little exercise book, just like the old days, and scribble down snatches of thoughts and conversations, quotes, anything that resonates, and attempt my first song. I have no idea how to put chords together any more or what works lyrically, but I have to write about what I'm feeling or I'll burst.

I need some help to learn how to play guitar again, I need a teacher. Richard from the guitar shop says, 'Well, it's got to be Nelson King, hasn't it?'

I'm standing outside a dinky little cottage on the outskirts of Hastings, flowers round the door and everything, my Squier in a droopy black plastic case on my back, feeling a fool. I ring the bell. Nelson King answers, friendly, smiling, longish hair, non-judgemental. I don't tell him about the Slits; as far as he knows, I'm just a woman who wants to play electric guitar. He's fine with that, not because he's a teacher, but because he's such an open-minded person, a true musician. I go to him every week and he shows me some scales and bits and pieces. I start to feel more confident, not about my playing, but about telling him my secrets. I confess I've written some songs and he wants to hear them. I can't sing, but I trust him so completely that I stumble through them anyway, it's excruciatingly embarrassing for me, but nothing is going to stop me doing this. He loves the songs, he can hear past all the mistakes and the out-of-tune singing and says I must sing them myself, not get somebody else to do it. 'I can hear a lovely voice in there,' he says.

To prove he's right he records me singing and playing in his home studio, adds a bit of bass and drums, and when he's mixed it, emails the track over to me. I rush upstairs to the computer in the bedroom and play the song. My voice is appallingly, sickeningly terrible. I can bear less than a minute before I shut it off. I'm crushed, he was wrong; my voice is awful and I can't do it. I call Nelson in tears and say I'm not coming to the lessons ever again, I've faced the truth, I'm rubbish, I give up. Then I go to the doctor and get antidepressants. I don't do this lightly. I've always been prone to depression, I'm melancholic, I've fought it all my life – last year it occurred to me to ask my mother, 'Mum, does everyone have a knot of pain and anxiety in their chest every day, from the moment they wake up in the morning until they go to bed at night, like I do?' She looked worried and said, 'No.'

I can imagine the pain and stress that's ahead of me now my marriage is falling apart and the stable family I've created for my daughter is disintegrating – I admit defeat. Give me the pills.

Nelson calls and persuades me to come over for one more lesson. When I get there he says, 'I'm not going to teach you chords or scales any more, you have a unique guitar style and I don't want to ruin it.' It's only because I trust Nelson with my whole heart that I believe him. I don't believe in myself, but I believe in his belief in me. He continues, 'I'm going to take you to some open mike sessions and get you playing live.' He must be mad. I can't stand up in front of people and play and sing. I would rather die. *Remember, Viv, the Year of Saying Yes.* So what if I die? So what if I'm crap and make a fool of myself? I know that no one ever does anything or gets anywhere without failure and foolishness. I've got to do it. Nelson has made me an offer I can't refuse, the bugger.

I do have one other supporter: my eight-year-old daughter. My little girl, who has never seen her mother do anything except housework and being a wife, accepts me sitting down at the kitchen table every night and trying to learn to play guitar and write songs. She thinks it's a wonderful thing for her mother to be doing. I involve her as much as I can in the process, asking her advice on lyrics, rhymes and middle eights. She's very musical and I value her opinion. Then one day as I'm struggling with the bar chords I get frustrated and let go. I thrash at the guitar, zinging up and down the strings, strumming wildly. From this outburst comes a strange but very Viv-like riff – oriental, modal, lots of open strings ringing – and I know I'm back. My daughter looks up from her homework and with an emotional catch in her voice says, 'Mummy, you were *born* to play guitar.'

That phrase, and the way she says it, sustains me for years.

19 BEL CANTO

2008

The better a singer's voice, the harder it is
to believe what they're saying.
David Byrne

I feel ridiculous going to my studio to rehearse, plodding through the rain and greyness of Hastings, electric guitar slung on my back. What a fool, what a fraud. I trudge out of the car park, past the pound shop, through the underpass, glance sideways out of my hood at the thrashing waves and empty bus shelters; could it be any grimmer? Still, I'd rather be rebuilding myself in Hastings than anywhere else. I feel as if I am on the edge of the world here, or at least on the edge of England. This is a town that people come to when they want to get as far away from other people as possible. This is a town of renegades, musicians, writers, artists, drug takers, teenage mothers and pyromaniacs. It's lawless, a frontier town, where anything goes and everything's acceptable, even failure. I fucking love Hastings.

Andy Guinaire, a friend and brilliant pedal steel guitarist – who played with the Faces amongst others – comes to an open mike night and tells me to buy a better guitar. 'That one sounds like you're rattling a drawer full of cutlery.' So I go and buy my first Telecaster for twenty-five years from Richard in Rye, a pink flower-print Fender Telecoustic.

I'm still going to the art school once a week, and I confide in Tony Bennett – the first person I say it out loud to – that my

343

marriage is over. He looks unfazed and replies calmly that he sees marriages fall apart all the time amongst his students. He explains that it's because you have to dig deep into yourself to make the work and you can't help but get to know yourself better, who you really are and what you really want. It's bound to have an impact all through your life.

I think back to Tony saying he recognised my voice when he heard me on the radio; I've always thought I have a very ordinary North London voice, but a few people have commented that the timbre of it is unusual. I don't think they meant it in a good way, just that it's a bit odd. Once when I was at a play centre with my daughter, a woman I hadn't seen for ten years came up and said, 'Is that you, Viv? I recognised your voice. You've got such a distinctive voice.' I decide not to take it personally but to use this oddness in my voice and turn it to my advantage. I'm no chanteuse, but if I'm true to myself, true to 'punk' ethics and use my voice naturally and honestly, maybe it will be enough that it's distinctive and personal like the songs. I start to let this idea roll around my mind. I go to the guitar shop, and this time I ask Richard if he knows a good singing teacher.

Sandra Scott. What a find. She lives in a black wood fisherman's cottage, with a canary-yellow front door, on the edge of Rye. Every time I go in, I feel like I'm being gobbled up by a fat, squat blackbird with a yellow beak. I tell Sandra I don't want to learn how to sing, I don't want to sound mannered, I don't want to change my voice in any way, I just want to learn how to open my mouth and let my voice come out. I'm so shy and scared that I can't make a sound. I spend a lot of the lesson time sitting in front of the log fire crying. Winter turns to spring and as the seasons change, I fall apart in front of Sandra's eyes and stitch myself back together again. She teaches me the bel canto method of projecting your voice through your nose and the front of your face using the chambers in your skull as resonators ('singing into the mask'). Most untrained people sing from their throats, which gives no resonance, no warmth, and is very weak. With bel canto you can still use your voice even if you're unwell, which is helpful because I always seem to have a cold.

I go to my studio every day and sing along with the exercise tape Sandra has given me. Up and down scales I go, that's all I want to do. Not songs, just work the muscle that is my voice. Even though I'm on my own I don't sing very loud, I stand with my back pressed against the white wall and make a tiny sound. Each day I make myself step further away from the wall until I have the confidence to stand in the middle of the room and project my voice all the way across, no longer caring if anyone is in the studio downstairs or what they think of me. I remember back to my squat in Davis Road, to the neighbours telling me to stop playing guitar, that it was unbearable to listen to, and how I got better, used my idiosyncrasies, made a great album. If I could turn my guitar playing around back then, surely I can turn my voice around now.

With new Fender Telecoustic

20 A MATTER OF DEATH AND LIFE

2008

What has to die in your life for what you are creating to be born?
Deepak Chopra

Midnight. I get out of the car and look up at the full moon. I feel so isolated and lonely that I talk out loud to it. 'All right, Moon? Who else are you shining on? Anyone like me? Someone who might love me one day? Someone I'll love?'

I lug my guitar up the path, past the spiky plants. During the day my daughter and I play around in the garden, running in and out of the bushes pretending they're monsters, but at night they can do serious damage to your eyes or face as they claw at you in the dark. I can hear the sea crashing relentlessly on the shingle beach.

The reason I'm walking up the path to my house at midnight with a guitar is that twice a week I drive three hours to a random pub and three hours back home again, to play two of my songs in public. I spend all my spare moments in the days leading up to one of these open-mike nights choosing the two songs I'll play. *Which ones can I play best? Which ones did I do last week? Which one first and which one second?* When I've made my choice, I practise the two songs over and over again for days.

Before I leave the house, I always make sure my daughter and husband are fed, that she's put to bed and I've done the washing up. My husband is furious that I'm going out and thinks of more jobs I have to do before I leave. I do them, but eventually I pick up my guitar and make a break for it.

Ruby, don't take your guitar to town.

During the long journey to the pub, I try to warm up my voice. The voice I have absolutely no confidence in. The voice I've been embarrassed about since I was a child – hating it so much that when I had to read a passage from the Bible out loud in assembly in the last year of primary school, I couldn't do it. I just stood there, my body paralysed, my hands gripping the lectern, my mouth opening and closing like a dying guppy, thinking, *I can't let them hear my voice, it's so deep and ugly, like a boy's.* I was frozen with fear. Eventually a kind teacher led me away.

The next time I dared use my voice was in the Slits – 'punk' was supposed to be open-minded and DIY but it was actually rigid and unforgiving and Ari was always very critical of our voices.

Driving along the coast road, singing along to the exercise tape, my voice sounds reedy and thin, sharp or flat, god knows which. I practise the lyrics, trying to memorise them, I think it looks terrible to have a sheet of paper in front of you when you sing. How is anyone going to believe you when you're reading from a script?

I steer the Audi into the car park of an ugly pebble-dashed building and manoeuvre into a space, turn off the engine and sit back in my seat. Do I really want to do this? It's not too late. I can turn the engine back on, reverse out of this place and drive home. I don't have to put myself through the humiliation. But for some reason, I do have to. It's like I've been taken over by an alien: I have no say in the matter. I get out, pull my guitar case out of the boot, put it on my back and walk mechanically up to the saloon-bar door. Inside my chest I have a heavy, bruised, sick feeling, like I'm going to the gallows.

I sit on my own at a sturdy dark brown wooden table, with a glass of mineral water on a beer mat in front of me, and my foot on the guitar case so nobody nicks my guitar. I think about Vincent, how he's probably swanning around in Cannes or at the Chateau

Marmont in LA. The bar's half empty, a couple of older guys with expensive guitars sit strumming in the shadows. A tall skinny man with a grey ponytail leans against the bar blowing some blues riffs out of his harmonica: they've obviously all been playing for years. I study the sticky orange-and-brown patterned carpet, so I don't catch anyone's eye.

I make numerous trips to the bathroom and wash my hands over and over again because they're sweaty with nerves. I look into the mirror and a nice, decent woman looks back, clean hair, lipstick, jeans, T-shirt. Middle-class. What the fuck is she doing in this godforsaken place with an electric guitar? Why isn't she at home with her husband and child, watching TV? Vacuuming? Tidying up?

I hear my name announced and run back into the pub lounge, grab my Squier (the Telecoustic's not very good live) and step up onto the small stage in the corner of the room. The MC tries to be helpful. 'You a folk singer, love? Joni Mitchell, that sort of thing? This is where you plug in. Do you know how to use a mike? Have you turned the volume up on your guitar? It sounds a bit too trebly, here, let me turn the treble down a bit for you.' He leans over and twiddles the knob on my guitar. I let him. My hands are shaking so badly that everyone can see.

I start to play. There are no monitors, the speakers are pointing away from me. I can't hear what I'm singing but I can hear what I'm playing from the amp directly behind me, and it's terrible. I'm embarrassingly awful. I am shit. But the songs are good. I know I'm crap, but I know the songs are good. And I have to get them out there somehow. They are little creatures clamouring to be heard. I'm compelled to do this. Beyond logic, beyond failure, beyond self-consciousness. There's an older lady with a tatty woollen bobble hat on, leaning on the bar, staring into her whisky. She doesn't look up. The guy with the ponytail smirks with his friends.

348

There's always someone laughing, sniggering, tutting. I shake with passion as the songs pour out. I make loads of mistakes, I sing wildly out of tune, I can't look up from my fingers or I will miss the guitar strings. Every second is excruciating for me and for the audience. Six minutes later it's all over. The compère jumps up and asks for applause for Viviane. He says kindly that it takes a lot of guts to get up and perform your own songs, that at least I'm not doing what everyone else does and playing cover versions. I unplug the guitar and walk through the tables to my seat. No one looks at me.

Something strange starts happening as I keep playing the open mike circuit. At every pub one or two people come up to me as I'm leaving – a fisherman, a farmer, the barman, another musician, a cool-looking girl – and say, 'You know what? You really touched me. I know what you meant with those words. You're the best thing I've seen in here.' And once, out in the middle of nowhere, 'You ever heard of a band called the Slits? You remind me of them.' These people help me to keep going. They see past my incompetence to the honesty of the material.

I reach the front door to my house and fumble about in my bag, looking for my keys. The outside lights are turned off. All the lights in the house are turned off too, my husband's gone to bed. Once inside I don't dare turn on a light, I feel so guilty and wrong for what I'm doing that I'm as quiet as possible. I clean my teeth in the kitchen because the electric toothbrush is too noisy. I undress in darkness by the side of our bed and slide in. I try not to think about the humiliation that I've just suffered performing to a bunch of guys who can play the blues. I'd love to sit up with a cup of herbal tea and a piece of toast and chat and laugh about my experiences with my husband but he's pretending to be asleep. I feel so lonely lying next to him, in this beautiful white house.

The blackness outside the windows stretches away into infinity.

Not even an owl hoots. The weight of the silence is suffocating. The marriage is suffocating. Sadness and shock press down on my chest. We've been together for seventeen years. We've been through so much. We've been faithful to each other. We've always had a good sex life. We were so very much in love. But here we are, like two little children cold and lost in the woods, curled up, facing away from each other, blaming each other, and making our lifelong fears of abandonment come true.

21 THE NEW SLITS

2008

All I want to be able to do is sing and play three songs to a consistent standard and never drop below it, no matter how tired I am or how bad the PA is. At the moment I veer between passable and absolutely atrocious and this aspiration seems unattainable to me.

Nelson has to get on with his own life, he can't keep coming to open mikes with me, but the thought of going to these pubs on my own twice a week is terrifying. For a lone female to walk into a pub – truck stop-type places some of them – in the middle of nowhere is a pretty daunting thing to do, but to stand up and play and sing your own bonkers songs, when everyone else is doing covers of 'Chasing Cars', is beyond brave, it's madness. To make sure I don't give up and because she believes in me, my friend Traci gets the train from London every time I play. I pick her up at Brighton, Hastings or whichever station is near the pub I'm going to that night, and she sits with me before I go on and giggles with me once I've come off. She's a true friend.

I'm getting bolder, trying out different songs, talking to the audience, making jokes. When I play at a pub in Lewes in East Sussex, a guy called Tom Muggeridge comes up to me afterwards and says he really likes my songs, will I play at a festival he's organising at Lewes Arts Lab in a couple of months' time? My first gig. I get a band together with Tom on bass and a drummer and violinist from Brighton that I've met on my travels. We rehearse a couple of times in a warehouse. A few things go wrong on the night, but it's a huge step forward and a thought pops into my mind as I'm up on stage: *I'm the singer*. I've made that transition from guitarist to front person, a massive leap for anyone in a band; if you start on an instrument, you never quite believe you've got what it takes to be the front person.

I don't take shit any more when I play. One night in front of a crowd of braying ponytailed old rockers I shout, 'Anyone here ever taken heroin? Made a record?' There's a stunned silence. 'Well I have, so shut the fuck up or go home and polish your guitar.' (They all had perfect, mint-condition guitars that you just know were only taken out of their cases once a week, polished and then put back to bed.) This time I don't take the inevitable 'too much treble' comment from the compère. 'It's meant to be uncomfortable,' I tell him and turn the treble up even more; I hope it hurts their ears. I begin to enjoy the tension between what the audience expects from a nice-looking woman and what they get – angry words and edgy guitar playing.

After a year and a half of playing open mikes, I'm in a large soulless modern pub in Brighton with an outside barbecue and a cocktail bar. I pour my heart out in my first song but no one takes any notice, they talk and laugh and shout. I've had enough; what I do doesn't work as background music. I change the words of my next song to 'Fuck, bollocks, cunt, shit, piss, wank' – and every other swear word I can think of – and repeat them over and over again until eventually the whole room goes quiet. When I have their attention I say, 'Thank you and goodnight.' That's the last open mike I play.

The New Slits gig is looming, I'm not nervous; what I've been doing in pubs for the last year, with a handful of people two inches from my face, playing my own material solo, is much more frightening than being on stage with a band. We go to Spain. It's such good fun to be with Ari and Tessa again, and to have the camaraderie of a band. When we arrive at the hotel, we all hang out in one room, lounging across the beds and talking. There's no group of women in the world that I have ever felt more completely at one with than Ari, Tessa and Palmolive (I wish Palmolive was here in the hotel room now), not just because of our shared history, but because we are all the same kind of woman. Ari talks about the trouble she's having in Jamaica, how there's a rumour going around Kingston that she's a CIA spy and because some people believe it, they're out to kill her. I don't know how she can bear the amount of pressure she is constantly under, and has been under since she was fourteen, all for looking a bit different and doing her own thing without compromising. She asks me to look at a lump on her breast, says it's been there for about a year. She knows I've had cancer and hopes I can give her some advice and reassurance. I touch it lightly, it's pretty big, the size of an almond. I have no idea if it's just a cyst or if it's a tumour; I tell her she must go to a doctor as soon as we get back to England. She says she doesn't like England, she'll have it looked at in Jamaica.

At the venue we have a big dressing room, food is provided and there are monitors on the stage so we can hear ourselves, it's all such a luxury to me. I love playing with the other musicians, I feel so much safer than I do when I'm solo. I feel a bit uncomfortable playing the songs though. The original Slits songs – although they stand the test of time musically – don't resonate with me emotionally any more, not now I'm doing my own stuff. And the new songs, which are Jamaican-dancehall influenced, don't resonate with me musically, even though they are really good. I can't relate to the songs as a player, I'd rather be in the audience dancing to them and having a good time.

The next New Slits show is in Manchester. I take my daughter out of school so she can attend the concert, and I only need to look down from the stage at her in the front row, her eyes fixed on me with a look of such glowing pride, to know that I've done the right thing by her. If a mother or father ever gets to see such a look, just once in their lives, on their child's face, they've as good as discovered the Holy Grail. During a dub section in the show, I play a couple of dissonant, abstract chords over the rhythm, but Ari runs over and shouts at me, 'Stop playing! Stop playing!' She hates it.

On the way back to London that night I look out of the car window at the motorway flashing past and decide I'm not going to play any more shows with the New Slits: I want to do my own thing. My little girl is curled up asleep with her head on my lap, I stroke her hair, I feel such love for her. I remember back to my love of the Slits twenty-five years ago, how devastated I was when it ended. I was like a dumped lover, I grieved for years but eventually I healed and hardened – not without scarring – because I had to. Ari made it impossible for the group to stay together, then years later she came back, like so many deserting lovers do; but for me, the time to make it work was then, not now.

Trace

22 FALLING APART

2009

You're not an artist, you're a wanker.
My husband

Husband issues an ultimatum, *Give up the music or that's it.* I tell him he's not asking me to choose between music and marriage, but life and death. So there is no choice. He thinks that by playing music I'm abandoning my family, welching on the deal (a deal that exists in his mind – I do the house stuff, he earns the money). I'm just a wanking, self-indulgent narcissist, a bad mother and a disappointing wife. He sounds like my father, 'Don't do it, don't talk about it. Never mention it again.' Except he goes a step further with 'You're useless, too old and what you're doing is a waste of time.' One afternoon, when a friend asks who I would like to be able to sing like and I answer, 'Karen Carpenter,' Husband guffaws with derision, spraying a mouthful of coffee across the table.

The two most important men in my life want me to deny who I am. As if it's shameful. I can imagine a century ago they would have said, *If you don't stop, I'll commit you to a lunatic asylum.*

I keep trying to paint what I'm doing in a good light to my daughter, but Husband is taking away all her enthusiasm by turning my passion into negativity. I believe without a shadow of a doubt that I'm a good role model for her. To see your mother sit down and learn an instrument from scratch, write songs, and eventually be up on stage singing them is a fantastic lesson in making a dream come true. But my husband, who is ten years younger than me, is a child of the eighties and he doesn't believe in hippy-dippy dreams coming true, he believes in earning money. I'm not making money. I may never make money doing this. He and I come from ideologically different times; I don't judge him for that. He doesn't want to support me financially or emotionally in this endeavour, I get that too.

I do something very unmotherly now, even though it feels as though I'm losing my daughter for the second time (the first time was after the cancer): I don't stop concentrating on my music. I collect her from school, I make dinner, I put her to bed – I don't tidy up, I don't have time – I'm present most of the time physically, but not mentally. To make this huge step I have to immerse myself in my work. Just like all artists (wankers) have to immerse themselves in their work, just like Husband has immersed himself in his work for the past sixteen years. He's stayed up all night figuring something out on the computer, sometimes for weeks on end. The difference is – *and it's a big difference* – that he was earning money for the family. I'm not. I'm getting back on my feet and I'm contributing to the family in other ways, but what I'm doing right now can't be measured in pounds and pence, and he's a pounds and pence kind of guy. I liked that about him.

We go to a party, it's full of couples we know. I look around the room and note that in every couple, one or both of the partners has had an affair, and yet here they all are, smiling and staying together. Husband and I have been faithful to each other and yet we are miserable and falling apart.

23 YES TO NOTHING

2009

Keith Levene is back in my life for the first time in twenty years; he's considered a great guitarist now. I knew he was great, but I just thought he was great amongst us lot. It's only recently that everything and everyone from back then is starting to be reassessed and often credited with influencing what's happening in music today.

We meet up in the BFI bar on the Southbank. It's as if we've never been apart. Immediate intimacy, deep talk, an emotional reunion, he sheds a tear. He really is an extraordinarily sensitive man. I tell him I've picked up the guitar again but I can't play it very well. He says, 'I'll teach you, Viv.' I'm so touched that Keith would help me again, even though it does seem to be a crazy thing to be doing, but he never was one to judge situations the way everyone else does.

And so I drive to East London once a week to play with Keith. The first time is excruciating. I'm scared of driving on motorways, I've lost confidence in every area of my life. When I get there, he says, 'Let's hear some of your songs then.' I get out my guitar, plug it in and sing and play a bit of a song for him. He's sitting about a foot in front of me. My voice shakes, my fingers stumble. But he gets it.

I've noticed a pattern forming in my life, it happens every time something doesn't work out – a friendship, the New Slits, my marriage – if I have the courage to walk away from it rather than stay and cling on for fear of the unknown future, it seems to take from four to six months at the very most for something even better to manifest in front of me. I think of it as saying Yes to Nothing. If your choice is either the wrong thing or nothing, however frightened you are, you've got to take nothing. Haven't you? Hasn't everyone?

No husband, no lover, no band, no money, no confidence.

Here goes nothing.

At my Hastings studio. Silk top – Kate Moss for Topshop; belt – Miu Miu; shorts – Sloggi. Father's gold medallion and the boots Vivienne Westwood insisted I buy in 1977

24 A RAINY NIGHT IN NASHVILLE

2009

> How often have I lain beneath rain on a
> strange roof, thinking of home.
> William Faulkner, *As I Lay Dying*

The Raincoats have invited me to support them on a short tour of America in September. *Say yes, Viv.* They're popular in the States, so we'll be playing big venues. I've never played more than three songs before when I've been solo; in America I'll have to do a whole set. I rehearse every day at home and a couple of days before we leave I ask six friends to come and critique my set at Enterprise Rehearsal Studios in Denmark Passage, the sort of place that has drawings of cocks all over the ceiling. I play seven songs and say a bit to introduce each one. They give me some useful feedback, and then we go downstairs to sit in the sun, where we bump into the New Slits, who are also rehearsing here. A bit awkward with Ari but everyone else is cool about it.

At the airport my suitcase bursts open: CDs, pedals and clothes spill out all over the white marble floor. I rush off to an airport shop and buy two huge suitcases to spread the load, I'm way over my weight limit and have to pay extra. Gina Birch, the Raincoats' singer/bass player, laughs her head off and says nothing's changed. 'You always had a huge suitcase stuffed full of clothes in the seventies!'

Two days to go before the first show, I stay in my room and practise like mad, then I discover that the treble knob and the lead input on my guitar are broken. I have to track down a guitar shop in San Francisco and get it mended just before the soundcheck.

I arrive at Mezzanine, a large 'industrial chic' venue, and make my way to the backstage area. *Am I allowed back here?* I've forgotten everything about playing a big gig. I've forgotten to write a set list, what to ask for in the soundcheck, what I need in the monitors, everything's foreign to me. There's a list of performers and their stage times pinned up on the dressing-room door. My name is on it. *Oh no, this is real, not a dream. I'm not going to wake up. I actually have to go out there in front of hundreds of people and play and sing.* I fight down the panic whilst I wait nervously in the wings and all too soon it's time to go on. I walk out onto the stage feeling like a child in her first play. I stare out at the crowd, they stare back at me. I've got to get a grip of myself or I'll turn into a frozen statue and have to be dragged off like I was in my primary-school assembly. A nervous gabbling voice races through my mind, *I know what to do I'll rush through the set cut out a couple of songs make it really short won't do any of the talking no introductions I'll . . . No. I'll do what I planned to do. It's now or never, otherwise I'll never learn.*

I take a deep breath, and off I go. I do my chats and play the songs with all my passion and the audience love it. They're open and receptive, they laugh (at the right bits) and call out to me, I could stay up here communicating with them forever. By the end of the set, I'm reluctant to leave the stage.

Tonight we play the Echo in LA. A guitar string breaks just as I'm about to go on. I never break guitar strings – I can't remember how to change a string and haven't got any spares. The duo Rainbow Arabia are here, they take me backstage and introduce me to a guitarist who kindly gives me one of his spare strings.

One particular song in my set, 'In Vitro', is very hard for me to sing, a difficult melody change happens twice in it. I always dread the change and often sing it out of tune – but a weird thing happens each time I play it in America: the right notes come into my mind a split second before I have to sing them. It's amazing what the brain can do when all your senses are heightened.

Afterwards we go back to the hotel, no raving for us, everyone calls their family back in England. I've been told not to call; I will wake my daughter up and it's too expensive. The rest of the band think it's odd and rather sad that I have no contact with home; this is the terrible place Husband and I have got to in our relationship.

I've arranged to play three small solo shows during a gap in the middle of the tour. First Chicago, a nice little gig organised by my friend Jon Langford from the Mekons, then Austin, Texas, where I meet a cute young Christian couple at my gig and go to church with them the next day, just to see what it's like. It's like *High School Musical*, held in a large school hall with a rock band and the words to the songs projected behind the speakers. The hall is rammed with a thousand young people. Then off to Nashville. Exciting, such a musical town; maybe Jack White will come to my show. I'm picked up from the airport by friends of a friend and taken to a motel. I have a few hours until the soundcheck. I sit on the beige bed in the beige room, god I feel lonely. I miss my daughter so much I don't know what to do with myself. I can't bear the ache in my heart. Now I understand why musicians on the road take drugs, take lovers; right now I'd take anything to kill this unbearable loneliness. I pull the beige curtains aside and stare out of the window across a never-ending car park. It's pouring with rain, blue neon light from the hotel sign shimmers in the puddles. A slick wet bruise of tarmac. Black and blue desolation.

What am I doing here for god's sake? If something happens to my baby, how long will it take me to get to her? How many hours am I away? Fourteen. My thoughts start tunnelling down into a rabbit warren of nightmare scenarios: *If she gets ill, she could die in four-teen hours, I won't be there beside her when she needs me most.* I imagine her calling out for me, *but where am I? In a shitty motel, looking out over a car park in Nashville, for what? To play a bunch of three-minute songs.*

Time to go to the gig. Three people turn up. Well, this is a test. Disappointed and dying inside, I promise myself that when the tour ends I'll never leave my daughter again – fuck the songs and the self-expression. I play and sing my heart out for those three people. My little audience and the bar staff are very into it, they say they feel like they witnessed something very special. (*They did, that show was the most intense and intimate of the tour.*) Back at heartbreak hotel, I receive an email from one of the three people in the audience saying he hopes I can find it in my heart to give god another chance ('I don't believe in god' is a lyric in one of my songs). I climb into bed and text my dear friend Traci telling her that I've had it. She calls me and we talk until I fall asleep, a friendly voice on a rainy night in Nashville. Feels like it's raining all over the world.

Off to New York tomorrow, I can't wait to see the Raincoats again, they have become my family for these two weeks. All the money from selling my merchandise is nicked out of my bag at the airport.

I arrive at the Knitting Factory in New York exhausted, haven't slept for two weeks – from nerves, not from having a crazy time – but because I'm so tired I'm very relaxed; that's the great thing about touring, you get to know your material so well that you can sink into it and play around with it. My last song, 'Confessions of a MILF', goes down well; I get very emotional during it, feeling the adrenalin pump through my body, right up into my brain as I close my eyes and let go. There's a young boy squealing with excite-ment at the front of the stage, and I hear a girl laugh knowingly

362

when I sing the line 'There's no place like home' from *The Wizard of Oz.*

The next day I see Palmolive; she is still close to the Raincoats and they've invited her over to stay the night at the hotel. We get caught by the hotel manager bundling mattresses into the lift – we all want to sleep in the same room together. I see Palmolive's cheeky face light up as she charms her way out of trouble, just like the old days.

Gina shows me an online review of my show, the first time someone has written about me playing live. I've reprinted it below, not to toot my own trumpet but because the writer explains what I'm doing more objectively than I can. This review gives me the courage to keep going and helps wipe that terrible night in Nashville from my mind. Until I read this I really wasn't sure if I was mad or not. Thank you, Carrie Brownstein. (Sounds like a Gertrude Stein book or a Woody Allen movie title.)

On Friday, I saw Viv Albertine of The Slits, Softpower (featuring Mary Timony) and The Raincoats play at the Knitting Factory in Brooklyn. How do I feel? Lucky.

As I wrote last week on this blog, The Raincoats influenced nearly every musician that sprang forth from Olympia and countless other similar towns and scenes across the US. Needless to say – or perhaps I *do* need to say it – so did The Slits.

So, at the Knitting Factory on Friday, watching *not* The Raincoats (who were fantastic, by the way) but Viv Albertine, I realized I hadn't really witnessed fearlessness in a long time, at least not at a rock show. As one of my friends put it, more succinctly: 'This was one of the punkest things I have ever seen.'

If there is a voice in music that's seldom heard, it's that of a middle-aged woman singing about the trappings of motherhood, traditions and marriage. A woman who isn't trying to please or nurture anyone, but who instead illuminates a lifestyle that's so ubiquitous as to be rendered nearly invisible. She places in front of you – serves you up – an image of the repressive side of domesticity, the stifling nature of the mundane, and turns every comfort and assumption you hold on its head. It raises questions that no one wants to ask a wife or a mother, particularly one's own. Are you happy? Was I enough? What are you sacrificing, and are those sacrifices worth it? And when someone is brave enough – honest enough – to confront the difficulty of it all, the strange, often irreconcilable dichotomy of being a mother and an artist, a woman and an artist (and why should it be a dichotomy?), frankly it's scary as hell. It makes people uncomfortable. And this sentiment of unease, especially coming from a woman in her 50s, sounds somewhat silly, even juvenile. Why? Because after a certain point, we're supposed to feel settled, or at the very least resigned.

I haven't even mentioned that Albertine's guitar playing is beautiful and unsettling in its strangeness. It's not simple, but rather a distortion of the facile. Sort of like the subjects of her songs.

I'll say it again: I felt lucky to be there.

Seen anything punk in a while?

Review by Carrie Brownstein (guitarist formerly for Sleater-Kinney and now Wild Flag), 19 October 2009, for Monitor Mix

25 LIBERATION

2009

> For now she need not think about anybody. She could be herself, by
> herself. And that was what now she often felt the need of – to think . . .
>
> Virginia Woolf, *To the Lighthouse*

My father has been taken to hospital; he was heard calling out
for help in a feeble voice by his neighbour who, kicking the front
door in – not easy, my father is so paranoid, it was reinforced with
planks of wood, steel plates, three locks and a padlock – found
him lying on the sofa emaciated and dehydrated. I fly to France to
see him, missing Neil Young at the Hop Farm Festival. I'm overcome with a sense of duty for some reason. I sit on the edge of his
bed and hold his hand: he has a very strong grip. Maybe he's going
to be fine. I call my daughter and she chats to him on the phone,
which perks him up, makes him smile. But later he starts ranting
in French. I don't know what he's saying, he sounds angry, I ask
him if he wants me to leave, he grips my hand even tighter and
says, 'No, no, no.'

The two French doctors in charge of my father look at me
snootily and ask how could this have happened, an old man dying
alone in his apartment with no one giving a damn? I bring them
documentation to show I hired a male nurse to visit my father
three times a week – much against his will. My father told him not
to come any more, without my knowledge. He was closing down,
letting the light bulbs burn out one by one until his apartment, his
mind and his body went dark.

It's my third visit to the hospital. After I've checked in with the doctors I go and see how my father's doing. He shouts out, '*Maman, Maman!*' over and over again. The man in the next bed answers, '*Je viens!*' My father is placated for a few minutes, he thinks she's coming. Here he is, at the end of his life, calling for his mother. Could there be any more proof of her power? Even while dying he manages to be ugly and obnoxious. He keeps coughing up huge lumps of dark yellow phlegm and spitting it with great force across the room. It goes in all directions, I never know where it's going to land next. I dodge around the room, desperately wanting to leave, I'm frightened I'll catch something. A cleaner comes in and I mutter, '*Je suis desolé,*' I'm so embarrassed that she has to clean up this mess; she starts to mop up the slimy lumps spattered all over the floor and gets spat on. I feel terrible. I stand right in the corner by the door, a huge pellet of gob flies towards me, I duck out of the room and go home.

Back in England I get a phone call. 'Hello? Viviane Albertine?' French accent.

'Yes, speaking.'

'I am sorry to have to tell you, your father, he has died today.'

I don't say anything. I hope I'm conveying shock and sadness with my silence, because I think it would be terrible for the doctor to know I'm feeling nothing.

I have to go back to France and sort out the practicalities. To sort out a parent's death is bad enough, but in a foreign country, in a foreign language, it's daunting. But there's no one else to do it – my sister lives on the other side of the world – so I take it one step at a time, put one foot in front of the other, and get on with it. If I actually thought about what was ahead, I would panic.

So: *first step* – fly to Toulon. *Second step* – check into a hotel. *Third step* – go to the hospital. They tell me to find a funeral director. I go to the morgue in the basement, they give me a card with the address of a funeral director in Toulon. *Fourth step* – get a taxi to the funeral parlour. I muddle through the meeting with the funeral director. I really like the thick glass 1930s door to the office and keep staring at it. When he leaves the room for a minute I take a picture of it on my phone. *Fifth step* – buy cleaning materials and rubbish bags and clean the apartment. This takes a whole week, working morning to night in thirty-degree heat. My father was a hermit and a hoarder; his apartment is the cave of a hermit and a hoarder. It's crammed full with newspapers, boxes, bottles, biscuit wrappers, paper bags, tins, tools, clothes, letters, everything you come across in life. Ceiling-high towers of newspapers, mazes of cereal boxes, there's hardly an inch of floor space. Even the wardrobes are full of empty cake wrappers, all smoothed out and laid one on top of the other, thousands of them. He sure did like his madeleines. There are hundreds of old containers put aside for possible reuse. I can't rush through these towers of debris though, because three-quarters of the way down a tottering pile, sandwiched between a cake wrapper and a pizza box, I find his passport, or a lovely old family photograph; I even come across his will in an old biscuit tin. Every single piece of paper has to be sifted through. As I go through the flat, room by room, I think about his life; I can see a shape to it now it's over. Now it has a beginning, a middle and an end.

He was born in Corsica to a rural family, he was the youngest of five children, pretty, blond and indulged. The other kids resented him. He was a bit Asperger's, didn't quite fit in. He joined the Free French Navy and met my mum at Queensway ice-skating rink in London during the war. They married and emigrated to Canada, then Australia. They had two girls and came back to England. He trained to be an engineer. He was always an outsider. Divorce. Loneliness. Mental breakdown. Moved back to Toulon. Lived alone for the rest of his life, all bitter and twisted, bent over and muttering to himself. What a waste of a life. Well, not me. That's not going to be my story. But how can I possibly be normal when I've come from this sort of a parent, these embarrassing genes? I pack, bag up and scrub furiously, gradually erasing the crazy man from the apartment. But I can't erase him from my blood. Neighbours call it 'the mad house'. I am the daughter of the mad man who lived in the mad house.

Sixth step – go back to the morgue. I have to take some clothes for them to dress the body in. I choose the most normal garments I can find, although they were normal back in the seventies, not now. I select a beige corduroy jacket, dark jeans, a blue shirt and navy tie. At the morgue they ask if I want to see him laid out. I say no. I'm not going to go and stare at a dead bloke. It's morbid. But sitting in the white reception room – watching the young men and women glide past in white clothes with silent white rubber shoes, like a scene from the film *A Matter of Life and Death* – I start to feel sorry for him. How sad to be lying there, all dressed up in your Sunday best, and no one wants to come and see you, no one wants to say goodbye. I tell the mortician I've changed my mind, I will see him. I sit on a tiny gilt chair and look at him. The first thing I notice is how rigid his jaw is, clamped together in bitterness and resentment. He's very thin. Disgustingly thin. I'm shocked; I think to myself, *I will never glorify or aspire to thinness again. It is abhorrent.* They've cut his long straggly hair and swept it back off his face, he looks quite distinguished, noble and handsome with his strong Roman nose, high cheekbones, silver hair and smart clothes. Like a French university professor. And I have a little cry. Because for a few minutes, right at the very end, just before he goes up in a puff of smoke, my dad looks like the kind of dad I always wanted him to be.

Seventh step – my daughter and I go to the funeral at the crematorium. We dress in black and huddle together as we hurry past another funeral, this one full of family and friends, cars and flowers.

I'm aware of how pathetic we look, just the two of us, mother and child, following a coffin. The French pallbearers share a joke as they hoist the coffin up onto a trolley. I scowl at them. The funeral is dramatic, extremely florid emotive music plays at top volume as the two of us sit in the baroque room with the coffin, paying our last respects. The music changes to a sombre, doom-laden dirge, the doors to the oven open and the coffin trundles into it, there's a fanfare as the doors close. My daughter is overwhelmed by the pageantry of it all and sobs her heart out. I wrap my arms around her and take her outside, past the big funeral and all the mourners, into the hearse and back to the hotel.

In his will, my father leaves me £17,000. In France you have to leave your money to your children. It's the law. I use this money to hire a lawyer and get myself out of my marriage. Husband wants out too. The rest I put aside to make an EP one day. (The last time I was left money was when my grandmother died and I bought a guitar.)

26 SEX AND BLOOD

2009

'Well, now that we have seen each other,' said the unicorn,
'if you believe in me, I'll believe in you.'
Lewis Carroll, *Through the Looking Glass*

I stumble through life in a state of shock and terror as my husband
and I start divorce proceedings. I don't know if I can do this. Can
I live alone again after seventeen years? Can I pay the bills, mend
the leaks and tax the car? Earn money? I have forgotten how to
survive on my own. I talk to other divorced women and they say
it all comes back. Married women tell me I'm making the worst
mistake of my life and this is a terrible age to be divorcing: 'You'll
never get another man.' A very sophisticated, honey-highlighted
blonde divorced mother from my daughter's school confides in
me outside the swimming pool: 'When you'd rather live in a tent
in a field than in your nice house with your husband, that's when
you're ready for divorce.'

My marriage is over. My husband and I have been living in the
same house – but apart – for six months and I can't stop thinking
about sex. I have an urgent desire to shag someone, and this is for
one extremely important reason – *I am sure as hell going to do it
before he does.* Very mature.

For seventeen years I've been with one man and I don't know if
I can bear someone else's hand on my skin or to undress in front
of a stranger; whether my body will be attractive to someone else;
what to do or how to move with a different person. It's as if I've

only talked to one man for seventeen years and now I have to learn how to talk to a different one. It's scary, but I'm not going to let Husband get in there first, so to speak. And deep down I hope it will hurt me less when he has sex with someone else if I've done it first (*this worked, by the way*). So, I have a very strong urge to fuck someone as soon as possible, but not anyone, a specific type of someone; someone unthreatening, with poor eyesight, and – due to my immense insecurity – someone who will be grateful.

I choose a man who is very keen on me but, more importantly, he's not intimidating in any way physically. He's not handsome or fit. He looks like a minicab driver (his description of himself, not mine, but I have to agree) – not a taxi driver, they're quite a different genre, edgy, could even be sexy. He is perfect for my purposes, I feel safe enough to give it a go.

I've done it. We lie together naked, tangled up on the sofa. The room is dark except for a puddle of pale light from the full moon on the oak floor. A warm sea breeze wafts in through the open glass doors.

I am off somewhere in my head, congratulating myself: *Haha. I did it before you. Na na nana na.*

The minicab driver interrupts my thoughts.

'You're very wet.'

I reach down between my legs and touch myself. I *am* wet. Not 'turned on' wet. Absolutely soaking. I lift my hand up to have a look. It's covered in blood.

In the moonlight, our limbs appear luminous white and the blood splattered all over them looks black. Sticky black blood. It seeps into the sofa cushions and drips down onto the floor, like we've spilt a tin of molasses over our laps. Here it is haunting me again, my old enemy, Blood. Bugging me again. Bloody bloody Blood. Always there when I don't want it and never there when I do. I jump up, a river of red gushes down my legs. We're in the middle of a bloodbath, like the prom scene in *Carrie*. In my mind I can hear Carrie's mother screaming, '*The curse of blood is punishment for sin!*'

There's no obvious physical reason why this has happened. It isn't my period, we haven't had rough sex and he doesn't have a massive cock, so what's wrong with me? It must be true, I'm being punished for the sin of having sex without love, for being so shallow and for daring to think I could leave my marriage, go out into the world and live a liberated artistic life. This is punishment for being a bloody, feisty, witchy woman.

I fake nonchalance, excuse myself and go into the bathroom to take a shower, completely forgetting about the blood-spattered guy in the living room. I turn the water pressure up high. Hot water smashes into my face and pours down my body, but even this vicious shower can't obliterate the nagging thought at the back of my mind . . .

It can't be. Can it? Please, not now. Not now I'm at the beginning of a new journey, striking out on my own. Not after all the risks and courage it's taken for me to get this far.

Please god, not the return of fucking cancer.

I go straight to my consultants, Professor Jeffrey Tobias and Dr Anthony Silverstone, the two men at UCH who saved my life in 1999, and they whisk me into hospital for an internal investigation. I'm pumped full of anaesthetic and come round to Dr Silverstone telling me that I am extremely sensitive inside but there is no return of the cancer.

Six months later I go for another check-up with Dr Silverstone, he's known me for ten years now, watched me come slowly back to life. I say to him, 'I still haven't met anyone.' And in his wonderful reassuring voice he replies, 'You will. One day you'll find someone who will look after you.' I hold back the tears until I'm outside the consulting room. He may as well have said, 'One day you will find a unicorn.'

27 FLESH AND MILF

2010

I'm recording again. This is something I never envisaged, I thought that life was gone. I thought I was an imposter who'd been found out. But here I am, in the Levellers' studio in Brighton for two weeks, making songs. The weirdest thing of all is that I sort of know what to do. Even though I haven't listened to music properly for twenty-five years, I know what I want the instruments to sound like, where I want backing vocals and where to put a bridge or a pause. I'm exhilarated, I can't bear to go to the bathroom because I don't want to miss one second. Dylan Howe (a great drummer who plays with Wilko Johnson, has his own group and is the son of Steve Howe from Yes – funny how he's had another distant influence on me) is on drums; he's also producing the record. I couldn't do it without him, his strength, knowledge and enthusiasm carry me through. Sometimes I'm so exhausted I can't think any more but Dylan never tires.

The first track, 'I Don't Believe in Love', I wrote the day I found out my father had died. I'd grieved a long time ago for the lack of a decent father in my life, but I didn't realise until he was gone that I was still holding out a little shred of hope it would all be all right in the end. *He's gone and now I'll never have a good father,* I moped to myself. I thought about what effect it may have had on me, having a father who didn't or couldn't love. Have I ever been able to truly love a man? Has a man ever loved me? Fuck love. I don't believe in it any more. Look at most of the couples I know, they're not in love, they're scared of being alone, financially entwined or hanging on to a partner to try and convince the world they're acceptable human beings. I can't think of one couple I'm envious of. When a woman I know comes up to me and says, 'I'm so sorry to hear about your marriage,' I think, *No, I'm so sorry to hear about* yours. *At least I had the courage to get out.* On the day of my father's death, I decided that from now on I'm only going to believe in things I can see and touch, no more woolly concepts like love and religion.

Once I've made the EP, good things start to happen. Gina Birch introduces me to Thurston Moore backstage after a Sonic Youth show at the Forum in Kentish Town. He's interested in what I'm doing now and asks me to send him the recordings, says he'll release the EP on his Ecstatic Peace! label, which he does.

Jane Ashley invites me to come and have a look at Mick Jones's Rock 'n' Roll Library in Portobello Road and suggests I play a short acoustic set there next week. I'm very scared but I say yes. Mick comes to watch me, I can see him smiling at the back of the room. Afterwards he says he wants to record one of the songs I played, 'Confessions of a MILF'.

With Mick, the Rotten Hill Gang, Zoë and Dylan after recording 'Confessions of a MILF'

374

We record it a week later. I wear a black skirt and my Vivienne Westwood boots. Mick has asked the Rotten Hill Gang along to play on my track. I'm so touched that all these guys – plus Dylan Howe – have turned up to play on my song for nothing. We go through the track a couple of times before we start recording. This is one of the best days of my life and it all happens because of Mick. He was always very generous about my music.

28 THE MIDFIELD GENERAL

2010

> Better that she had kept her thoughts on a chain,
> For now she's alone again and all in pain . . .
> Stevie Smith, 'Marriage, I Think'

My daughter and I move back to London. She goes to a comprehensive school. Like I did. I'm not ashamed of myself any more, or worried that she will be like me. She fits in at the school and I fit in with the parents. Now I've got to get out and about, go to anything I'm asked to, build a social life. There's a party at Gaz's club tonight. I haven't been to a club for years. I go with a friend. Mick Jones is there and quite a few other people from West London that I've started to see again. It's not so bad. I can be single.

I'm wedged between a couple of guys I vaguely know, just about finding enough things to talk about. Give it ten more minutes and I'll go home. I've done my duty, gone out to Soho for the evening and survived. That's how out of practice I am, to get through an evening is like an assault course.

The guy to my left, long hair, shades, says he and a few friends are going back to someone's house in a minute, do I want to come?

I say, 'No thank you, I've got to get home.'

'Go on,' he says. 'We're going to do the midfield general.'

Should I know what that is? At the risk of sounding completely naïve, I ask him what the midfield general is.

'It's a mixture of MDMA, ket and coke, and my friend, Dave,' he points to an out-of-shape, middle-aged bloke next to him, 'chops it up and blows it in your arse with a straw. It's fantastic. Goes straight into your bloodstream.'

I decline. He tries again. 'Last time we did it, all these girls', he gestures towards three dyed-blonde West London posh girls of a certain age, 'knelt down in a row with their pants down, arses in the air, and Dave went along with the straw doing one after the other.' I must look horrified because he says, 'Oh, don't worry, he's like a doctor, he doesn't check you out, he does it all the time.'

I say it's really not my thing, I don't take drugs, but thanks anyway, I must be going.

He gets annoyed. 'Oh, you don't drink and you don't take drugs? Yeah great, you'll die a beautiful corpse, but you'll be lonely. And you'll never meet a guy. Only queers don't drink.'

I can't wait to get outside onto Oxford Street and catch the bus home.

Touring France. I translated all my song titles into French – this is 'Never Come'. Still in the 1977 Vivienne Westwood boots. Jacket Vivienne Westwood, 2011

29 BEAUTIFUL PSYCHO

2010

> I had heard that madmen have unnatural strength.
> Bram Stoker, *Dracula*

I play a show one frosty February night in Camden Town. After the gig I'm hanging out with a bunch of mates in the downstairs bar. I'm buzzing, not on drink or drugs, just happy. I look across the crowded room and see this face, and I think, *That's my kind of face*. Not because it's a handsome face, because it's a *familiar* face. The Mediterranean skin, the dark eyes, a slight innocence to the expression, the shape of the chin and the brow. Maybe he reminds me of my dad. I try not to look at him again. I just get on with enjoying the evening.

My friends are giving me a lift home in their truck and they keep texting me, they're waiting outside and are impatient to leave – so I pick up my guitar and make my way through the crowd to the exit. My gait stiffens slightly as I pass the nice-looking guy and I try to look nonchalant. To my amazement he looks me straight in the eye as I pass and says in a gentle voice, 'Goodbye.' This is no ordinary goodbye. It's a meaningful goodbye.

Outside I rush up to Trace and complain, 'It's not fair. No nice guy like that would ever approach me at a show and ask me out. They're too shy and respectful.'

She says, 'Go back in and give him your phone number.'

I'm appalled. 'No way. I can't possibly do that. He might have a girlfriend. It's embarrassing.' Then I think, he did *kind of* make a move. I turn to my friend Barry who's standing next to us and say, 'You do it.'

Giggling away together and trying not to be noticed, Barry and I peer through the pub window to make sure he approaches the right guy. 'Him in the black jacket,' I point and then duck below the window. I can't believe I'm doing this. Barry goes in with my number scribbled on a piece of paper. And I go home.

The next day I get a text from the guy at the bar and we arrange to meet at a tearoom in Camden. I've never done this before – well, not since I was sixteen. Have I lost my marbles completely? Am I in a divorce-induced hysteria? But I really don't want to sink into a man-free solo existence: must get back on the horse.

I dress down and opt for a V-neck slate-grey Donna Karan jumper, jeans and boots. I'm feeling a bit nervous as I walk past Sainsbury's . . . better stop at the cash machine and get some money out. Can't expect him to pay, a bit presumptuous.

I walk into the tearoom. A young guy is standing at the counter, wearing a V-necked dark blue jumper, jeans and boots. He looks at me questioningly. I panic and look wildly round the room. *This can't be him. For god's sake, Viv, what were you thinking? He's gorgeous.*

But it *is* him. We sit down with a pot of tea between us and start to talk, I like his voice, he's from New York. How many warning signs does a girl need before she backs away? Well, post-divorce, a bit green and lacking in confidence, quite a few.

He waves his arms around in a nervous manner: Keith Richards, Nick Kent and Captain Jack Sparrow come to mind. A sort of druggy twitchiness. He tells me he was a junkie in the past. But that was a long time ago. *I admire his honesty.*

He calls homosexuals 'fags'. *Must just be a New York thing.*

As he walks me home, he tells me it's important never to give way to oncoming pedestrians, he sees it as a jungle out there,

'You've got to establish your dominance.' *He must have grown up in a tough neighbourhood, poor thing.*

He would like to see me again. 'Don't make it too long,' he says softly.

OK, a couple of things about him are a bit weird, but I can handle weird, can't I? Wasn't I in the Slits? Didn't I hang out with Sid Vicious? I've known all sorts of weird people. That's who I was, and that's who I'm trying to find again, so this must be what I'm supposed to be doing: reconnecting with the sort of creative, interesting people I hung out with back then. Right?

We go on lots of dates. He's funny and has precise and discerning musical taste, which matters to me. I take it slow, try to be sensible, we don't kiss or touch for ages, months. He's on best behaviour, and eventually I start to relax and we get physical. But things in the bedroom are turning out to be a bit strange.

I can feel he's holding himself back sexually. Controlling himself. It crosses my mind that maybe he's holding back because if he lets go, he'll get violent. He keeps trying to put off sexual encounters. Says he's almost ready, can I give him another fifteen minutes? Is he on medication? Viagra? Why won't he talk to me about it? I've told him all my problems, it's not like I'm in a hundred per cent working order myself. He can't come. He can keep an erection but he can't ejaculate. I'm totally confused. Is this what men are like nowadays? Is it an age thing? I'm so new to the dating scene that I don't know what to expect, what's normal. Eventually one night he does come, but he has to rub himself so hard against my dry stomach that I fear his penis is going to split open. Is this the result of years of masturbating? Maybe he can't come inside a vagina because it isn't tight enough. I don't think I'm too bad inside, I had a Caesarean, but there's no way he'll get the kind of pressure he can get from rubbing *that* hard (inside anyone's front bottom anyway).

As he relaxes with me, he starts to show his aggression more. He shouts and throws things, flies into a rage if I remark that one of his stories doesn't add up or contradicts his previous version, he can't leave the house without getting into an argument with some-body on the street. And there are more warning signs.

He has no friends. Not one. 'Oh, they've all settled down and moved away,' he explains. *Well, I suppose this can happen, everyone pairing off, having kids, moving to the country. At the same time.*

When I'm not there, he doesn't sleep at night. 'I can't bear the thoughts in my head.' He stays awake until four or five in the morning and then curls up on the floor and falls asleep in front of the electric fire. *How cute, like a little wild animal.*

We have a play fight, but he can't control himself and presses his fist hard against my throat. It hurts for about three days. When I ask him about it he's shocked and upset that I would even consider that he did it on purpose. *He seems so sincere, I must have imagined it.*

We do have some good times, he cooks for me a lot – he only has one plate, one knife and one fork, but I like that he doesn't care about possessions and he lets me have them whilst he uses a bowl and a spoon. He's got loads of great vintage guitar pedals, he's techy, a geek. I love that in a guy. Also, I can turn up on his doorstep, any time day or night, and he's happy to see me. This is good: sometimes I work strange hours and not many men can cope with it.

But I'm crying a lot. This isn't what was supposed to happen. I didn't leave my marriage to be upset all the time. What kind of role model will I be for my daughter if I'm in an unhappy, unstable relationship? I want her to be strong and have self-esteem. She hasn't seen me upset about this guy yet, and I don't intend to let her. I'd better sort myself out. A couple of times I end it, but the day after an outburst he's always so calm, intelligent and rational, so loving, I think I've imagined the whole thing and I go back. I'm so insecure about my ability to attract someone, so desperate to prove that I wasn't the one in the marriage who was difficult to get along with, that I'm in denial. He's quite clearly insane.

Eventually I face up to the facts and tell him calmly one evening that I'm very sorry, I can't go on, it's not working, I wish him well, and head for the door. *Quite grown up and civilised*, I think to myself proudly – I could easily have ranted and raved and had a blazing row about his peculiar behaviour, but instinctively I feel it's better not to rile him.

He starts hissing at me to be quiet, not to make a noise. 'The guy upstairs will think I'm attacking you.'

Eh? Where did that come from? I ignore him and collect my stuff.

'I'm begging you to be quiet, Viv.'

The guy's really losing the plot here; or is it me? Am I going insane? No, keep a grip on reality, you haven't raised your voice. He says it *again. Christ! If he's that worried about noise, I'll give him something to fret about.* I purposely bang the front door open as I struggle out with my suitcase.

That bang is like a starting pistol. He's straight off the blocks and flying at me with a demented expression, eyes blazing with furious hatred, arms outstretched, hands in a strangling position. I've never seen anything like it before. Not on any murderer in any movie. They don't come close. Not a patch on the real thing.

Before I've even blinked, he's snatched both my wrists, gripping them tightly together whilst dragging me back into the room. With his free hand he grabs a clump of hair at the back of my head and forces me to the floor, down onto my knees, pushing my face hard into the carpet, somehow he's twisted my hands behind my back. All this happens in a second. He has the superhuman strength of a crack addict, the speed of a commando and the reflexes of a pretty boy who's been in the nick and had to watch his arse – which he's hinted to me has happened to him.

I sense utter madness, blind rage and a very practised hand, and decide with a calmness that is necessary for survival not to make a sound. Not to move a muscle. I go completely limp and acquiesce. You don't argue with crazy. And I don't want to give him one tiny reason to beat me to a pulp.

So this is how I come to find myself, a middle-aged mother of a twelve-year-old girl – wearing a stripy blue-and-white sailor-style Sonia Rykiel cardigan with an appliquéd red silk heart on it, knee-length red linen skirt cut on the bias, bare legs, hair in a scruffy ponytail and blue Havaiana flipflops – on my knees, with my face pressed on the floor, in a poky bedsit above a Chinese takeaway in Camden Town, held down by a man fifteen years younger than me who has the strength and unpredictability of a lunatic. A man I've introduced to my mother and my daughter, cooked for, laughed with, worn my best dress for and attempted to amuse. *Jeez, there's just no pleasing some people.*

Because I feel that to struggle will ignite his blood lust even more, all I can do is stay alert and grab the opportunity, if it arises, to escape. I'm playing each second as it comes, all my senses heightened like a trapped animal. But then he does something even more unexpected, although he has me under control, at his mercy, making no noise, offering no resistance, he jerks my head up and twists it into a vicelike headlock, digging his fist into my eye and cutting off my breathing by clamping his forearm around my throat. Uh-oh. Now we're entering even darker territory. *This is it, I'm going to get my head kicked in.*

My beautiful innocent daughter's face floats into my mind. I see her soft peachy skin, big round green eyes, button nose and rosebud mouth, and I feel ashamed. I talk to her across the ether, *I'm so sorry, baby. So sorry that your mother is so stupid. I've let you down. If I get out of this alive, you will always come first and I will never put you at risk of losing me again. I love you, darling.*

I steel myself and wait for the blows.

They don't come. He lets go. I see the madness drain from his face, like someone's stuck a straw in a coconut and sucked out the juice. He's completely calm. I'm not. I'm furious. Now I know the danger has passed, I explode. 'I knew it! I knew you were a violent nutter!' He wants me to sit down and talk about it but I want to get out of there as quickly as possible. I fly down the stairs, out onto the street and home.

It takes three days until I start to shake. Three days for it to become real to me. Until then, I go about my life as if nothing's happened.

It hits me in Berlin. I arrive at the Michelberger Hotel. My room is like a white womb almost completely taken up by the bed. I lie down on it. I'm meant to be meeting people to look around Berlin before my show but I can't move. I just lie there shaking, flashbacks going off like fireworks in my head. Maybe it's the distance from London and being away from my daughter that's let me think about how near I came to something quite terrible. How I was groomed. How he waited. His patience and lies, soft voice, gentle manners, his pretence at respect, all drawing me in. It's all so obvious now. I've been had.

I manage to do the Berlin shows, no problem to get myself into the zone, it's a relief to forget for half an hour. I'm a bit highly strung though. A German boy waiting outside the first venue asks me to sign his autograph book, he shows me that he's already got Ari and Tessa's signatures. Then he says he asked them to sign some spare pieces of paper, would I sign them too? I sign them. Now he wants me to sign some more blank bits of paper. I get suspicious. I ask him if he's coming to the show. He says unfortunately he can't come. He's busy. So I take the bits of paper I've signed and tear them up into little pieces and throw them on the ground. Not the ones with the other girls' signatures, but all the extra ones. It happens quite a lot now, people waiting outside venues wanting autographs, with no interest in coming to the show, ghoulishly collecting memorabilia so they'll be all ready and organised to pop it straight onto eBay when you die.

What astounds me is, for a short while, *I miss the psycho*. I'm deeply ashamed of myself, but now I have an insight into battered wives and why they go back. The cycle of abuse is hypnotising; the intensity of the love they pour over you, followed by violence, contrition, your forgiveness and embarrassment, and then they love you again. But I'm never going back. And just to make doubly sure, I tell everyone I know what's happened. Even my mum. Poor Mum, will it ever end? My catalogue of mistakes. I can't be seen to forgive this man. Silence and shame are your enemies in this situation. I tell everyone where he lives, the different names he uses, everything about him, so if anything ever happens to me – *anything* – they'll know where to find him.

30 LIVES WELL LIVED

Malcolm McLaren
22 January 1946–8 April 2010

I haven't been invited to Malcolm's funeral but I'm going anyway, I feel strongly about it. I know it will be full of people who never even knew him.

I hadn't seen him for years, then I heard he'd died. Not Malcolm. He was so impish and mentally alive. I realised what a huge influence he'd had on me, his views on life, his playfulness, the way he made everything he did into an adventure. Even going to the bank or a business meeting he turned into an event. He made mundane chores into happenings.

For the funeral I wear a black chiffon dress with tiny green dots by Phillip Lim and black Prada Mary Janes. I don't try and look edgy, I just want to look nice. Be myself. It's in One Marylebone, the church building on Marylebone Road. We file in silently and fill up the pews. I recognise a few people, but not many. Paul Cook and Glen Matlock are here; Steve Jones is in LA but sends a joke about Malcolm taking the cash with him.

Vivienne's son by her first marriage, Ben Westwood, gives a sweet, honest speech about what it was like growing up with Malcolm around. How Malcolm was always trying to get rid of him and wanted Vivienne all to himself. It's funny and affectionate. A few other people give speeches and a pattern emerges: he surrounded himself with very organised, hard-working people. His girlfriend from New York, Young Kim, makes a big impression on me. They were together for twelve years, she's elegant, intelligent, restrained, tactful, loving. If Malcolm can have a long relationship with a girl like that, he can't be all bad. Then Vivienne gets up. She's dressed in one of her own asymmetrical suits. She says a few throwaway things about Malcolm giving the boys piggy-backs and making paper aeroplanes and then launches into a tirade, it's not quite clear if she's criticising him or people in general. She's saying stuff like, 'What's the point of being a rebel if you don't do anything with it? It's all just fashion.' Malcolm's lying there behind her in the box. I imagine him stretched out with his feet pointing up wearing red Anello and Davide tap shoes – which I heard he used to wear when he was at art school – and his curly orange hair. I look around the church but everyone is staring ahead blankly. Vivienne moves on to saving the planet. She's in mid-flow when this voice shouts from the back, 'Capitalist!' Vivienne doesn't hear the voice and goes on talking, he shouts it again, 'You're a capitalist!'

Vivienne stops and leans down to a flunky by her side, 'What did he say?'

I can just imagine the flunky replying, 'He said you are a capitalist, ma'am.'

She asks the flunky, 'Who is it?' The flunky whispers something. Vivienne straightens and squints into the darkness, trying to focus on a face at the back of the church. 'Bernie?'

He shouts back, 'Bernard!'

Vivienne bends down to the flunky again, 'What did he say?'

'He said, "Bernard," ma'am.'

Vivienne looks up and says, 'Oh, very well, *Ber*nard then.'

This is hilarious. Bernie Rhodes, the Clash's ex-manager, storms down the aisle to the front of the church, his face strangely puffy (he reminds me of David Gest), shouting that he knew Malcolm better than anyone, knows what Malcolm was trying to do, it was him, Bernie, and Malcolm together who did it all, changed the world and blah blah blah, inserting himself into the narrative of

Malcolm's life. It's like the marriage scene from *The Graduate*, with Dustin Hoffman banging on the glass shouting, 'No! Noooo!' And I think, *Malcolm would be having a right laugh at all this.* Bernie stands in front of the coffin, addressing the pews and rambling on for ages. No one stops him. He's ranting away right in the middle of the funeral. I have to be held down by my friend, Mark, to stop myself jumping up and putting a stop to it. Why doesn't anyone cart him off? I am mindful of Malcolm's sweet girlfriend sitting in the front pew, she's probably finding this all very upsetting and disrespectful. Vivienne is pacifying Bernie now, 'I know what you mean, Bernie,' she says, nodding sagely. Vivienne doesn't mind people standing up to her; it's when you have no opinion that she can't tolerate it. Bernie eventually runs out of steam and the funeral continues.

Sitting here, remembering how Malcolm thought and lived, I feel more affected by him dying than when my father died. That's how much his ideas have infiltrated and influenced me.

Steve New
16 May 1960–24 May 2010

A month later I'm at Steve New's funeral. This is more like it. Packed with people who actually knew and loved him. Lots of girls. He loved women. There's even a paragraph in the words he wrote for his funeral thanking all the girls he's ever known for being in his life. His family play some music he's been working on, it's the sort of sound I imagined him making, dreamy and technically complex. He was a great guitarist, a prodigy, very intelligent, very beautiful and iconoclastic, he remained himself to the end and he never licked anyone's arse. Ever.

Ari Up
17 January 1962–20 October 2010

My phone pings by my bed in the middle of the night: I've got a text. That's funny, I never usually leave it on, must have forgotten. I'm not pissed off, I'm awake anyway, woke up at five o'clock. It's from Vice Cooler, the Raincoats' drummer, who lives in LA. *So sorry to hear about Ari.* It can only mean one thing. She's gone.

Baby Ari went first. She was the youngest of all of us, not just of the Slits but the whole scene. Grew up in front of us. Had more energy than all of us put together, even at the end. I thought she'd get better: she had a will of iron, of course she'd beat it. How ridiculous of me, I know about cancer, it's not about your will, it just depends what type you've got and how bad you've got it.

Ari emailed me a couple of times recently, I didn't take enough notice of the emails. In the first one she invited me to the New Slits' London show, her last London gig; she knew it was her last. I couldn't be bothered to come up from Hastings, was too bogged down in divorce shit. She invited Poly Styrene too. Poly and I talked it over, 'Shall we go or not?' Of course we would have gone if we'd known she was dying, but we assumed that if she was playing gigs she couldn't be too ill. I don't wish I'd gone so I can say, *I was at Ari's last gig*, or anything ghoulish like that, it would have been to show her I cared for and respected her.

The next email from her was very sweet, a couple of days before she died, telling me where some photos of the Slits were, saying I should get them and have them. I still didn't twig. I wrote back a couple of lines saying I'd get onto it.

I think of Ari every time I practise guitar, especially when I'm playing with a metronome to work on my timing. I think how she would love to still be alive, to still be making music, she was a truly dedicated musician, music was her life. Ari was an artist and an artist needs love more than anyone, she needed loads, but I don't know if she got enough on a one-to-one level. Everything came second to her music, even family. You have to be selfish to be an artist; your family just have to accept that. It's not personal, it's not that you don't love them. What an artist gives their family isn't routine and their constant presence, they give vitality and ideas, independence and creative thinking. That's what I think Ari will have passed on to her sons and to many people who never knew her. As each month and year goes by after her death, I feel warmer towards her and I realise more and more what an amazing woman she was.

Poly Styrene
3 July 1957–25 April 2011

I saw a lot of Poly. We'd meet up about once a week because we both lived in Hastings. We'd have a coffee and talk about music. We were in pretty similar positions, coming back after years of silence, except she had some hits and is better known than me.

I saw her sitting outside a cafe when I went back a couple of months ago. She said she could hardly move, felt like her back was broken, but the doctor wouldn't take her seriously, said she was mentally unstable. Her face was grey and twisted from the exhaustion of bearing constant pain. In the end, her friend Naz, a photographer, called up the hospital and demanded they send an ambulance immediately or she would sue them and tell the press. The ambulance came straight away and later that week Poly was diagnosed with cancer. She was put straight into a hospice.

Before she was ill, Poly and I went to see her daughter sing at Cargo in London; I drove and played her my new EP in the car. She was amazed, she hadn't wanted to come back to music because she felt she'd moved past the 'punk' thing, but when she heard my songs she saw there was a way to record and do gigs again that was compatible with being an adult. She thought I was crazy at the beginning of the car journey – 'Why would you want to do that?' – but gradually she got it. She saw I wasn't trying to be young, she could hear that in the songs, I was myself, writing honestly about my life now. I sowed a seed, not by lecturing her, just by doing it. I'm glad she got her drive back and made her album, *Generation Indigo*, before she died. She got on with it immediately and finished way before I completed my album. She was a real doer.

When I visited Poly in the hospice we held hands the whole time, she had soft, young, girlish skin, and we had such a laugh, laughed our heads off about boys and sex and all that bollocks. Before I had cancer I was a bit uncomfortable about illness, but not now. I think Poly felt very relaxed with me. She still had hope that she was going to get better.

I texted Poly a couple of days later that I was thinking of her, and got a message back saying she had just passed away. At her funeral I thought, *It's true the good die young, I'm going to try and be good like Poly, that's what I'm going to take away from knowing her.*

31 THE VERMILION BORDER

2010–2012

You design your music to accommodate the level of skill that you have available to you.

Brian Eno

Making my record, *The Vermilion Border*, is like being a kid and getting all my mates over to help build a tree house out of bits of wood that are lying around. We bang it together bit by bit, only stopping if I run out of money or need to write another song. It takes a couple of years. I set up a crowd-funding account with Pledgemusic to help pay for the recording, the money dribbles in and I make sculptures and drawings to send to the pledgers.

Working at the kitchen table, 2012

I bump into Jah Wobble at a party, I haven't seen him for twenty-five years; he's just written his autobiography, *Memoirs of a Geezer*, and we talk about playing together. I hustle and hassle him and make it happen; we record two songs at his publisher's studio in Soho ('Traum Palace' and 'Bury the Bones'). A couple of weeks later at a gig, I meet Jim Barr, the bass player with Get the Blessing and Portishead. I act confident and say I'd like to work with him. He's a very open-minded person and says yes. I send him the track 'Couples Are Creepy' and he records a bass line for it.

Now I have Wobble and Jim on my record, the thought pops into my head, *This could be a theme: I've already got two great bass players, why not keep going in that direction and have an interesting bass player on each track?* Another bass player I would love to work with is Jack Bruce, how ridiculous is that. I only had about four LPs when I was fifteen and one of them was *Disraeli Gears* by Cream. Someone at Pledgemusic knows Jack so I send him an email, and lo and behold he replies and says yes too.

I choose a drummer who I think will suit Jack, Charles Hayward (formerly of This Heat – one of the best bands in the world), and on the recording day Jack arrives right on time. We all have a laugh together and when he's nice and relaxed I say, 'Let's go into the studio and play through the song.'

'Have you got a demo for me to listen to?' says Jack.

I try to sound positive. 'No, we've only just learnt it.'

He looks surprised. 'Wow. That's old-school.' There's a pause, the air suddenly seems very thin and I take a deep breath. Then he smiles: 'OK!'

Phew. Got past that awkward little moment.

'What key is it in?'

I don't know! I don't know anything about keys. I'm way out of my depth here. 'I've no idea,' I say, keeping my voice steady.

'Don't you care what key I play in?' says Jack.

He thinks I'm an idiot.

'Cool!' He beams.

Jack asks what sort of thing I would like him to play, I talk about opium dens, Morocco . . . but he laughs and says that to him the song sounds like those music-hall performers from the 1930s and '40s, Wilson, Keppel and Betty, who did funny Egyptian dancing in a sand tray. He plugs in his Gibson bass guitar shaped like a violin, we dim the lights and watch him through the glass window of the control room. As I lean against the mixing desk, listening to Jack play, I feel spiritually elevated, his playing pulls me down into sadness, soars up into joy and rattles me through every emotion in between, that's what he does with his bass playing, he paints an emotional picture.

And that's it, the end of the session. Jack says that if I ever need him again he'll be there like a shot, he hasn't enjoyed a session so much in years.

The bass players on my album are: Tina Weymouth (Talking Heads, Tom Tom Club), Jah Wobble (PiL), Jim Barr (Portishead), Jack Bruce (Cream, Blind Faith), Jenny Lee Lindberg (Warpaint), Danny Thompson (John Martyn, Nick Drake, Pentangle), Norman Watt-Roy (Ian Dury, the Blockheads), Winston Blissett (Massive Attack), Glen Matlock (the Sex Pistols), Wayne Nunes (Tricky), Gina Birch (the Raincoats) and friends, Toby Strain and Phil Oakey.

32 FRIENDLY FIRE

2011

Behind every successful woman is a man who tried to stop her.
Graffiti on the wall of the women's lavatory,
the George Tavern, East London

I'm on my mobile in Waterstones in Camden Town, arguing with my 'manager', Pete Panini, about my book. He's telling me he's found a twenty-three-year-old music journalist who he thinks should ghostwrite it for me. She's never written a book before, just articles.

I start off quite calmly, 'Pete, I've asked an editor I know to oversee my writing. Give me a chance, just three chapters and if it doesn't work out, we'll do it your way.'

'Well, if you want the book to be shit,' he replies.

I try again. Mustn't get ruffled, god forbid a woman should appear to be difficult in business. 'I know I can do it, I've already started writing and I've found my voice, I'm really excited.'

'What's *my* role? I have no role if you do it that way,' he says.

Aah, now we're getting to the nub of the problem.

'Anyway, your new agent won't want to represent you any more,' he continues. 'Faber probably won't want you either.'

I swear at him. He hangs up.

'Excuse me, madam, but I'm going to have to ask you to leave the premises.' I stomp out of Waterstones, security guard at my heels, and onto Camden High Street. Dodging through the traffic, I stop in front of Marks and Spencer and lean against the window shaking with fury. My so-called 'manager', who in all the six months he's been 'managing' me has never once come to one of my gigs, is now telling me that I'm a shit writer and can't write a book about my own life.

I knew I'd have a fight on my hands when I came back to music but I never imagined I was going to be taken down by one of my own team. That's the end of that relationship.

I'm scared he might be right. I can't write. The book will be shit. But I ignore my fears. I feel a fool, I'm sure the answer will be 'no' – but I call my new agent and the editor at Faber and ask if they would still be interested if I wrote the book myself. They are. I can't overemphasise how difficult and embarrassing it was for me to make those calls, but I'm so glad I did.

33 FALSE START

2012

We've been filled with great treasure for one purpose: to be spilled.
Yoko Ono

Why do I bother pounding around Regent's Park three times a week, going to the gym, keeping fit? It's not like I've got a boyfriend to roll around with. It's not like anyone cares what I look like. It's exhausting trying to keep it together at this age. Constantly tweezing, waxing and moisturising, running, stretching and all the rest of it. Aaargghh! I trip over a tree root and smack down onto the hard dry earth. I fall so heavily that I'm winded, my tracksuit bottoms are ripped and my knees have gaping wounds jam-packed with little stones. But I'm not giving up and going home after all the effort it took to drag my arse over here, I'm going to run my usual course just to show god, myself, my non-existent boyfriend and anyone else who may be looking down on me from above that I cannot and will not be beaten.

My friend Joanna Hogg, the filmmaker, calls whilst I'm lying in bed the morning after the fall. For twenty-five years, since we first met, our friendship has kept bubbling along. We support each other by meeting up every now and then to appraise our lives. We've both been through slumps, but we buoy ourselves up and give one another creative goals to achieve. It's an unusual and productive friendship.

Over the past few weeks we've been discussing the new feature film Joanna's about to start shooting, bouncing ideas around for casting. It's getting perilously close to the first day of filming and she still hasn't found the right people to play her two main characters. Joanna has her pick of actors, but she likes working with non-actors.

'Viv, I'm going to ask you something, please say no if it's something you really wouldn't want to consider.'

A little glow ignites in my sternum, not quite pleasure, not quite anxiety.

'How would you feel about playing the main character in the film?'

I say yes. Not only because I've got used to saying yes to challenges since the Year of Saying Yes, I also know that if Joanna thinks I'm right for the film, I'm right for the film. I trust her judgement completely. This is an amazing thing to happen to me, like when you find love. It's wonderful and terrible at the same time: wonderful because something you thought could never happen has happened and terrible because all you can think is, *Am I up to it? Will I fuck it up?*

I've just sold the family house (I got it as part of the marriage settlement, unlike my mother – after her divorce we had to move into a council flat by the gasworks in Turnpike Lane, women were not allowed to take out mortgages on their own then, they needed a man's permission), and during the next two weeks I pack everything my daughter and I own into cardboard boxes, call the removal company, bring the move forward two weeks and we move out the day before filming begins. I thought I wouldn't want to leave this big house I was so proud of, but as I shut the front door for the last time, I feel nothing. We can't move into our new home yet, so I install my daughter at my mother's. Tomorrow I'm going to start living with the man playing my husband at a house in Kensington – this house is also the main location for the film – for the next six weeks. I'm meeting him for the first time tonight.

I stop packing for half an hour and meet Joanna and the man in a pub up the road. This is what an arranged marriage must be like; the first meeting laden with hope, expectation and dread. The main thing is, I must feel safe with him, I don't want to spend six weeks alone in a house with a creepy guy. I walk into the Lord Stanley and he's leaning against the bar with Joanna. His name is Liam Gillick, he's an English artist who lives in New York. He talks a lot but I can't understand most of what he says. It's convoluted. He speaks like an academic giving a lecture, so I ask him to speak more simply. He drinks a lot of wine and his nose goes red but I don't feel threatened by him, so I know we'll be OK. When he goes to the bog I whisper to Joanna, 'Please will you ask him to clean his teeth before we kiss?' She assures me she will. I haven't kissed a guy for a year.

I arrive at the location at 8 p.m. with all my bags, an assistant helps me unload the taxi and then leaves me and Liam alone. Tomorrow we start filming. I'm going to stay the night in someone else's empty house, with a man I just met. How weird. He suggests we go to the pub. We sit outside under an electric heater and discuss life, art, having children. As we talk, I realise that an old friend of mine went to Goldsmiths art school with him. I text her to ask what he was like. She texts back: *VERY ambitious*. Meanwhile Liam is telling me what a lovely big cuddly socialist he is. I don't care that he's ambitious, lives in a fancy penthouse and has round-the-clock nannies for his child, I just think it's funny. I start to tease him about it but he explodes. He's not at all amused. I think I'm being quite flirty calling him a Thatcher's child and a careerist. (I have been off the dating scene for seventeen years.) I thought we'd got to a place during the evening where we could say stuff like that to each other, wind each other up with a smile, but I've hit a raw nerve. He goes mental, jumps up off the bench, practically turns over the table, grabs his (designer) coat – face bulldog

400

angry and red, chest puffed out – and says he's not doing the film, it's not going to work, he's going to pack his bags and fuck off back to New York.

As I watch Liam scurry off up the street in a huff, my mouth in an O shape, I dimly recall Joanna saying something like 'Be gentle with him' the last time I saw her. She knows me only too well. I'd better sort this out or the film isn't going to happen. I run after Liam and try to placate him; I explain that I was only teasing and I really like him. I put my hand on his arm, he shakes it off like I'm a leper and hisses, 'Don't touch me.' He looks disgusted by me. Wow. I go back to the house and watch him pack. He's still snarling and hissing, 'You're not smart enough to play my wife,' and, 'You're lazy and unprofessional.' (Because I haven't Googled him yet.) 'I don't want to be in this bourgeois film anyway.' It seems to matter very much to him how he is perceived in the 'art world'. On and on he rants. I give up trying to pacify him and say, 'I understand if you think the film's not right for you and I'm not the right person to play your wife, you have to do what's best for you and your image.' His expression softens, he stops packing, says he's not going to leave the film after all, he's going back to the pub and he'll see me later.

When I hear the front door close, I sit down on the top step of the spiral staircase and cry. Then I get angry. *I'm not going to be bullied and told I'm not good enough by any more men. I've had enough of it. I'm not doing the film, it's not worth having a nervous breakdown over.* I pick up my guitar and my bags, call a cab and go home to mother.

34 FEELING THE WEIRD

2012

Always go too far, because that's where you'll find the truth.
Albert Camus

'Never mind, dear. Didn't they think you were very good?' Mum isn't being mean, it's just that to be asked to play the lead in a feature film is so far out of her life experience, she can't imagine how I could possibly do it. She assumes I've been sent home because I was crap.

In the morning I talk to my daughter: she wants me to go back and do the film. She's so proud and excited about it, and Joanna's promised her she can be an extra in a scene with Tom Hiddleston. She doesn't want to give that up.

I go back to the house in Kensington and come across Liam in the kitchen. I give him a hug. We get on with the job. I make a pact with myself to commit to the challenge ahead and give it everything I've got, I'll deal with the consequences later. It's very *very* important I get this right, more important than my pride.

The crew are friendly and easy to get along with. You'd think doing something as huge as being the lead in a film would be overwhelming. It isn't. I've been a director and an editor, I understand the language, how to start and end scenes, how it might edit, how to repeat movements and dialogue. Even if none of this knowledge is relevant in this particular film, knowing it stops me feeling out of my depth. I'm not sure I could be in an ordinary film and learn lines, but I can improvise, I'm confident about that. What I'm not confident about is my body, or my face. Joanna doesn't want me to wear any makeup, and here's the camera inches from my face (and thighs), god knows what kind of lens Ed Rutherford, the director of photography, is using. I have absolutely no control over what I look like. I feel like Blanche Dubois in *A Streetcar Named Desire*, when Stanley Kowalski grabs her face and holds it under a bare light bulb to see how old she really is (Vivien Leigh said that was the most painful scene she had ever filmed). On the first day of shooting I'm acutely aware of my age and the rarity of a movie camera lingering over an older woman's face in films. Usually it's a young woman's face the camera loves, it almost caresses her: *isn't she beautiful, isn't she perfect.*

At first I think portraying the character 'D' in the film isn't that big a leap for me: I know Joanna well, I know her films and her aesthetic, but the challenge reveals itself stealthily; D is a slightly out-of-sync reflection of myself, it's disturbing and unsettling that I'm so close to her – but not her. The events I'm portraying in her life have just happened in mine: moving away from the family home, trying to create within a relationship, fear of change – although I'm much feistier than D. I start to lose track of where she ends and I begin.

One of the references Joanna mentions to me for my performance is the film *Jeanne Dielman, 23, quai du Commerce, 1080 Bruxelles* (1975) by Chantal Akerman. I saw it at film school and loved the naturalism and thought how revolutionary it was to show such ordinary everyday chores as peeling a potato in real time in a feature film. Joanna also gives me Robert Bresson's book *Notes on the Cinematographer* (1975) and it helps me trust my own judgement. 'Prefer what intuition whispers in your ear to what you have done and redone ten times in your head,' Bresson writes.

The role is physically very demanding. I'm in almost every scene, working every day, six days a week, running up and down stairs, in and out of rooms, around the local streets, on my feet all the time, thinking, remembering, calculating, improvising, and I'm pleased that I kept myself fit in those dark times when there seemed no point, especially as I'm naked in five scenes.

Still from the film Exhibition

I couldn't do the sex scenes if I had a boyfriend, it would be a betrayal. Just before the first one, Joanna and I discuss what sort of knickers I should wear. Not sexy black ones, this is a long-term marriage; I try a pair of white ones but we agree they're 'too Bridget Jones': we settle for a plain flesh-coloured pair from American Apparel. The crew are nearly ready, Liam's on the bed, I'm wearing nothing but the knickers and a white towelling robe, when my body gives me the signal, a clutching feeling in my stomach, that diarrhoea is imminent. I rush down to the ground-floor loo, the most private one in the house, although even this one isn't very private, it's right next to the front door, which is open and a bunch of the crew are sitting outside drinking tea and eating biscuits.

I wash myself about a million times and go back upstairs, I feel weak and fragile as I climb onto the bed. *How glamorous, if only the audience knew.* This is the first time I'm going to be touched by Liam (playing 'H'), he's just woken up and was drinking again last night. I think he's nervous, cold, clammy, alcohol-scented sweat oozes out of his pores. I've showered twice, cleaned my teeth twice, washed my hair and down below, I'm spotless. Joanna tells us the shape of the scene – which boils down to H wants sex, D doesn't – and off we go. I haven't been touched by a man for over a year, this is so strange, a man I don't know touching me intimately, with another group of men I don't know watching me, the microphone dangling over our heads and the blank shark eye of the camera lens recording it all. I'm half appalled and half aroused. To cope with the situation I employ the same trick I used throughout the IVF and cancer investigations, I float outside my body and watch what's happening from above.

Later during filming I realise I'm acting two people all the time: one is the repressed character D, and the other is the free-spirited actress Viv, who takes her clothes off and isn't fazed by emotional or sexual scenes with a man she doesn't know, in front of a group of strangers.

By the time we get to the last sex scene, towards the end of the six-week shoot, I have to make a huge effort to get into it. I'm exhausted, all wrung out, I've given every last drop of myself. I talk to Tom Hiddleston about readjusting to normal life, tell him I don't know what's real and what's the character any more. Tom says, 'You're feeling the weird, that's a good thing, good for your performance.' I also receive good advice about de-roling from the actress Mary Roscoe, who has worked with Mike Leigh. Mary says that Leigh advises his actors to make contact with family and friends at the end of each day, to change clothes, go to the pub, do things that remind you who you are.

One of the last scenes we shoot takes place in a country house. The room is cold and completely dark, there's no bed, just a mattress in the middle of the floor. Joanna tells Liam and me to curl up together under a blanket. I put my head on Liam's shoulder, he wraps his arm around me. I start sobbing uncontrollably. Joanna asks me what she should do, I say, 'Keep filming, I'm not going to be able to stop.' It's the position we're in that's affected me so deeply. Just how Husband and I used to snuggle up together when we were happy. I cry continuously for the next four hours, the first time I've cried since the break-up of my marriage.

35 ALONENESS

2013

Silence is so accurate.
Mark Rothko

I'm sitting at my dad's ugly, dark brown, chunky-legged dining table, the sort of substantial piece of furniture Victorians would have appreciated. I'm wearing an old black vest with big armholes showing a bit of side boob, not in a good way, more in an 'I look like my old man' sort of way. I point out to my daughter how many butterflies are flitting around the lavender bush outside the French doors, just like my father did to me. The warm air and the sound of cicadas rattling their feet makes me feel good. Every time I visit Toulon, I buy a naïve painting by a local artist from the flea market – rough bold strokes suggesting pine trees, waves, the rocky coast – they hang on the whitewashed walls in dark brown frames.

I used to think my father was so selfish and uncompromising, not making the effort it takes to find new friends. I was sociable back then, turning up every summer with a boyfriend or a couple of girlfriends, but now I'm too outspoken for most people, they think you're rude if you tell the truth. 'Punk' was the only time I fitted in. Just one tiny sliver of time where it was acceptable to say what you thought. Perhaps I was lucky to have that. After a divorce friends seem to just melt away, like they're frightened they'll catch it off you. Or maybe it's just that your face doesn't fit at dinner parties any more. Anyway, it is a truth universally acknowledged

407

that a single woman in possession of a decree absolute must be in want of a few good mates.

I hear children across the road splashing in a swimming pool. I can smell lavender and pine. Citroëns putter past the front gate. My wooden shutters, painted eau de nil, bang in the breeze: is the mistral coming? It often comes in August, it can last three days or three and three and three days, that's what the French say. I get up and wedge an old red towel between the shutter and the sill. Everything I imagined when I used to visit my father, how I would change the flat, paint it white, retile the floor, make it look clean and simple, I've done, and now I stay here for two weeks every summer.

I walk along the streets lined with fading villas; there's the raspberry villa, the vanilla villa, the pistachio villa – and dog shit everywhere. The French love their dogs. I'm always suspicious of people who adore animals, they often don't care much for humans.

As I near the flat, I imagine how it would feel if I had a boyfriend, holding his hand, brushing past the purple blooms of the overhanging bougainvillea. How nice it would be. Or would he be in a bad mood? How would he feel about me having a quick swim in the morning, strolling home to eat goat's cheese with fresh tomato on a baguette, then writing all afternoon? Would there be arguments about how I spend my time?

Maybe I'm better off without a boyfriend, no matter how much I'd like one. I find what I do difficult; if I could avoid it, I would. I'd much rather be sitting on the sofa cuddled up to a guy watching box sets, cooking a meal for him when he comes back from work, telling myself love is more important than anything in the world, worth neglecting my music and writing for, than be self-disciplined and write songs on my own all day. It's scary standing in front of audiences singing and playing, struggling to keep a band together, hustling for gigs and money. If happy domesticity came my way, I'd probably grab hold of it and never let it go. I think of what my mum said to me when I was lamenting my loneliness to her last week: 'Do you really want to be owned again?'

I'm invited to lunch with two French women, they're ten or fifteen years older than me. One is in a relationship, the other is alone. One is annoyed by and resentful of her partner and embarrassed to be seen with him, the other comes and goes when she pleases. Here it is, laid out in front of me, the two options: with someone and irritated by them (I think most people in long marriages have a touch of Stockholm Syndrome) or alone and free. Neither appeals. There's got to be a third way.

Bored, bored, bored if you're in a relationship, lonely, lonely, lonely if you're not; Ari told me that when we were in Spain together. I remember feeling her lump. Should have taken control, done more to help her.

36 AN ORANGE

2013

> I seem to have run in a great circle, and met
> myself again on the starting line.
>
> Jeanette Winterson,
> *Oranges Are Not the Only Fruit*

I picture my journey through life as a circle, as if I am travelling around a sphere, like an orange. I started at the bottom and began to climb up the side, becoming more confident as I went along. Sometimes life got difficult and I was hanging upside down, traversing it as best I could. When I reached the top, I tipped over and began to go down the other side. This part of the journey seems to be going faster. I find I'm drawn to behaviours and people that remind me of my past; even if they're difficult, they're familiar. I recognise some of my parents' traits creeping into my character. My true nature – which I suppressed in order to function and succeed as an adult – is surfacing again. I'm shy and inclined to introversion. Still I keep on travelling to the underside of the orange, no way to stop it.

This is where I am at the moment – Winter 2013

A great relationship with my smart, beautiful daughter, my
  sister and my mother.
A couple of good loyal friends.
A small income and a home/room of my own.
The freedom to create.

I never sit outside my house not wanting to go in, rather I hate
to leave it.

I've rebuilt my health.

I'm a good weight (no more FFFs).

Occasional confidence that I can cope with anything.

Occasional despair and loneliness, no big deal, not as bad as
flu.

Lovely pool of talented musicians to work with.

Playing some great shows.

Wonder who to put as next of kin on hospital forms.

I still believe in love.

CLOTHES MUSIC BOYS

This is not a comprehensive list of the clothes, music or boys I was into, but it gives a flavour.

NB: I haven't shagged everyone in the 'Boys' sections. Many are included either because they were a musical influence, I fancied them or they were just around at the time. I haven't included the unpleasant ones.

1963–66: Home and Primary School

Clothes: Black patent T-bar shoes, long white socks and shirt-waisted dress for parties. Maroon twill and gabardine school uniform. White ankle socks, blue leather Clarks sandals, hand-knitted cardigans, Woolworth's jeans and T-shirts for playing in Highgate woods. Purple cord skirt and jacket and 'Donovan-style' purple cap, black leather knee-high boots, op-art dress from C&A, op-art pendants, long hair parted in the middle, homemade capes. Crocheted tights, Levi's, elephant-cord mini skirts from Kids in Gear, Carnaby Street. Hair: dried over the open oven.

Music: Hymns, 'Bobby's Girl', 'Seven Little Girls', 'Rawhide', 'My Boomerang Won't Come Back', 'Sea of Love' by Marty Wilde (all given to me by my cousin Sally). The Swingle Singers, Georgie Fame, the Beatles, the Rolling Stones, the Small Faces, the Kinks, Them, the Walker Brothers, the Yardbirds, the Moody Blues, Bob Dylan, Dusty Springfield, Marvin Gaye, the Four Tops, Otis Redding, the Troggs, the Beach Boys, Dave Berry, Percy Sledge, Tamla Motown, Sandy Shaw, Marvin Gaye.

Boys: Lucien (Albert) Albertine, Colin and Raymond, John Lennon.

Clothes: Ex-military stuff from Laurence Corner. Fluorescent pink tights from Mr Freedom, black mini skirt, shrunken black angora jumper from jumble sales. Black suede over knee boots, striped T-shirts and stripey tights, all from Biba. Cheese-cloth maxi skirts, and T-shirts from Kensington Market. Shoes and boots from Terry de Havilland and Anello and Davide. Hand-studded Wrangler denim jeans, tight denim jacket. Platform boots and shoes from Ravel. Maria Schneider perm (*Last Tango in Paris*): Molton Brown.

Music: Ska (through skinheads at school), protest songs, Pete Seeger, Bob Dylan, Country Joe and the Fish, Taj Mahal, Richie Havens, Ewan MacColl, Nick Drake, Tim Hardin, John and Beverley Martyn, Steve Miller Band, Gil Scott-Heron, Hawkwind, Cat Stevens, Carole King, Thunderclap Newman, Melanie, Philadelphia Soul, the Doors, Captain Beefheart, Fleetwood Mac, King Crimson, the Incredible String Band, the Soft Machine, Henry Cow, Edgar Broughton Band, White Noise, the Pretty Things, Pink Floyd, Neil Young, James Taylor, the Small Faces (*Ogdens' Nut Gone Flake*), Marvin Gaye (*What's Going On*), David Bowie (*Hunky Dory*), Syd Barrett, glam rock, pub rock (Kilburn and the High Roads, Dr Feelgood), Northern Soul, Frank Zappa (I knew every Zappa song like it was a pop song, same with Syd Barrett), Cream, Traffic, Bob Marley and the Wailers, Steely Dan, Sparks, Tim Buckley, Sly and the Family Stone, Sam Dees.

Boys: Mark (Magnus) Irvin, Maurice (Amsterdam), Nic Boatman, Ben Barson, Rory Johnston, Steve Mann (influential DJ at Dingwalls), Russell Hunter, Brandi Alexander, Jan Hart.

1975: Hammersmith and Early 'Punk'

Clothes: Narrow-legged jeans, home-printed T-shirts, customised leopard-print and lurex clothes from jumble sales. Baby-blue handmade cowboy boots, Converse trainers. Tight, fitted, checked jacket, shrunken T-shirts. Mohair jumper from jumble sale, combat trousers. Brown leather bomber jacket. Hair: Keith at Smile.

Music: Roxy Music, the New York Dolls, David Bowie, Patti Smith, Esther Phillips, Lou Reed, Can, Kraftwerk, Jonathan Richman, Mott the Hoople, the Ramones, Iggy and the Stooges.

Boys: Rory Johnston, Mick Jones, Keith Levene.

Summer 1976–79: The Flowers of Romance and the Slits

Clothes: Sex: black leather jeans, rubber stockings, pink patent boots, tits T-shirt, cowboy T-shirt, mohair jumper. London Leatherman: studded belts and wristbands. Customised black string vest with Durex fringe. Old black leather jacket. Dr Marten boots, Spalding and Converse trainers, torn boys' T-shirts, tutus, little girls' party dresses, customised fringed tights. Leather mini skirt. Hair: Keith Levene.

Music: Velvet Underground, Ramones, Iggy (*The Idiot*), Bowie (*Low*), Lou Reed (*Metal Machine Music*), Eno, Patti Smith, Suicide, reggae (dub and lovers' rock), the Sex Pistols, the Heartbreakers, the Clash, musicals, *Dionne Warwick Sings Burt Bacharach*, the New York Dolls, the Ramones, Television, Richard Hell and the Voidoids, Black Uhuru, sound systems (Jah Shaka, Sir Coxone, Moa Anbessa, Stereograph), the Carpenters, bit of disco – Gorgio Moroder, the Bee Gees – Linton Kwesi Johnson, reggae played by Don Letts (DJ at the Roxy).

Boys: Mick Jones, Johnny Thunders, Keith Levene, Joe Strummer, Paul Simonon, Sid Vicious, John Lydon, Don Letts.

1979–81: Simply What's Happening *Tour to the End of the Slits*

Clothes: Ethnic fabrics from Brixton, Stephen Linard, Betsey Johnson, Scott Crolla and Georgina Godley, Vivienne Westwood. Converse trainers, Dr Martens, Santini and Dominici Mary Janes, Vivienne Westwood boots. Hair: matted.

Music: Reggae (lovers' rock and dub), 'world music' and jazz (Fela Kuti, Sun Ra, Eddie Harris, Olatunji, Dollar Brand, Don Cherry). Improvised music (Company, Steve Beresford, Derek Bailey, Fred Frith, Maarten van Regteren Altena, Tristan Honsinger, Anthony Braxton, Evan Parker, Lol Coxhill, Han Bennink, John Zorn, Steve Noble), Parliament, Chic, Bootsy Collins, This Heat, PiL, the Last Poets, Dionne Warwick, the Pop Group, Rip Rig and Panic, Dennis Brown, Dennis Bovell, Pharoah Sanders, Miles Davis (*Bitches Brew*), Ornette Coleman (*Dancing in Your Head*).

Boys: Steve Beresford, Gareth Sager (the Pop Group), Dick O'Dell, Bruce Smith, Budgie, Dennis Bovell.

1982–84: Lost, Teaching Aerobics

Clothes: Boring.

Music: None. Listened to LBC and BBC Radio 4 (talk-only radio stations).

Boys: None.

1985–95: Film School, Directing, Fall in Love

Clothes: 1980s stuff. Lots of money, always down South Molton Street – Alaia, Romeo Gigli, Katharine Hamnett, Margaret Howell, Donna Karan, Sybilla. Shoes: Manolo Blahnik, Patrick Cox, Stephane Kélian, Robert Clergerie. Hair: Daniel Galvin.

Music: Jeff Buckley, Prince, Madonna, Philip Glass, Radiohead, Beth Orton, Nirvana, BAD, Mazzy Star, Van Morrison, Abdullah Ibrahim, Neneh Cherry, the Sugarcubes, lots of tribal and ethnic music – Romanian, Inuit, African.

Boys: Jeb Loy Nichols (good mate), Malcolm McLaren, Oliver Curtis (from film school), Dom Lobo (cute runner), the Biker.

1996–2007: Marry, IVF, Cancer, Become a Mother, Family Life

Clothes: 7 for All Mankind jeans, T-shirts from Velvet and Whistles. Agnes B, Joseph, Prada. Addicted to TK Maxx. TAG watch. Gucci for evening. Tod's loafers, Prada boots and trainers, Hunter wellies and Nick Ashley puffa jacket for walks on beach. Wetsuit. Hair: Aveda.

Music: Pop because of daughter (all the *Now . . .* series; chart music really good at this time), Mika, Gossip, No Doubt, Keane, Bon Iver, Fleet Foxes, Kate Bush, Yoko Ono, the Libertines, Macy Gray, Mazzy Star, Guillemots, the Yeah Yeah Yeahs, Devendra Banhart, Aaron Neville, the Ting Tings, Albert Hammond Jnr, Björk.

Boys: Husband, doctors (Dr Anthony Silverstone, Prof. Jeffrey Tobias, Dr Shah), Vincent Gallo (sort of a doctor).

Clothes: Black Gap jeans, Prada jackets/boots, Clarks desert boots, Topshop, James Perse T-shirts, Phillip Lim, Acne, Christopher Kane for being fancy. David Preston boots. Sue Ryder/Oxfam/charity shops. Lots of vintage shoes and clothes. Not into bags. Hair: local salon in Hackney, or Kennaland when I can afford it.

Music: Still listen to Syd Barrett, Marvin Gaye, Tamla Motown, and all the old jazz, blues and soul stuff. Chris Watson (*El Tren Fantasma*), Apparat, Warpaint, Micachu and the Shapes, Leila Arab, Steve Mason, Oval (Markus Popp), the XX, Beach House, Broadcast, Kate Bush, Scout Niblett, Beyoncé, Robert Wyatt, Chuck D, Lauryn Hill and Yuka Honda.

Boys: Made friends with men again through working with them, which is nice. Kissed a few frogs – surely not many more to go now until I find a prince. Well, at least no more nutters (please, god), I've kissed enough of those . . .

ILLUSTRATIONS

Side One

Side Two